AFRICA
EMERGENT

AFRICA EMERGENT

Africa's Problems Since Independence

John Hatch

Henry Regnery Company•Chicago

To Julius Nyerere and Kenneth Kaunda, whose visionary yet practical leadership is showing Africans the way to overcome the problems bequeathed by European colonialism.

CONTENTS

Acknowledgements

A book of this kind, which is the product of relationships with Africans over a period of 25 years, obviously owes much to a host of informants. They are far too numerous to name and it would be invidious to select. They include academics, Ambassadors, architects, businessmen, doctors, drivers, engineers, factory-workers, farmers, High Commissioners, journalists, miners, ministers, peasants, public servants, teachers, waiters, wives, writers, unemployed. I am grateful for the time they have all willingly given to my often ignorant enquiries.

If I were to select one category for special thanks it would be that of personal assistant to Presidents and Prime Ministers. These men and women, who always remain modestly in the background, carry an enormous load of responsibility, have their mental faculties constantly stretched and work all hours of the day and night. Yet they have always found time to give me those special insights which they can uniquely offer.

My book also owes much to the work of other writers. Rather than interrupt its continuity by footnotes referring to their treatment of each issue, I have preferred to compile an extensive bibliography divided according to the subject of each chapter. I should like, however, to pay my tribute to the work done by other authors on every aspect covered in this book.

Finally, but by no means least, I offer my warm appreciation to Mrs Gillian Hollings for her help in typing, bibliography arrangement and indexing. This the ninth book of mine in which Mrs Hollings has participated; my debt to her is incalculable.

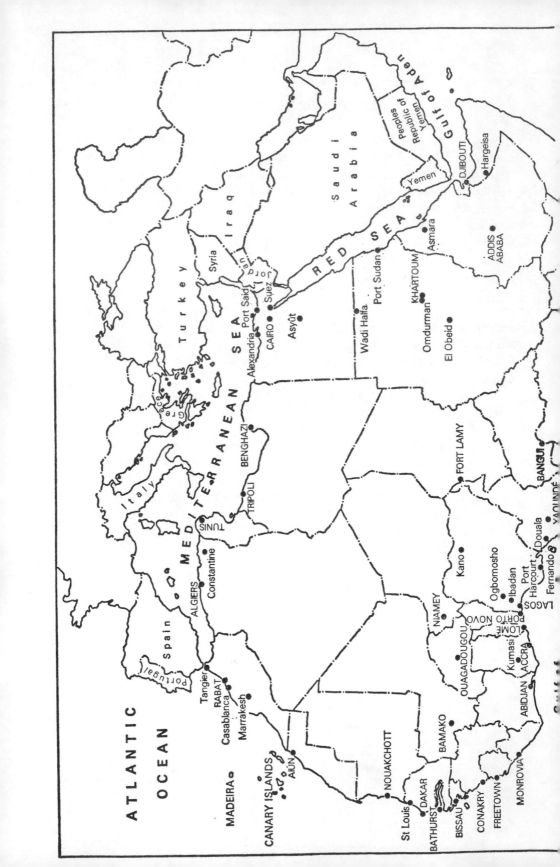

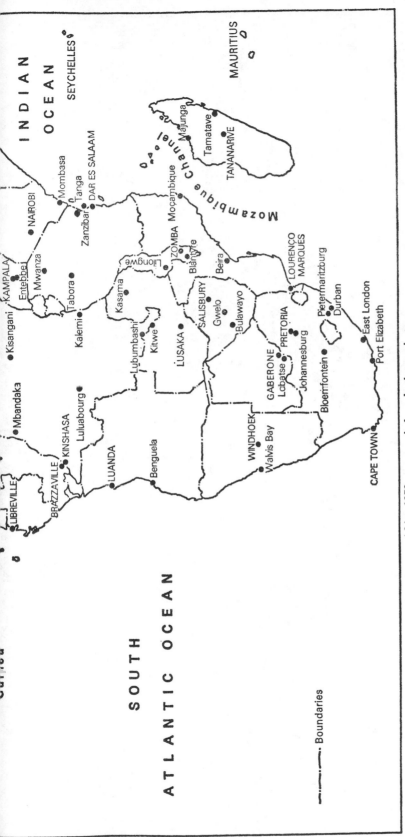

Africa 1973: state capitals and other main towns

Boundaries

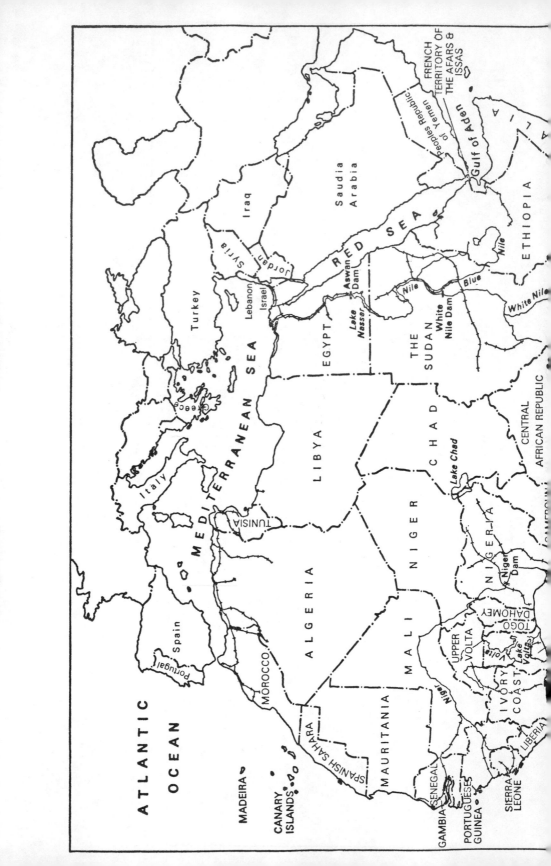

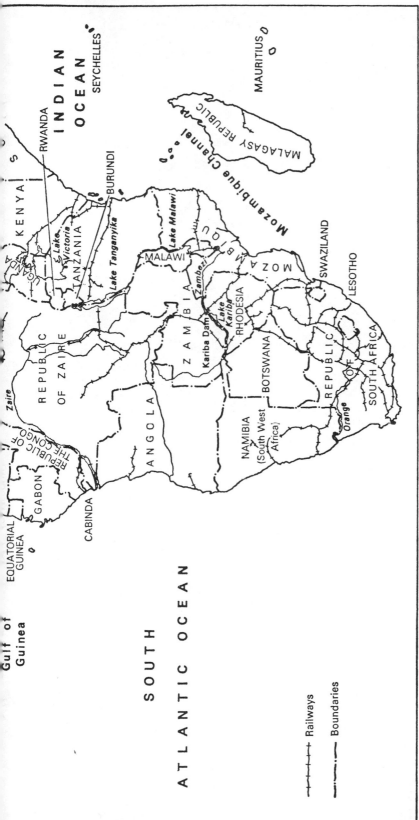

Africa 1973: the states, main rivers and railways

Railways
Boundaries

The 1960s: Decade of Disillusion

The 1960s can be termed the decade of African independence. For the first time in a century some 300 million Africans came to live under governments of their own people. This was the culmination of a generation's anti-colonial campaign. What did the peoples of Africa anticipate from the replacement of European by indigenous legislators? To what extent were their expectations fulfilled, in which ways frustrated? What factors brought satisfaction, which influences produced disillusion?

For some years after World War II it was fashionable in European imperial circles to assert that there was no such thing as African public opinion. The theory propounded was that the vast majority of Africans were too ignorant to understand politics and that the few who expressed political views were merely agitators seeking to further their personal interests. It was claimed that only the European colonial officials knew the thoughts of the ordinary African; they reported that Africans were content with their lot, having no desire to lose their colonial rulers. The claim was made throughout colonial Africa, but was especially insistent where a substantial number of Europeans had settled. Thus it was audible at crescendo in South Africa, only slightly less loud in the Rhodesias and Kenya, but more diminuendo in west Africa.

The proposition that Africans held no political views provided a justification for imposing imperial policies on them. This was particularly the case when the British government co-operated with European settlers in creating the Central African Federation in 1953. Despite African protests and consequent accusations in the British parliament that the will of the people was being over-ridden, Churchill's government, Sir Godfrey Huggins and Sir Roy Welensky all claimed that the ordinary African approved of their action. Not only did they maintain that federation would further African interests, they professed to know that the mass of Africans did not wish to meddle in politics but were content to leave them in the hands of the Europeans whom they trusted to act on their behalf. When challenged to provide an opportunity for Africans to express their own views, they fell back on the lame argument that they would not understand the process of voting.

If this colonial-government/white-settler assessment had been correct, the conclusion of colonial rule and its replacement by independent government would have represented nothing more than the victory of a tiny African political class over the colonial rulers. It would have signified simply a change in the power base within a small, closed administrative establishment. Yet the resistance displayed against the Federation, and in Kenya, South Africa, Rhodesia, the Portuguese territories and throughout the Magreb against local white rule, demonstrated the falsity of the claim. Ordinary Africans did have views on their future. Peasants, town-workers, miners, farmers, were not content to leave their destiny in the hands of white masters. Nor were they simply swayed by the rhetoric of political agitators. They held their own aspirations for a changed life, even if, inevitably, their ideas as to how to attain their objectives were vague and sometimes unreal.

I can testify to the reality of African public opinion from personal experience. During the 1950s I made four extensive tours to various African regions. I travelled throughout south and central Africa three times, in the east and west twice and the north once. These were not fleeting visits by plane to a few capitals or cities. Most travelling was done by road, allowing conversations in villages or isolated homesteads, in shanty towns as well as professional suburbs, in bars, schools, universities, factories, mines, cattle compounds as well as parliaments, ministerial drawing-rooms, chiefs' houses and palaces – even in a number of gaols. Indeed, in southern Africa it was apparent that I met many more Africans on each visit than most local Europeans encountered in a lifetime.

During the course of these journeys during the 1950s I attended meetings of Africans in such diverse locations as Cape Town, Durban, Johannesburg, Alice, Serowe, Mbabane, Maseru, Gaborone, Lilongwe, Kitwe, Dar es Salaam, Machachos, Nairobi, Entebbe, Kumasi, Accra, Enugu, Ibadan, Lagos, Cairo. Sometimes they were small gatherings of local villagers; in Dar es Salaam one meeting was estimated at 30,000, drawn from all over the country.

Did Africans of the ante-independence era entertain any common hopes? Were any visions shared between the peasant living on family subsistence, the town-dweller dependent on odd jobs, the migrant miner, cocoa-farmer, teacher or farm-worker?

The answer is bound to be given with reservations. It may be partially subjective. Yet I found that in all the countries I visited and amongst almost all the people to whom I listened, certain common expectations and views were widely held.

First, there was a general, virtually universal desire for self-government.

Apart from the handful of individuals who feared that they might lose their privileged employment with colonial Europeans, Africans wanted the laws and regulations governing their lives to be framed by Africans instead of by aliens.

Superficially this might appear to be nothing more than a re-statement of the platitude that a wave of nationalism swept the continent during the 1950s. Nationalist sentiments did arise in some countries during this period, but they seemed to me to be little more than a veneer. Most Africans I met wanted to be free from the interference of European rulers and administrators; but although they might cheer nationalist leaders when they visited their district, they were much more concerned to control their own local affairs than to see black ministers replace white around cabinet-tables. Their main objection to European rule was that the foreigner did not understand their ways. His orders frequently infringed the mores of the group, the institutions he imposed often paid no attention to local custom and diminished the authority of natural rulers, the values and ethics insisted on were alien to the people. In short, Africans wanted to live in their own ways, to return to the kind of society they had evolved themselves.

Secondly, universal resentment was expressed against racial discrimination. Throughout the continent Africans were treated as second-class human beings, and sometimes as third-class. Under colonial rule a white skin was the qualification for major privilege. Where whites had settled, there were usually Asians or Coloureds. They were accorded minor privileges, but the African was always relegated to the bottom of the scale. In the three-tier system he resented the favours accorded to Asians and Coloureds immediately above him even more than those of the whites whose life-style was beyond his reach. Even in west Africa, where there was no substantial Asian or Coloured community, the business or commercial activities of the Lebanese, Syrians and other aliens caused indignation. In all cases, Africans felt a deep resentment against being forced to live in what appeared to them as an undignified posture in their own land.

Thirdly, many local grievances and aspirations were expressed. The most frequent was concern over lack of schools. A passion for education seized Africans during the 1950s. Where a locality had no school – and this was common – its inhabitants felt that their children were being deprived of their fair opportunities. Even where a school existed, the charging of fees was felt to be unjust. Schools took precedence, but there were also complaints against lack of roads, clinics, transport, houses, jobs, whilst in many areas there were bitter complaints against the prices paid for the goods produced for sale.

Finally, a curious dichotomy was apparent in the relationship between countryside and town. In some areas it had become a form of initiation rite for young men to do a stint as a migrant worker in urban employment – in the mines or at any odd job he could pick up so as to experience town life. Some girls would refuse to marry any boy who had not gained this experience. The older people, whilst recognizing the advantages gained by those young men who saved money from their wages and brought it back to the village, were worried about the effect of town habits and values imported into traditional communities. They heard of the promiscuity, homosexuality, drug-taking, violence, urban diseases and alcoholism which were becoming rampant in town societies. They saw the diminution of respect shown by returned youths.

Thus a conflict of interests marked the attitude of rural inhabitants – the vast majority of Africans – towards this migratory practice. The antagonism felt towards the impact of urban irreverence was also aggravated by a growing sense that the towns were being given preference over the rural areas in the allocation of resources. It was evident from the conversations I heard that during the 1950s hostility between town and country was growing at an ever-increasing rate.

The relevance of these widely held views to the post-independence era became immediately apparent as soon as the conversation turned to the nationalist movements or anti-colonialism. The desire for colonial rule to be brought to an end and for indigenous government was virtually universal.

It was accompanied by a general sense of common African purpose, a sense of Africanness which it was felt should permeate every aspect of the continent's life and establish the character of Africa in the affairs of the world. To some extent the anti-colonial nationalists were successful in engendering a feeling of nationality, a patriotism which saw its goal as the achievement of independence. The resurrection of African state names like Ghana, Mali, Zambia, Zimbabwe, provided an illustration of this concept; the use of African languages, flags, national anthems, supplied others.

Nevertheless, the most significant factor in the relation between the views of the 1950s and the post-independence situation was the expectations aroused. Popular opinion amongst Africans universally assumed that the resentments they felt and the aspirations they entertained would all be resolved by independence. They believed, almost without question, that once Africans replaced Europeans as legislators, they would be able to return to their own mores in the villages with improvements in facilities. Discrimination would disappear, not only between people of different skin colours, but also between rural and urban inhabitants, and a new life would flow for their children, based on the old values but devoid of the old miseries.

It was this burden of expectation which African governments had to bear as soon as independence had been achieved. The 1960s saw most of the continent emerge from the colonial era, the establishment of sovereign states, newly independent governments striving to fulfil these multiple expectations. Governments or régimes in Africa should be assessed as elsewhere: not by the criteria of other societies, but according to how they satisfy the demands of their own people, together with consideration as to how they affect the interests of others. It is by concentrating on the expressed needs of the African peoples and the degree to which their governments supplied them that we can most validly analyse the first decade of African independence.

Events during the 1960s largely destroyed the euphoria aroused by independence, replacing expectancy with cynicism or resignation. A score of régimes, created in the fine flush of anti-colonial nationalism, were unconstitutionally overthrown. The use of violence, actual or threatened, supplanted political processes over large areas of the continent. The goal of Pan-African unity, for many nationalists a central objective of the anti-colonial campaigns, receded beyond the horizon, a forgotten Utopia. Instead of national prosperity, anticipated from the collective national efforts released by independence, stagnation in the countryside, massive unemployment in the towns and ostentatious luxury for a tiny minority became the general experience. Detention without trial, public executions, inter-communal massacres, commonly succeeded the colonial authoritarianism against which nationalists had inveighed. Freedom to organize trade unions, political parties or co-operatives, to publish newspapers or to hold public meetings, was widely curtailed. Violence, theft and rapine spread through town streets and country paths. Corruption became rampant, graft commonplace. Africa seemed to be fast imitating not only the societies of New York, Chicago, Dallas, Hamburg, Marseilles or London, but also those of Johannesburg, Cape Town, Salisbury and Bulawayo.

The bubble of expectation burst because it was filled with romantic vapours rather than realities. Africa is not inhabited by supermen but by ordinary human beings. They were not going to become saints when colonial rule was replaced by self-government. Colonialism, with all its faults, was never the sole cause of African poverty, of inequality, of inefficiency, nepotism, corruption. These evils flourished in Africa as in all other continents because there were men and women seeking to practise them. The colonial system may have encouraged certain people to use such methods of self-seeking; so have many systems established since independence. There was never any reason to believe that the parliamentary, judicial or administrative structures developed in Britain, France and Belgium would serve the needs of totally different African environments.

The main element in the century of colonial rule over Africa was European ethnocentricity. This arose from the legacy of the nineteenth century. The concept of those Christian humanitarians who followed the lead of men like David Livingstone was that European responsibility lay in bringing "enlightenment" to Africans. And "enlightenment" to nineteenth-century Europeans was synonymous with commerce, monetary exchange, technology, with the Christian religion cementing together these elements of civilization.

Thus the main impact of European imperialism on Africa was to stimulate market economies where they existed and create them where they were absent, to encourage or compel the cultivation of cash crops, to introduce European machines like internal combustion or railway engines, and, where possible, to substitute Christian churches for indigenous religions. The effect was to assault African cultures, though they were too strong to be destroyed.

By the mid-twentieth century this process had advanced so far that it was considered proper to introduce Africans to the European political institutions which had evolved out of Europe's industrial revolution. European and African liberals hailed this development enthusiastically, urging it forward at ever-greater speed. Africa was seen as becoming a microcosm of liberal Europe, with her expanding trade, investment and capital, her European social and educational mores, her parliamentary, judicial and administrative institutions. These burgeoning European models would be held together and directed by an African middle class, replete with suits, ties, umbrellas, brief-cases, and with sound European advisers in their shadows.

What the liberals of both continents had forgotten during the euphoric decolonizing days of the 1950s was that this structure of society had only taken root in a few countries – in Britain, in some areas settled by the British, and in Scandinavia. It can hardly be regarded as "European" if one recalls the history of that continent over the past century. Moreover, it has produced its own social evils. Indeed, at the very time that this system was being urged on Africans, important sections of European and American society were questioning its democratic validity, and some totally rejecting it. They had discovered that its materialism, its violence, its competitiveness, its impersonal nature, were souring the quality of their lives.

In the light of these considerations, it could hardly be expected that this social system, when exported, would meet the needs of African states.

Black and white liberals rejoiced in the achievement of independence which created a succession of sovereign states during the decade from the mid-1950s. They looked forward to Europe's colonies being transformed into stable, prosperous, parliamentary régimes. There was reason in their welcome for the end of colonial rule, because alien government can only retard genuine social development. But liberals thought of political independence as a panacea, whereas it could be no more than an opportunity to face the social and economic problems which colonialism had obscured. Not surprisingly, when these problems had to be met many of the instruments bequeathed by the colonial powers were found to be inadequate. In discarding them Africans frequently disappointed the romantic expectations of their liberal friends in Europe.

Many Africans as well as Europeans had endowed political independence with extravagant significance. Kwame Nkrumah was no doubt tactically right to assert, "Seek ye first the political kingdom"; but his failure to use his political kingdom to effect radical changes in the socio-economic life of the Ghanaian masses was symptomatic of the general nationalist inadequacy after independence. For the purpose of the anti-colonial struggle national mobilization had been achieved. Inevitably, nationalist propaganda had emphasized the barriers which colonial rule raised to the economic and social development of the African peoples. Lively expectations were thereby raised that once independence was achieved life would become richer and more bountiful. In fact, independence raised problems which made life for many harder and more insecure.

Most of the anti-colonial nationalists had been too busy organizing the campaign against colonial rule to give much thought to the post-independence planning of their countries. Their most crucial weakness was a blindness to the foresight of certain elements within the imperial states. It was natural for nationalists in the midst of their anti-colonial efforts to assume that they were fighting an implacable enemy determined to maintain European imperialism until compelled to withdraw by the force of their subjects' attacks. In fact, few colonial situations in Africa answered this description. With the exceptions of the Magreb, Kenya, and the Central African Federation, force or the threat of force played little part in British, French or Belgian decolonization. Once Ghana had been granted independence in 1957, more through negotiation than by coercion, it became only a matter of time before those colonies and protectorates directly controlled by the British parliament similarly gained indigenous rule. The French dependencies followed the same path rather in imitation than from their own anti-colonial pressures. The Belgians were quick to recognize the advantage of reversing their previous colonial policy and accepting the Anglo-French prescription.

What most African nationalists failed to observe was that many European capitalist concerns foresaw this trend of events and adapted their policies to meet it. It may only be through hindsight that we can now see that once Britain had decided that it would be too costly in life, resources and reputation to stave off Indian independence, the demise of the British Empire appeared on the horizon. Similarly, the French defeat at Dien Bien Phu made it impossible for France to hold on to her African empire while Britain was withdrawing from contiguous territories, whilst the Belgians had few delusions of grandeur and were certainly never going to be left holding an island of European imperialism surrounded by black-governed states.

The major European companies operating in Africa did not wait for hindsight; they used foresight. Reading the signs correctly, they estimated that imperial rule in Africa was approaching its end and made their dispositions accordingly. Unilever, the Société Commerciale de l'Ouest Africain (SCOA), and the Compagnie Française de l'Afrique Occidentale (CFAO) in west Africa, for instance, turned over most of their traditional collection of raw materials to local agents and concentrated on the production of consumer goods for local markets. They began to recruit indigenous staff on a serious scale. Airlines combined with hotel groups to invest in the tourist potential of east Africa. In the centre of the continent, the copper companies of the Congo and Zambia – then Northern Rhodesia – were more hesitant. They had to estimate whether the experiment of forming an alliance between the dominant whites and a putative black middle class would endure. They took the precaution of establishing relations with the expanding African trade unions and encouraged a handful of Africans to take staff posts. Once it became clear that the Federation would disintegrate into separate states, companies invested covertly but deliberately in friendship with nationalist leaders and their organizations.

The fact was that the commercial and financial organizations were not concerned whether Africa was ruled from Europe or by her own people. Their concern was confined to their opportunities for making money. In some ways it furthered their interests to see African countries becoming independent. Provided that they had won influential friends amongst the African élite, they would not only be spared the hostility shown towards colonial companies, but might well be enabled to extend their economic empires. In the Ivory Coast, for example, the number of Frenchmen trebled in the years following independence. Meanwhile, the finance company Lonrho vastly expanded its operations all over the continent during the post-independence decade.

Of equal significance were the attitudes of multi-national companies and international consortia. Again there appeared new opportunities for rich dividends once the restraints of colonial discrimination were removed. One example was the building of Kwame Nkrumah's famous Volta Dam. Finance for it was made available from Europe and across the Atlantic. Investors secured the enormous advantage of enthusiastic encouragement from Nkrumah and his colleagues, who believed, with some reason, that it could be of vital significance to the development of their country. Yet the scheme revealed two crucial factors which illustrate the dangers of this kind of operation. In order to maximize profits the dam was built by capital-intensive methods. It therefore did little to ease the unemployment problem, whilst setting wage standards which inevitably stimulated the growth of a tiny, but socially dangerous, labour aristocracy. Secondly, instead of using local bauxite for the smelter, raw material was imported. As the administration of the alumina company remained overseas too, ultimate control was never centred in Ghana. Instead of providing a base for the creation of a heavy industrial complex which could have served all west Africa, this massive scheme remained basically a foreign investment, dependent for its capital, material and skills on alien decisions. The international investors were not going to risk nationalization!

Thus the attainment of independence, celebrated euphorically by African nationalists and European liberals alike, handed powers of political decision to indigenous rulers but left control over the basic issues on which those decisions had to be taken in alien hands. African presidents and ministers could decide in their cabinets to build more schools, hospitals or roads; what they could not do was to determine how national income was to be increased to meet these needs. That depended on investment decisions of boards in London, Paris, New York or Brussels, or on the world price of commodities like copper, coffee or cocoa, equally controlled from abroad.

The mistake made by African nationalists was to concentrate solely on the transfer of political office. They thereby left themselves unprepared for the complex dilemmas remaining when colonial rule was removed. A few Europeans and Africans showed sufficient foresight to warn of the impending dangers. The Fabian Colonial Bureau, for instance, tried to persuade its former chairman, Arthur Creech Jones, when he became Colonial Secretary, to consider nationalizing the Northern Rhodesian copper mines; but he, with the characteristic liberalism of a British social democrat, held that this was a matter for Rhodesians to decide. Thomas Balogh warned Nkrumah of the dangers inherent in the methods being used to build the Volta Dam; René Dumont similarly was urging

Africans in the French colonies to eschew imitation of French cultural patterns and concentrate on raising the productivity of their farmers. But these were lone voices, drowned in the roars of political acclamation.

A few African voices were also to be heard warning of the problems to be faced after independence. Nkrumah himself constantly beseeched his colleagues to set an example of austere living, but to little effect. The slogan Nyerere gave his Tanganyikan nation was "Uhuru na kazi" ("Freedom and work"). Perhaps the most profound warning came from a young Malawian, tragically killed in an accident before he could impress his intellectual insight on his country or continent.

I first met Dunduzu Chisiza in Gwelo gaol in 1959. He had been imprisoned by the Federal authorities along with Hastings Banda. Chisiza immediately impressed me; instead of complaining about his incarceration, he was using the time to read and think out the problems of Africa's future. His only request to me was to secure him a number of books he needed for his studies.

Dunduzu Chisiza, writing in 1960, had this to say about the dangers facing his fellow-Africans after independence:

(a) It throws into sharp relief basic economic and social problems hitherto eclipsed by the over-riding problem of foreign domination, and (b) it creates its own problems, but (c) it also gives the new rulers power with which to tackle the problems. However, to recognize that the future of free Africa is fraught with problems is one thing; to have a clear idea of what those problems are likely to be is quite another matter.

The fact was that the African politicians who had led the successful assault on colonial rule succeeded their erstwhile masters in the seats of political power, but they found themselves and their countrymen ill-prepared for the crucial tasks which faced them. Most of these nationalist politicians had already experienced limited forms of decision-taking, for various kinds of restricted self-government had been practised before imperial authority was withdrawn. In the British territories Africans had been elected to parliaments and appointed ministers in charge of departments of state during the immediate ante-independence years. Although the governor, answerable to the British government, remained the ultimate authority until the moment he handed over the instruments of authority, these African ministers secured genuine experience in taking decisions, dealing with civil servants, practising collective responsibility in Cabinets and answering for their actions to parliament.

Yet, in one sense, this experience was a handicap in facing the problems of independence. Not only was much of the time in this limited self-government taken up with politicizing, both in pressing for early sovereignty and in party conflicts, but the politicians were indoctrinated into an acceptance of alien institutions. Ministers were taught to consult their senior civil servants, usually colonial officials. As in Britain, "consultation" was frequently a euphemism for acceptance of advice from a body of men with infinitely more experience and often more power than political ministers. Moreover, these civil servants were inevitably thinking in terms of colonial policies laid down in Whitehall and maintained the British assumption that all civil-service policy is non-political by nature.

It was assumed, for example, that national economies would continue to rely on a mixture of external aid and European or American capitalist investment. Expansion of national income could only be achieved by increased exports of primary products, like cocoa, sisal, copper or cotton. These would follow the traditional routes from producers to coast and thence to world markets, usually to Britain herself. Resultant profits would accrue to foreign shareholders, with any surplus from the export trade either being used to finance imports or being banked in London. Social services would normally be subordinated to commercial growth, whilst the educational system would be patterned on the hierarchical pyramid characteristic of British education. It was anticipated that a black owning class would slowly grow, taking control of the reins of authority, as in nineteenth-century Britain. In the meantime, expatriates would remain in positions of influence, if not of control.

This was the outlook on which most advice tendered by British officials to the embryonic African ministers was based. It was designed to create a thread of continuity from colonial to indigenous rule, and to a considerable extent it succeeded in this task. Upon independence, African governments in the former British territories had already been well indoctrinated in British colonial policies; the legacy of institutions, economic instruments and advisers bequeathed by Britain left them little option but to follow the roads constructed by their colonial rulers.

The example of Tanganyika illustrates the situation particularly well, for Tanganyika had been lightly administered compared with most British dependencies. Consequently, what was found there at the time of independence was seen in exaggerated form elsewhere.

Despite the paucity of British administrators in the country, the fact that the Germans had been in charge before 1918, and the influence of both the League of Nations' Mandates Commission and the United Nations' Trusteeship Council, on independence in 1961 Tanganyika was a British-dominated country. It had an elected parliament with a two-party system, even though only the Tanganyika African National Union was able to win any seats. Its educational system was divided between primary, secondary and university, the examinations and curricula all being drawn from Britain. Its army had British officers, its senior civil service was staffed by Britishers and its trade unions had been tutored by the British Trades Union Congress.

Tanganyika had also been left with an eighteen-month economic development plan. This was simply designed to continue conventional British economic policy, increasing exports of the few cash crops like sisal and coffee, attracting overseas investment and building an infra-structure which could be utilized by foreign firms.

Even with a united nationalist movement and with fewer colonial administrative roots to excavate, it took Julius Nyerere and his colleagues some six years to reshape the structure of their society to meet the real demands of independence. They were able to accomplish this more easily than, for example, their Kenyan neighbours, where British administration had been much stronger and deeper, where more European interests were involved, and where the British cultural influence was much greater. Yet even Nyerere and his associates found themselves imbued with British assumptions. It was not until a mutiny had uncovered military resentments that they removed the British officers. Unco-operative attitudes from the peasants forced them to abandon the notion that an infusion of money could increase productivity in the countryside. The need for concentration on agriculture taught them that the educational system would have to be radically changed to train most young people for life in rural areas. Their own first development plan foundered on the conventional assumption that economic progress could only come from quick industrialization and foreign capital.

The Tanganyikans learnt these and other lessons remarkably quickly, but they had to learn them through experience, often bitter, dangerous experience. They found that they had to discard most British concepts, from their own minds as well as in their society. If this was difficult for the unified, aware Tanganyikans, with little wealth to cause envy or materialist ambition, and with but a veneer of British culture, how much tougher it was in countries which had wealth to covet, strongly embedded British values and deeply entrenched British institutions? In west Africa, for instance, the British cultural impact had lasted twice as long as in the east.

In many senses the French cultural influence was even stronger than the British, for the French had a more conscious, assertive conviction in the cosmic superiority of their culture. They regarded their colonial subjects as integral members of Greater France, as potential or actual black Frenchmen. Not only did they take French cultural patterns into their colonies, they took many colonial Africans to Paris, integrating them into French political, intellectual and literary society. Indeed, in one department of national life, French colonial subjects were crucial. The French army depended heavily on colonial recruits. In consequence, tens of thousands of Africans from the French colonies saw service in Indo-China (Viet Nam), in Algeria or in France itself.

As a result of African adherence to General de Gaulle during the war, African representatives participated in writing the constitution of the Fourth Republic and were then elected to all its institutions. Sitting in the French parliament, African leaders were brought into contact with the political parties of the metropolitan power where they found themselves wooed as allies. This influence extended back into the colonies themselves, where various French parties played a part in the establishment of colonial parties like Félix Houphouet-Boigny's Rassemblement Démocratique Africain and Léopold Senghor's Indépendents d'Outre-Mer.

Indeed, de Gaulle himself attained a remarkable charisma amongst French-speaking Africans. From his sponsorship of the Brazzaville Conference in 1944 to his Communauté concept of 1958 and then his settlement of the Algerian war, the General became the father-figure of francophone Africa. This enabled him to command widespread African support for his foreign policies; it also induced many French-speaking African leaders to model themselves on him.

Trade-union links were even closer than those of politics. Because the colonial policy of French governments prevented independent trade unions from being established in the colonies, branches of metropolitan unions were formed. And because the French trade-union centre, the Confédération Générale du Travail, was dominated by communists, the influence became political as well as industrial.

The concept of black Frenchmen extended also into intellectual and artistic life. Poets, writers and artists from the colonies were welcomed into Parisian society irrespective of skin colour. Many became as French in their outlook as anyone born in Paris, Lyons or Marseilles.

Of course, racial discrimination existed in the French empire as in the British. Africans never attained equality with white Frenchmen in political representation; colonial rule was often oppressive; the concept of Greater France only extended to an élite in the colonies. Nevertheless, the integration of the African élite certainly extended much more profoundly into French society than was evident in British practice. Whereas, by strictly separating colonial institutions from those of Britain, the British tacitly presumed an eventual creation of African nation-states, many French African leaders explicitly rejected this objective.

Until the British colonies rapidly accelerated their pace towards sovereignty at the end of the 1950s, the idea of independence was anathema to French politicians and rarely considered by French African leaders. As late as 1958, General de Gaulle was engaged in creating his

Communauté, in which the French colonies would have become autonomous in domestic responsibilities alone, participating with France in a common pool of foreign policy, defence and economic affairs. All the French African leaders but Sékou Touré of Guinea approved the concept. Indeed, so far had integration of the African leadership penetrated into French political life that Houphouet-Boigny of the Ivory Coast had been France's Minister of Health and then one of the General's four state ministers.

The French leaders were swept into following the independence trend largely by the example of British Africans whom they feared would dominate the continent as rulers of sovereign states. In their haste to catch up with their rivals, French African leaders even allowed their two great federations, in the west and the centre of the continent, to disintegrate. By so doing they condemned themselves to dividing their resources between the twelve tiny constituent nation-states in place of the more viable federal structures which could have economized on personnel and pooled their wealth for a combined effort on development.

In 1960, therefore, when most French colonies became independent, the new French-speaking states were already deeply rooted in French traditions. Their educational system was wholly drawn from France, their civil service had been organized by the French, their soldiers had been trained in the French army, their economies were controlled in Paris.

The French intended that these ties should be maintained. Their bright hopes for the Communauté might pale, but they still considered their former colonies to be an essential part of the Greater France concept, particularly as long as General de Gaulle remained in office. From the time of the German victory in 1871, France had been obsessed by the need to increase her population, expand her military resources and gain reliable overseas allies. Bismarck had encouraged her to build an African empire to divert her thoughts from "revanche". She came to feel that her status as a Great Power depended on her imperial strength.

In the post-World War II era, when decolonization gained momentum, France desperately attempted to transform her empire into a Communauté which would have allowed her to secure the rôle of a nucleus surrounded by a group of satellites. Her attempt came too late, being overtaken by the independence epidemic spreading from British territories. But General de Gaulle, even more convinced than his predecessors that a French independent international rôle depended on an overseas accretion of strength, determined that sovereignty should not be allowed to detach his former colonies from the French camp. He showed his intentions clearly when defied by Sékou Touré in Guinea. The French exodus from that country when it decided on independence in 1958 served as a stern warning to any other African country contemplating severance from de Gaulle's embrace. French officials simply stripped Guinea of the entire colonial apparatus, files, equipment, even electric light-bulbs. The rest of French Africans heeded the warning. On their independence in 1959–60, their defence and economic arrangements with Paris ensured that they would remain as firmly aligned to French policies as when they had been formally ruled by French governments.

So, after independence, the French could ensure the adherence of their former colonies whenever such support was needed, at the United Nations, within the European Economic Community, in selling arms to South Africa. In Upper Volta 86 per cent of investments were French; in Gabon a successful coup d'état was reversed by French arms; in Niger the majority parliamentary party was overthrown by French-supported chiefs; even in Senegal, which had been represented in the Paris parliament since 1914, French favours for the influential Islamic marabouts, combined with price support for her essential groundnuts, ensured compliance. With financial aid to balance budgets, thousands of French teachers preferring teaching in Africa to military service, a virtual monopoly of investment, expert personnel of all kinds, and available French troops, the sovereignty of most French-speaking African states was always conditioned by the will of Paris during the 1960s.

The most outstanding French success was in the Ivory Coast, as might be expected from the career of its president, Félix Houphouet-Boigny. With an economic growth rate of over six per cent, a per capita annual income of some £66 (compared with about £30 in Nigeria, or £14 in Niger, for example),* budget surpluses and rising investment, the Ivory Coast appeared to be one of Africa's few post-independence successes.

Yet below the surface the picture was rather different. The number of Frenchmen in the country about trebled after independence. Their income increased faster than the domestic product. The large corporations enjoyed high and rising profits, largely repatriated to France. Most of the boom conditions were due to a rapid increase in exports: cocoa, coffee, citrus, timber, mainly grown on large estates. This type of economic growth brought little benefit to the vast majority of the African population. Indeed, despite her agricultural expansion, the Ivory Coast remained a net importer of food, unable to supply even the needs of her own people. There were some Africans who, in co-operation with European investors, became capitalists themselves, but they were very few. The

---

* Where either US dollars or pounds sterling are quoted in the text, the following average rates of exchange apply:

1960–1966	$2.80 to £1
November 1967 (devaluation of £)—December 1971	$2.40 to £1
December 1971 (devaluation of $)—June 1972	$2.60 to £1
June 1972 (floating of £)—February 1973	$2.35–$2.40 to £1
February 1973 (devaluation of $)	$2.45 to £1

Ivory Coast boom mostly benefited foreigners from France or from other EEC countries. Dividing the gross national product by the number of inhabitants provided a per capita income higher than that of most African countries: but the reality of life for the vast majority of Ivoreans was very different.

Meanwhile, the Ivory Coast remained France's lynchpin in securing support in Africa for her foreign policies. The long association of the Ivorean president with Paris, together with the number of French personnel, ensured that the Ivory Coast would consistently support the policies of French governments. As she also had considerable influence amongst other French-speaking, or francophone, African states, particularly those in the Entente, Upper Volta, Niger, Dahomey and Togo, her value to France was considerable.

A few ex-members of the French African Empire tried to resist the post-independence embrace of their former master. Guinea has already been mentioned. After the failure of an attempted federation between Senegal and Soudan, the latter, adopting the federal name Mali, tried to follow a similar path to that taken by Guinea. Later, Congo-Brazzaville also attempted to assert her independence from Paris. We shall examine some of these efforts later, but none of them can be said to have shown much success during the 1960s.

The outstanding exception to the practice of providing experience in national government before independence was seen in the Congo. The Belgian government took a very different attitude from the French or British. In fact, its policy was, to some extent, a reaction against its fellow imperialists. The Belgians feared that the modern education given to the tiny African élite in France, Britain and, later, in Europeanized African universities, would stimulate resentment against colonial rule and produce a group of agitators. They therefore prevented their African subjects from studying in Belgium (except in the church), avoided the establishment of any university in the Congo, and confined their education almost entirely to primary and technical classes. They were consistent, however, in providing better mechanical and manual training for Africans than anyone else in the continent.

In order to insulate their subjects still further from organized criticism of their régime, the Belgians also excluded Africans from political activity. In this they could hardly be accused of racial prejudice, for the same prohibition extended to the many Europeans who settled or worked on contract in the Congo. Policy was determined in Brussels and administered by Belgian officials – although, as in Belgium itself, the Roman Catholic Church and powerful companies wielded considerable influence on decisions.

Theoretically, Belgian policy was aimed at eventual independence for the Congolese, but the prospect was envisaged to be so far beyond the horizon that it was not worth considering in practice. The philosophic concept underlying Belgian colonial policy was that Africans should be trained first for the lower reaches of economic life in order to build the foundations of a modern nation-state from its base. In practice, both the church and the companies felt that their vested interests in the colony might well be threatened once Africans became politically minded. Moreover, from 1953 the existence of the white-ruled Central African Federation to the south, with its Copper Belt contiguous to the Katanga mining complex, held out the eventual prospect of a massive state in central Africa, endowed with vast wealth and dominated by the multi-national mining corporations.

This concept of imperceptible evolution to distant independence was suddenly shattered in 1958. Just across the River Congo from Kinshasa (then Leopoldville) lies Brazzaville. In 1958 General de Gaulle visited this capital of the French Congo and declared that his colony was to be granted self-government. Shortly afterwards an All African Peoples' Conference of nationalist parties was held in Accra; Patrice Lumumba led a delegation of Congolese rebels to it. The Belgian government suddenly awoke to the fact that their policy had been overtaken by events in other parts of the continent. This realization was soon confirmed when riots broke out in Kinshasa, with nearly 200 Africans losing their lives.

It was now that an astonishing reversal took place in the Belgian government's 60 years of colonial policy. Within less than two years all the precepts of the past were thrown away. In June 1960 the Congo was given sovereign independence. Africans took responsibility for the government, with Joseph Kasavubu as Head of State and Patrice Lumumba as Prime Minister.

But, of course, the legacy of the past 60 years could not be reversed. The Congo entered independence a mere month after her first elections. No political party was more than two years old. There was no more than a handful of graduates in the country, hardly any secondary schools, no African doctors, lawyers or engineers. In the civil service chief clerk was the highest grade attained by any Congolese, and in the army no African had risen above the rank of NCO. But the European companies were still there, controlling the economy; and Belgian soldiers remained stationed in their bases around the country.

The tragedies which followed the Congo's independence were more than predictable; in these circumstances they were inevitable. If the country had been wholly agricultural it might have been possible for traditional authorities to have co-operated in order to work out some form of continuity in government until modern institutions had been devised and experience gained in directing them. But, like most of Africa, the Congo had a dual economy and a multiple government. The importance of the modern economic sector to outsiders soon became apparent when the Western powers immediately intervened in the chaos which succeeded independence. The multiplicity of governing institutions, from national government through urban and local authorities to tribal and village administration, had already undermined traditional forms of authority. Yet the Congolese had been given no opportunity to learn how to administer this complex system.

Thus, at the birth of the independence era, British Africans were handed a legacy of British institutions, accompanied by indoctrination in their innate superiority to other systems; French Africans were expected to retain their francophone culture and obey the voice of Paris; whilst the Belgian Africans were simply abandoned to a fate for which they had been allowed no preparation. Meanwhile, in other parts of the continent, the Magreb remained dominated by the Algerian war against the French government and settlers; Egypt continued to seek domestic reform in the midst of her distracting conflict with Israel; Ethiopia occasionally wondered whether modernization could be introduced without destroying her ancient feudalistic traditions; and Liberia continued to combine a Victorian social façade with barely concealed American economic dominance. In the south, Sharpeville tore a huge gap in the apartheid blanket covering white totalitarianism, the Central African Federation desperately sought to postpone its death-pangs and the Portuguese began to realize that the farce of naming their colonies "overseas provinces" would not suffice to deceive their African subjects.

It was from the failure of these constitutional instruments to meet the realities encountered after independence, together with the by-products of these European legacies, that the tragedies of the 1960s arose. Burdened with the consequences of these experiences Africans have to meet the even greater challenges of the 1970s.

Coups and Revolts

News from Africa in the 1960s was dominated by the horrors of warfare in the Congo and Nigeria, by frequent coups and counter-coups, and by constant arguments over racial attitudes in the south. This does not represent any objective order of priorities. From the viewpoint of African interests it may well be that the social experiments in Ghana, Guinea, Tanzania, Zambia and the Ivory Coast, the efforts to keep Nigeria's communities together after the war, the anti-colonial wars against the Portuguese, or relations with Western capitalism, Communists and the rest of the Third World, have greater significance. Nor should it be forgotten that there were other wars, in Eritrea, the Sudan and Chad, for instance, which tragically affected the lives of large numbers of Africans. Meanwhile, relations between different African states and between their leaders were changing, whilst throughout the continent millions of inhabitants were constantly seeking to balance the security of their traditions and the disturbing compulsion to experiment. All these factors profoundly affected life in Africa; yet they were not of the nature from which news-stories are made.

It was characteristic of the media that the events which were described to the public outside the continent involved violence, brutality and death. Yet, whilst this instilled a false view of the continent to outsiders, the significance of these events themselves cannot be ignored on that account. In one sense the stories of the Congo and Nigeria had a special importance for Africans. The spate of coups and revolts certainly presented them with new problems. And few Africans would repudiate the significance of the racial maelstrom in the south.

The Congo saw the introduction of military politics into independent black Africa for the first time. It is true that in 1952 Colonel Gamal Abdel Nasser and his Free Officers had overthrown the Egyptian monarchy by military means. That success undoubtedly influenced the army in the Sudan. Six years later General Ibrahim Abboud seized power there, instituting a military régime. Yet at this time Arab Africa had only tenuous political communications with its southern fellow Africans. In the British, French and Belgian territories eyes were still fixed on metropolitan systems of government, parliamentary régimes being accepted as the ideal objective to succeed colonial rule.

In the Congo, African military power was witnessed for the first time as a political factor. The mutinies of the force publique against its European officers which immediately followed independence, together with the subsequent strikes for higher army pay, cut right across the traditions taught by the colonial rulers. It had been assumed and accepted under imperial tutelage that military forces remained outside the political arena. (This principle certainly formed part of British and Belgian metropolitan traditions; it had dubious validity in France.) What neither the African nationalists nor the colonial rulers had realized was that until political authority was firmly established, those commanding guns would also possess potential political leverage. As colonial rule itself had been based on a monopoly of force, the precedent for military politics was already established.

It was Colonel (later General) Joseph Mobutu who showed African soldiers how they could transform their potential power into reality. During the political, administrative and military chaos which followed independence in 1960, and with no more than a couple of hundred men, he took over the capital, Leopoldville. Mobutu thereby set a pattern for his fellow African soldiers which has influenced them ever since. He showed that the officer who can secure the allegiance from sufficient troops to capture the key installations of a capital city can take control of the country. As, in 1960, the army had disintegrated into small armed bands, and as no one had more troops under his control than Mobutu, it only needed political will for him to effect a simple fait accompli.

Yet, at this stage, there remained considerable attachment to the colonial tradition of non-political armed forces. Mobutu did not use his troops in 1960 to establish a military government. He intervened to stop rival politicians tearing the country to pieces. Having taken power in Leopoldville it was not long before Mobutu brought back the Kasavubu faction of politicians, first into collaboration and then into full political control. Army officers did not yet visualize themselves as ministers forming governments. They still held to the convention that this was the responsibility of civilians. It was not until five years later that Mobutu used his armed forces to take power on a long-term basis, though even then he still used the services of those politicians whom he favoured.

The second lesson learnt by African military commanders from the Congo example was the importance of securing external support or connivance for their intervention. Mobutu was able to gain the adherence of his handful of troops in 1960 because he had been supplied with the money to pay them by the United Nations. He was also helped to gather around him a loyal group of paratroops by a Moroccan general serving in the United Nations' force. Through this supply of cash and training expertise from international sources, Mobutu built the power to take a decisive part in shaping the political destinies of his country.

There were African soldiers in the Congo at this time, members of the United Nations force. In particular, there were contingents from the Ghanaian and Nigerian armies. They witnessed the power which lay in military hands when civilians were unable to operate the political institutions with authority. They saw at first hand that the colonial convention that the army was non-political did not have to be accepted in all circumstances. They noted how little resistance was raised to a determined, purposeful military intervention in political or constitutional fields. Their ideas about their rôle in their post-colonial states were profoundly affected.

It was not only in relation to Mobutu and his army that international intervention became apparent in the Congo. Previously it had been assumed that external influence in post-independence Africa would remain the prerogative of each colonial power. There was little surprise when the Belgian army emerged from its bases in the Congo to protect its nationals from the anger and brutality of Congolese troops. The Belgians might be criticized when they appeared to be supporting Moise Tshombe's secession in Katanga, but this was also to be expected from an imperial power unwilling to surrender its colonial mineral wealth. But when Congolese affairs became a matter of bitter dissension at the United Nations, and then the Americans and Russians began to intervene in the country itself, Africans realized that they were no longer insulated from the conflicts which were dividing the world.

The Americans were active in supporting a College of Commissioners composed of graduates and students which Mobutu established in 1960 to run the country under his direction. The Russians provided transport planes for Lumumba to attack secessionist Katanga. West and East were deploying the Congo situation at the United Nations and in the country itself for their own Cold War purposes.

But beneath this political conflict lay deeper reasons of economic significance. For what Africans also learnt was that the greatest danger from external intervention lay in those countries which possessed wealth of international importance. In the year before independence the Congo produced 69 per cent of the world's industrial diamonds, 49 per cent of its cobalt, nine per cent of its copper, six-and-a-half per cent of its tin, substantial quantities of uranium and 25 per cent of its palm oil. All these are vital industrial and strategic materials. Almost all of them are produced in Katanga, the province which borders Zambia, then (as Northern Rhodesia) part of the Central African Federation. It was no coincidence that Katanga tried to break away from the rest of the Congo and set up an independent existence with the help of the huge Belgian companies whose financial base is New York; nor that the Russians were prepared to help Lumumba to prevent this operation.

It was the murder of Lumumba which finally tore the veil from African eyes. There may have been, and probably was, a Lumumba myth amongst Africans. Yet, despite his unpredictable temperament, he represented the concepts of African unity, of an Africanism which would unite the inhabitants of the new state and repel the intervention of outside powers. Africans throughout the continent began to suspect the United Nations of being manipulated by the Western powers when the General Assembly recognized the delegation representing the Mobutu/Kasavubu alliance in November 1960. This decision led the Lumumbists to leave Leopoldville and attempt to build power from their base in Stanleyville (now Kisangani). Lumumba was captured by Mobutu's soldiers and imprisoned. However, his lieutenants, Gizenga and Gbenye, soon succeeded in setting up a rival government in Stanleyville, and this represented a direct threat to Mobutu, Kasavubu and their College. Fearing that the Lumumbists were demonstrating a strength which would have to be internationally recognized and that Lumumba himself might be released, the Leopoldville authorities decided in January 1961 that he should be transferred to Katanga. No sooner had he and his two fellow prisoners arrived there than they were murdered.

To Africa it now seemed clear that there was a massive conspiracy to deprive the Congo of any chance of unity, to return the country to direct or indirect colonial rule. A wave of anger swept across the continent. Lumumba in death came to represent considerably more than he had ever done in life. His murder became the symbol of a new cult, given the name "neo-colonialism". Much of Africa awoke to the fact that it could no longer expect to be treated as an international child, but had been thrust into the rough and tumble of the adult world. In future, Africa, like Asia, Latin America or Europe, would have to be prepared for foreign intervention whenever it seemed that one of the interests of a Great Power was involved in any part of the continent.

It was not long before the contagion of the Congo began to spread. At the beginning of 1963 President Sylvanus Olympio was shot by a group of Togolese ex-servicemen from the French army whom he had refused to employ in his national forces. In October of the same year Colonel (later General) Christophe Soglo intervened in the political conflicts in Dahomey, deposed President Hubert Maga and took power himself. In January 1964 mutinies in the armies of Tanganyika, Uganda and Kenya were only suppressed with the aid of British troops. A month later the

French army restored President Leon M'ba to his office in Gabon after army lieutenants had achieved a coup d'état.

So it went on throughout independent Africa, through the shocks of the Nigerian coups, the military deposition of Nkrumah, the removal of Modibo Keita, to General Idi Amin's coup against Milton Obote in Uganda in January 1971 and that of Colonel Ignatius Acheampong which removed Dr Kofi Busia from Ghana a year later. Even such traditionally stable states as Ethiopia, Morocco, Senegal and the Ivory Coast were affected, although in their cases the attempted coups were abortive.

It might be that these unconstitutional actions were contrary to the political traditions brought by the Europeans and, as they thought, instilled into African society. Yet they were not entirely foreign to African tradition. It had been customary in many African communities to change authority if the ruling individual or group appeared to dissatisfy the needs and desires of the people. Members of royal families or of rival lineages had frequently seized governmental power by force.

In modern times, however, armies had become professional. Moreover, they were only bound to governments by the ties of a political tradition which was alien to Africa. Colonial rule had been based on the deployment of military and police force, behind which there always lurked the overwhelming power of the metropolitan state. Many colonial soldiers were actually African: over 370,000 Africans served in the British army in World War II; 15,000 Africans fought for the French in Indo-China; 30,000 in Algeria, others at Suez. The colonies themselves were patrolled by armies in which the majority of the other ranks were Africans and the officers European.

At the time of independence these colonial armies were handed over to African governments. Usually the white officers recognized a duty to obey the new government's orders, but the African soldiers felt but scant allegiance to those who had led the anti-colonial campaign and now occupied the seats of office. Sometimes they came from different, often rival, communities, especially when, as was common, soldiers were recruited from particular tribal groupings. Some politicians were less well educated than newly appointed African officers. They certainly did not share the esprit de corps which characterized the military community.

In any case, the soldiers had rarely participated in the independence effort. Usually they had been on the other side, defending colonial rule against the nationalists. They had been taught a military ethic. They had been trained as the security forces of a colonial system which was essentially authoritarian. They had absorbed the contempt for politicians shared by colonial armies and administrators. The colonial tradition, based on the British public school and the French military administrative systems, was essentially hierarchical and authoritarian. As the Duke of Devonshire, when Colonial Secretary, put it: "The code which must guide the administrator in the tropics ... demands that in every circumstance and under all conditions he shall act in accordance with the traditions of an English gentleman." And the closest ally of the administrator was the soldier, black or white. Together they formed the colonial government, without question or argument.

This syndrome of powers was not, of course, peculiar to colonial rule or to Africa. It had been dominant in much of Europe before the war. It returned to France in 1958. The coup of the generals in Corsica, combined with the menacing temper of the army in Algiers, threatened a military domination of the French nation. De Gaulle's accession to power resulted from what was virtually a coup to forestall naked military government. And when the generals found that de Gaulle was not simply their puppet, they tried to overthrow him by another putsch three years later. It was largely in order to avoid being faced by the power of the army victorious in Algeria that de Gaulle entered into negotiations with the Algerian leadership.

Thus the African soldiers had European examples as well as the experience in the Congo to signpost the path to military intervention in national politics.

There was one further factor promoting the concept of the military community as an independent entity in society. Most of the African military leaders had a close relationship with each other. In the British territories they had trained together at Sandhurst; in the French they had both trained and fought alongside each other. Thus the actions of a group of officers in one state would be likely to influence those of their friends or rivals in others. Once Mobutu had taken his army into political fields, it was only a matter of time before officers in other states experimented with political action. And for each officer group which did so, there were former companions of military colleges and battlefields likely to be taunted with lack of virility if they did not follow suit. The chain reaction of military politics has lengthened ever since.

African armies had been influenced during colonial times by their experiences in taking security measures against the nationalists who inherited power at independence. They also continued to rely on the colonial state for their training, military advisers and equipment. Consequently, they tended to be critical of any policies adopted after independence which stepped outside the colonial tradition or were contrary to the interests of the former imperial power. Their sympathies were therefore usually conservative, even if their actions were unconstitutional. They could be compared with the attitude of many British Conservatives towards Ulster just before World War I. Usually, therefore, though not always, their coups were tacitly or overtly approved by the West. As this became apparent, other armies were encouraged to intervene, secure in the knowledge that they could expect recognition and support from powerful European states and the United States. Towards the end of the 1960s and into the 1970s, every African crisis brought the probability of military intervention.

Those who had been thoroughly indoctrinated in the concepts of the colonial systems were shocked by the appearance of military men on the political stage. But these consisted mainly of the older generation of professionals, lawyers, doctors, civil servants and academics. The younger people, who had grown to adulthood under independence, and especially those who had been affected by the experience of student radicalism in Europe and America, held no stake in the constitutions inherited from colonial states. They identified themselves with the international revolt against neo-colonialism, with those in Europe and Asia whom they saw fighting against Great Power intervention.

These younger people had no desire to encourage the army to intervene in politics – with the exception of that considerable section in the ex-French states who were ex-servicemen. But they recognized the incompetence of governments and did not feel that allegiance to constitutions common to their elders. They were quite prepared to use violence to overthrow the status quo. If they had no particular confidence in the ability of the army to improve on civilian government, they often recognized the younger army officers as their classmates or members of the same age-group. These young people were certainly not going to risk their lives to defend a constitution in which they did not believe against intervention by soldiers.

Little concern was felt towards the military coups during the first half of the 1960s. Most of them were unsuccessful. The 1964 mutinies in east Africa were recognized as trade-union pressures for better pay, promotion opportunities and Africanization. There was some consternation at the apparent ease with which the Tanganyikan army threatened Nyerere's government, hitherto considered the most stable in the continent. In Africa, the deposition of Ben Bella by Colonel Houari Boumedienne in 1965 was widely deplored, though in many European circles it was welcomed. The assassination of Sylvanus Olympio in 1963 brought no pleasure anywhere. Yet these were outstanding exceptions; they were offset by the general failure of military intervention, the apparent absence of political ambition amongst the soldiers even after they had achieved a coup, and, in the Sudan, of the actual return of power to civilians by the military régime.

It was from the beginning of 1966 that the military menace assumed serious proportions. Rumblings of new military ambitions were heard from late 1965. In October the army in Burundi overthrew the Monarchy. Next month General Mobutu once more intervened in the Congo, bringing the conflict between Kasavubu and Tshombe to an end by taking power himself with army support. In the same month General Soglo stepped into the Dahomey political arena for a second time, dismissed the politicians and set up a government dominated by soldiers.

The year 1966 started with military coups in the Central African Republic and Upper Volta. But it was the action of soldiers in Nigeria in the same month which really shook the world. Here, in Africa's most populous country, Britain and the West believed they possessed their most precious investment in parliamentary democracy, middle-class entrepreneurship and political stability. Nigeria was constantly cited as the outstanding success of Britain's colonial legacy. Yet in one short night Nigeria's federal prime minister and finance minister, together with two of her regional prime ministers, were assassinated. The guns of Nigerian soldiers had swept away the model imitation of Britain in Africa.

Radical voices had scarcely found breath to express the axiom that chaos must inevitably arise out of neo-colonial politics, when the second stroke fell. A month later soldiers in Ghana followed the example of their Nigerian companions. Taking advantage of Nkrumah's absence in China, a section of the army seized Accra and deposed the President. The fall of the pioneer of African independence, the symbol of African unity and resistance to neo-colonialism, certainly the best-known African in the world, brought applause from conservatives but confusion to radicals. Nkrumah disappeared into exile from the stage he had dominated for 15 years. In both Nigeria and Ghana the army was not content to overthrow the existing régime and hand power to a rival set of politicians. In each country the military forces established their own government, soldiers taking political decisions advised only by civil servants. The army was no longer satisfied with changing policies and political personnel; it now took charge of the political system itself.

The military actions in Nigeria and Ghana seemed to open floodgates to African armies. During the following five years at least one military coup took place every year, sometimes several. Moreover, the character of the coups had changed. Army officers had now found that it was possible for soldiers to govern, with the help of civil servants. This might enable them to escape from the self-renewing cycle of replacing one set of politicians with another, only to have to repeat the process when no improvement resulted. It also allowed soldiers to acquire the fruits of political office, to become presidents, ministers, ambassadors, to dispense patronage.

Yet, even so, the pattern was not entirely uniform. In Sierra Leone, for instance, whilst the 1967 officers' coup took power from the politicians, in the following year a counter coup from the ranks restored Siaka Stevens and his majority party to office. In Ghana, too, the army government deliberately prepared the country for elections which enabled it in 1969 to return power to civilians. The fact that Dr Busia's civilian government lasted only two-and-a-half years before another group of officers deposed it demonstrated the intransigence of problems which neither civilians nor military could solve, and the continuing power of those with guns.

It was in Nigeria that military intervention had the most spectacular and tragic consequences. The coup of January 1966 brought General Aguiyi Ironsi to power with a military government. Six months later Ironsi himself was deposed and murdered. The succession fell on General Yakubu Gowon. After failing to agree on a peaceful settlement of the country's constitutional structure, the army leaders themselves went to war the following year. General Gowon led the federal side, Colonel Odumegwu Ojukwu the secessionist Biafrans. For two-and-a-half years the land was torn by fratricidal strife, in which millions of people suffered from starvation, terror and death. To the outside world Nigeria became the symbol of African savagery, of the inability of Africans to govern themselves. Inside the continent the civil war symbolized the final collapse of the colonial legacy, the menace of external intervention, the dangers of Africa lapsing into the kind of mass warfare which for so long had characterized Europe. For several years, too, the Nigerian war shattered all prospects of African unity as various states supported one or another of the combatants. The fact that within a year of the war's conclusion these breaches were healed and reconciliation pursued within war-torn Nigeria itself rated much less news-space than the conflict and suffering.

Criticism of Africans from the outside world was not, however, confined to military intervention in politics. If it had been, it would have been received with more tolerance in Africa itself, where there was often acute embarrassment over the way in which armies used their coercive power without reference to any popular will. African leaders strove desperately to find means of excluding soldiers from political intervention without endangering national security.

If anything, criticism of African events in the West was harsher over political reactions than against military coups. The overthrow of the colonial inheritance, the creation of single-party states, re-organization of trade-union structures, interference with the judiciary, nationalization of foreign companies, increases in the power of the executive, changes in the rôle of the civil service, and new electoral laws, all provoked condemnation from Western politicians, journalists and academics.

It is easy to see why this should be so. Conservatives, of course, started from the premise that Africans were unfitted for self-government. They therefore sought every opportunity to support their assertion. But liberals had believed that the anti-colonial movements of the fifties and early sixties which they had supported would result in the creation of what they could recognize as "democratic" states. They genuinely saw that colonial rule was fundamentally anti-democratic. They assumed that once colonialism had been defeated, independence would produce their kind of democratic system, based on adult suffrage, free elections, a multi-party system, parliamentary government with majority-party rule and an official opposition, an independent judiciary, a non-political civil service, autonomous trade unions and freedom of assembly, association and speech. What they failed to realize was that this kind of society had been built in Britain over many centuries, in special conditions and in a specifically British environment. It has been established in very few other countries. And it was created to sustain particular social institutions, generally based on an industrialized class structure. It displays either ignorance or arrogance to claim it as the only form of "democracy".

One can understand the liberals' concern over many events which occurred in Africa during the 1960s. Nor is it just to accuse them of criticizing Africans whilst ignoring the graft, violence, authoritarianism of America, Russia, Spain, Greece, Portugal and many other developed states; for they criticized these societies too. In any case, few Africans would wish to be compared with such societies. It is deeper factors which are at stake in the liberals' criticism.

At the time of independence most nationalist leaders would have liked to have been able to sustain the kind of liberal constitutions they had inherited. But the constitutions were simply skeletons. They did not possess the social flesh to give them life. Practice in parliamentary elections, in party systems, in the niceties of parliamentary government, had been ridiculously short. In the Congo the first serious election took place the month before independence. Even in the British territories it was usually only immediately before independence that the first fully representative election took place. Until that eleventh hour, almost all Africans had lived under authoritarian colonial government. They could hardly be expected to transform themselves into a sophisticated parliamentary electorate overnight.

Moreover, the character of the parliamentary system was alien to most Africans. Although their experience varied in different societies, in general African decision-making has not been based on dialectic, on the cut and thrust of debate, with majorities and minorities, governments and opposition. It has been much nearer the Quaker method of seeking "the sense of the meeting", of finding a consensus, searching for agreement rather than for polemical conflict. In Europe, party systems have usually developed from class divisions and their expression; class formation has hardly begun in Africa. Consequently, most parties were either of the mass congress variety, created solely for the purpose of securing independence, or they polarized around the only recognized divisions: the ethnic communities. In the first instance, they had served their purpose when independence was achieved; in the second, they involved the menace of civil war. In neither case did they lend themselves to the gentlemanly pursuits of "Her Majesty's Government and Loyal Opposition".

This political system could not meet the needs of post-independence Africa. It had been largely built during the European industrial revolution, from earlier historical roots. It was essentially based on the individualism, competitiveness and class conflicts of industrial capitalism. Political rights took precedence over economic egalitarianism or social justice. And such principles as equality of representation, freedom of speech or assembly, and equality before the law, had been realized only through struggles and conflicts in European settings. They had little relevance to the Africa of the 1960s. Moreover, although those in the foreground of British public life might still assume the system to be the quintessence of democracy, this was certainly not universally accepted, even in the West. The system itself was increasingly under question, particularly from the young, who queried the validity of its democratic content. They insistently questioned whether electoral equality alone could offer the individual personal freedom in an industrial society.

Africans began to ask similar questions, although in an entirely different environment. Most Africans had found their security in a variety of communities. The family was primary, but there were also age-groups, clans, villages, and ethnic groups. Each offered security throughout life and accepted responsibility for dependants after death. It offered a totality to human existence. This social structure may have inhibited a certain degree of personal initiative, aggression and ambition; but it also obviated many social tragedies and avoided a great deal of unhappiness.

At independence Africans were tacitly asked to abandon their traditional security for an individualized society created in other continents and in totally different circumstances. It is not surprising that its attractions only lasted a few years, particularly as Africans soon found that the votes they were allowed to cast did nothing to free them from the oppression of hunger, poverty or disease.

African leaders were forced to face this fundamental issue. They were expected by their people to reform conditions of life in the new nation — especially after expectations had been raised during the anti-colonial campaigns. They were also expected to retain the social securities traditional to African society. Often the two objectives conflicted. Meanwhile, the institutions bequeathed by the colonial power obstructed the achievement of both aims. Yet if they jettisoned them they would gain notoriety abroad where they had to seek the resources needed for reform.

It was from the attempts made to solve this basic dilemma that first Nasser, Ben Bella, Nkrumah, Keita, Touré, and then Nyerere, Kaunda and Obote became the butt of criticism in the West. Detention without trial under Preventive Detention Acts was naturally offensive to liberals intent on protecting the liberty of the individual. It had been common under colonial rule and was to be used by a British government in Ulster; liberals criticized those situations too. What they did not understand was that African leaders had to balance the arbitrary detention of a number of individuals against the chances of millions of their people securing the basic needs of life essential to the most elementary forms of freedom. Of course the power of detention was open to abuse and was abused many times. Yet, with security forces inexperienced in collecting evidence, widespread fear of intimidation of witnesses and an infant legal system, the choice was often between two evils.

It was noticeable too, that criticism was concentrated on those states which were trying to effect an economic revolution, to break away from dependence on foreign capital, to discard the social structures left by the colonialists. When Ghana, Guinea or Mali detained opponents without trial, the Western press wrote headlines; when the same thing happened in the Ivory Coast, Nigeria or Senegal, little notice was taken. When Nkrumah abandoned elections, Nyerere declared a one-party state or Obote drove out his chief opponent, the Kabaka, the Western media stridently denounced them as "dictators". When similar events took place in Kenya, the Congo or Malawi, there was virtual silence. Nationalization, of course, produced typical hysteria. Whether it was Nkrumah, Touré, Nyerere, Boumedienne, Kaunda or Gadafy, echoes were constantly heard of the virulence displayed towards Nasser over the Suez Canal in 1956.

The 1960s were years of revolt in black Africa. They witnessed a confused series of attempts to open roads to national consciousness, economic development and social justice, together with the building of institutional machinery capable of converging societies towards these goals. Often the efforts were diverted by personal ambition, particularist interest, foreign interference, natural calamity. They cannot be termed years of revolution, for only rarely were philosophies evolved from which the structure of society could be basically transformed, and in these rare cases only beginnings were made. Out of the welter of experiments, failures, successes and tragedies, which infuriated Western conservatives and dismayed liberals, a few lessons may have been learnt. Some hitherto unrecognized connections between action and effect may have been observed. Yet the basic problems remained. In order to comprehend the prospects for the 1970s, it is essential to analyse the efforts made by Africans during the 1960s in the context of the fundamental issues which face them.

If opinion outside Africa was generally critical of African civil wars, military coups and constitutional changes, over southern Africa, which also frequently filled the headlines, it was remarkably ambivalent. Throughout the world, except amongst American racialists, British right-wing Conservatives and fascists anywhere, the apartheid system of South Africa was condemned. Only slightly less condemnation was expressed for Rhodesia's imitation apartheid and Portugal's colonial policy in Africa.

This almost universal rejection of apartheid was, however, expressed almost entirely verbally, rarely in actions. The depth of its sincerity can be measured by a Labour minister's exhortation for increased British trade with South Africa, a Conservative Prime Minister's determination to supply the Republic with arms even at the risk of destroying the Commonwealth, the constant stream of weapons which flowed from France to the South Africans, and the massive capital invested by Britain, America and other Western states in the land of apartheid. Only at the beginning of the 1970s was any concern shown in the West for giving practical aid to the opponents of apartheid when the Scandinavians, the British Labour Party and some German Social Democrats began to provide a little help to the freedom fighters of southern Africa.

It was the drama of military coups, revolts and racial clashes which characterized Africa to outside opinion during the sixties. But Africans, and those genuinely concerned with Africa and its rôle in the evolution of human society, were repeatedly querying why the continent was so beset by conflicts, violence, suffering and bloodshed. They did not need to be told that this has often seemed endemic to the human condition; this increased rather than diminished interest in the African experience and its causes. To understand the events, to isolate their origins and to place them in the wider human context demands an examination of social, economic and political relationships as they proceeded along often tortuous paths through the post-independence maze. For it was from these that arose those more sensational vicissitudes which gave Africa her reputation during the 1960s.

D

3

"Tribalism"

In a world where Catholic fights Protestant in Northern Ireland, Pakistanis massacre Bengalis, Croats revolt against Serbs, American blacks wage a continual struggle against whites, Quebec agitates for separation from Canada, it seems somewhat superfluous to point the finger of "tribalism" at Africa. Tribalism, communalism, ethnicity, whichever nomenclature is preferred, has broken through the surface of "national" societies in all continents. In addition to the open conflicts, a variety of separatist movements, based on religious, linguistic or cultural affinities, have begun to agitate within nation-states, demanding some form of autonomy. The Welsh, Irish, Scots, the Flemish and Walloons, the Cypriot Greeks and Turks, the Malays and Chinese, the Hindus, Muslims, Tamils and Nagas, all illustrate this point.

So the tribalism or communalism which has been displayed in post-independence Africa is merely part of an international trend. As in other continents, it has often led to bloodshed.

In Africa communal separatism can be directly attributed to the imperial policies of European powers. When the continent was divided between the British, German, French, Belgian, Italian and Portuguese empires following the Berlin Conference in 1884–85, no account was taken of the African communities. Some were divided between rival Europeans, others were thrust within the same boundary, even though they had little in common and often a history of conflict with each other. The ancient state of Bakongo illustrates the former process. Eventually its inhabitants, despite their common language, customs and traditions, were divided between Portuguese Angola, Belgian Congo, French Congo and French Gabon. Nigeria is an example of the latter practice. There the Muslim Hausa-Fulani of the north were placed under the same administration as their traditional pagan enemies in the Middle Belt, the partially Christianized Ibo of the east, and the mixture of Christian, Muslim and pagan Yoruba in the west. Many smaller communities, such as the Efik, Ibibio and Ijaw peoples of the Niger delta, were also enclosed within this imperial frontier. Even the large tribal communities themselves were actually composed of many small groups, not all of which accepted a common allegiance.

These frontiers and the colonial states they delineated were therefore artificial European units, created by the imperial powers according to consideration of their own strength vis-à-vis each other; they bore no relation to the history, ethnic cohesion or traditions of the Africans living within them.

When African nationalism began to develop from a base of anti-colonial sentiment, its leaders had little choice but to accept the colonial boundaries as drawn by the imperialists. State machinery and infrastructure had been tailored by colonial rule to provide the administration of each unit. Education, political institutions, authority and economic instruments were all geared to each separate territory. Moreover, anti-colonial agitation and organization had to be designed to gain political power from each distinct colonial administration. For this purpose some sense of national consciousness had to be engendered. Many African leaders fully realized that the units they aimed to govern were artificial and often so heterogeneous as to invite separatist ambitions. But to try and redraw the frontiers at the moment of independence would have been to produce chaos; by the time that they had assumed office, vested interests in maintaining the boundaries of the state were too strong for adjustment to be feasible.

In any case, it was hoped that the mobilization of anti-colonial feelings itself would help to promote national consciousness. One crucial feature of anti-colonial agitation was the effort to engender and then express a popular will. This could only be achieved within the structure of a putative nation. As the appeal was made to the single, over-riding principle of self-government, it was aimed to create an allegiance superior to that of all smaller communities. The anti-colonialists based their tactics on what history had taught them was the method by which the nation-states had come into existence elsewhere. They deliberately set out to persuade their people of the advantages of a pyramidal structure of loyalties, in which allegiance progressively deepened as it rose towards the summit, with fidelity to the state taking precedence at the peak.

The Africans did not have time to wait for this process to be accomplished organically, as elsewhere. Not only had they to create the vision, however shadowy, for the purpose of their pre-independence political campaigns; but once independence was achieved, national consciousness became the keystone to survival for the new states.

The anti-colonialists gained a certain degree of success in projecting some concept of the principle amongst their followers. A sense of nationality was stimulated by such methods as creating an awareness of Africa's history, with particular reference to the medieval states. The adoption of ancient names for new states, like Ghana and Mali, formed part of this tactic. Glorification of the past is always partially spurious; but as an instrument for the stimulation of national pride it is universally effective. In Africa's case it was especially important in combating the influence of European history teaching which, in its ethnocentricity, had totally ignored African achievements.

This success perhaps only applied to the educated minority. Of equal and more far-reaching significance was the effort to extend the national concept to illiterate and semi-literate masses in town and countryside. Here the effect was more superficial. The usual tactic was to relate issues of grievance to colonial rule. This clearly raised dangers for post-independence governments which were inevitably expected to remedy them once colonial rulers had disappeared. Yet it served the purpose of nationalist campaigns. In towns like Accra or Nairobi the unemployed and ex-servicemen were given a nationalist focus for their discontent. In the rural areas Arab and Berber fought a common battle against the French in Algeria, whilst Nyerere was persuading a wide variety of Tanganyikan communities that their husbandry grievances could only be met by combining within his nationalist party.

Yet the extent to which this sense of responsibility had penetrated society may be judged from two examples. In 1956 a general election was held in Ghana over the issue of independence which was to follow in the next year. Nkrumah's party won, gaining a substantial majority of seats and 57 per cent of the votes cast. But as a mere 50 per cent of the electorate had voted, and as less than 30 per cent of those eligible had registered for the voters' roll, it can be seen that only a tiny proportion of the adult population was actually participating in the vital issue of independence. Political mobilization on the national stage had still only affected the minority.

In Tanganyika Julius Nyerere had built Africa's most widely diffused and unified nationalist movement. Yet when a republican form of government was introduced in 1962 and the population was asked to choose the first president, only about a quarter of eligible adults registered and just over 60 per cent of the registered electorate actually voted.

Ghana and Tanganyika were two of the most politically conscious African societies. If this was the degree of national awareness in them, how much lower it must have been in most of the rest of the continent. This should not be mistaken for an absence of political interest or involvement. The lesson was more subtly significant than that. Most Africans have traditionally been intimately involved in the governance of their societies. But, despite the experience of colonial administration and the exhortations of their nationalists, they continued to identify themselves with their local communities. To the majority, centralized national politics were remote, marginal to their lives. Which implied that as yet they also had little concept of the nation, and therefore but a weak sense of allegiance towards it.

The dominant feature of African social life was, and still is, that the vast majority of inhabitants find their needs catered for in global societies of comparatively small size. These are commonly called "tribes", but that is such a loose term, applied to so many disparate communities, that it has ceased to have any specific meaning. Probably "ethnic groups" comes closest to a valid definition of a diffuse subject.

Africans have always lived in a variety of small communities, forming a set of concentric circles of which the largest is the ethnic group. Extended families, age-groups, kinship bodies, clans, villages, all represent component parts of this largest group. In different parts of the continent the threads of relationship vary from tight webs to widely stretched fabric, according to the relative concentration of population. These groups are distinguished by a common language, historical experience, occupied land, technology and social institutions. In short, they can be termed "global" societies, within which their members find all their spiritual and temporal needs from before birth to after death. They are recognized as entities by their neighbours and have specific relations with other similar societies.

These societies are not static. There has been a constant merging, penetration, assimilation and hiving off over the centuries, whilst many of them have moved their location under pressure of land hunger, shifting cultivation or external dangers. Under colonialism administrators frequently interfered with them, supporting or deposing leaders, classifying them as though they were permanently stable, imposing new technologies and institutions. Yet they have remained remarkably resilient through the vicissitudes of centuries.

The nationalists were trying to create a new, alternative global society which could supersede the traditional. It is doubtful to what extent they succeeded before independence; but they had one important advantage. During the period of decolonization world prices for primary products were high. The revenues which accrued from exports therefore allowed the first generation of nationalists to offer tempting social and economic gifts. It seemed for a time that nationalist propaganda was valid, that as colonial rulers withdrew the new nation-states could vouchsafe considerable improvements in the necessities of life.

After independence, however, world prices began to fluctuate wildly. The general trend was downward, sometimes, as with cocoa and sisal, a very steep decline. If copper rose to new heights during the late sixties, providing Zambia and the Congo with unpredictable windfalls, it also fell catastrophically at the beginning of the seventies.

It seems probable that the effort to achieve supremacy of national over local allegiance would have failed in any case to secure widespread acceptance in such a short period. The imbalance of economic life and the economic patterns bequeathed by the colonial powers presented too many difficulties for the rewards of the national concept to be sustained for long. But the collapse of export revenues ensured its early demise. Expectations of continually rising social and economic benefits were quickly dashed.

The reaction was inevitable. People who had only been half-convinced of the superiority of national over ethnic allegiance, especially in the rural areas, returned to their traditional local security. Again, this was a universal trend amongst millions of peoples in all the continents who felt threatened by various aspects of mid-twentieth-century life; but its impact on newly developing states was particularly disruptive.

In one sense the impact of national government itself reinforced the trend towards strengthened ethnic ties. Because of the loyalties developed within these communities, responsibility was shared between all their members. This pertained throughout the extended family, so that there were virtually no widows, orphans, abandoned children, destitute aged. It applied to newcomers in the towns, where there was always a bed, food and money available from a kinsman. To varying degrees it was projected into politics, in general communities being solidly attached to a single political party, though there were noteworthy exceptions, as amongst the Luo of Kenya. Inevitably, therefore, when a national government had to be formed, ethnic influences entered into consideration. Not only did kinsmen expect to be appointed as ministers, but many more advanced claims to the many perquisites available for allocation by the group in office.

It came to be widely considered, often erroneously, that governments were formed by a particular ethnic group and that their patronage would be used in the interest of that community. This inevitably provoked jealousies and rivalry from those groups which believed themselves to be excluded. Because the national government possessed such concentrated powers in allocating social preferment, economic opportunity and employment, even at times in deciding between life and death, there were continual pressures to gain control of this new and powerful machine. As it seemed that the only road to secure command of government was through communal action, the very powers accorded to national governments at independence themselves induced a revival of ethnic consciousness. Paradoxically, of course, this trend led to a diminution in the much-coveted authority of government.

The rivalry of ethnic groups for control of authority can be seen as a continuity from tradition. It had often been customary for power in African societies to change hands as a result of group action. To many Africans the colonial era simply represented a period in which new and stronger rulers had succeeded in asserting their authority. When they departed another set of rulers replaced them. If they did not succeed in providing for the interests of the people, it seemed natural that they should be removed and another group given an opportunity. In consequence, in many states, changes in government were seen by the people concerned to be ethnic alternatives. In Sierra Leone, for example, the Mende of Albert Margai were replaced by the Temne of Siaka Stevens; in Ghana, Kofi Busia, supported by the Akan, succeeded Nkrumah and his coalition of Ga and Ewe. In no case was the identification between ethnic group and political party by any means complete; but it was sufficiently influential to be accepted as a crucial factor by a large proportion of the people.

The most successful leaders, at least so far as survival is concerned, were those who were skilful at ethnic arithmetic. Houphouet-Boigny in the Ivory Coast, Senghor in Senegal, Nyerere in Tanzania, Kenyatta in Kenya, and Kaunda in Zambia all retained power without a break from independence to the early seventies, partly because they were able to balance ethnic ambitions in their appointment. Ethnicity did not necessarily demand changes in government. It was only when one group believed that it was being discriminated against that conflict became inevitable. When resources are scarce and the building of a new road, a school, a water-pipe, the siting of a factory or hospital, is believed to be decided according to ethnic considerations, resentment may be provoked. It is then that local feelings tend to coalesce within the group, leading eventually to demands that central authority be changed.

The contrast in the experience of this ethnic problem can be seen most starkly between Kenya and Nigeria. In the early sixties most observers would have forecast that Kenya was the most likely new state to disintegrate under the centrifugal pressures of ethnic conflict. The anti-colonial campaign had been led from the start by the Kikuyu, culminating in the Mau Mau revolt. Although this had resulted in some dissension within the Kikuyu community itself, it had hardened the temper of the leadership and strengthened communal consciousness. Fear of Kikuyu domination was so strong within Kenya that before independence smaller groups insisted on a regional type of constitution. Meanwhile, there was no reason to suppose that other powerful communities would accept Kikuyu leadership. The Kamba, with a long military tradition, had shown ambivalence during Mau Mau. Most Luo had pointedly remained aloof from the conflict. Their most famous son, Oginga Odinga, had remained at liberty, whilst their most skilful politician, Tom Mboya, had seemed by some to be using the emergency as a ladder for his own fame. When one adds to this catalogue of potential discord the fact that many Kenyan Africans had fought against Mau Mau, the prospects of peace in post-independence Kenya seemed precarious.

Yet, most remarkably, under the universally accepted leadership of Jomo Kenyatta, at one time the personification of all most feared from the Kikuyu, Kenya created one of the best examples in the continent of multi-ethnic stability. The regional constitution soon gave way to unitary government, with a leadership drawn from all the major groups. Ronald Ngala, the arch-exponent of regionalism, became a trusted minister, along with his fellow-Kalenjin, Arap Moi. Paul N'gei, who had formed a largely Kamba party before independence, soon found satisfaction under Kenyatta's national standard. Mboya and Odinga from the Luo joined forces with young Kikuyu intellectuals, such as Charles Njonjo and Mwai Kibaki, as well as with others who had fought in the forests. There was a European, Bruce McKenzie, and an Afro-Asian, Joseph Murumbi, who actually became Vice-President. It would hardly have been possible to demonstrate more clearly that national sentiments had taken precedence over localism or ethnic rivalry.

Much of this comparative harmony was due to the immense prestige and skilful political diplomacy of the President, Jomo Kenyatta. He recruited men from different ethnic groups, deeply suspicious of each other, and welded them into a national team. He carefully balanced group representation and insisted that shares in development be allocated to every area. A most remarkable transformation took place in race relations. The man who had been viciously reviled by Europeans as an agent of Satan became the popular president on whom the white community relied for their security, a beloved fellow-farmer. If some degree of antagonism persisted towards the Asian community, it was almost entirely confined to its commercial activities and its alien allegiance, for it did not extend to Asians who took out Kenyan citizenship. Kenya thus demonstrated the possibility of drawing together all ethnic communities from within African society and including the non-African, into a national polity.

Only one serious rift appeared. When Odinga became dissatisfied with government policy and believed that he was being outflanked within the governing party, it seemed for a time that he might raise the Luo against the coalition. He resigned from the Vice-Presidency, in which he had succeeded Murumbi, and created a new party. Many Luo followed him, partly because of his standing in their community and partly because of suspicions that, despite the apparent national character of the régime, it was actually controlled by Kikuyu. But Odinga's revolt did not last long. It was suppressed by detention, but, more significantly, it was not long before its leaders came to make their peace with government and party.

It is true that this remarkable degree of unity centred almost entirely on the personality of Kenyatta. He was assisted by considerable foreign investment and lucrative tourism. Beneath the President there was constant intrigue to secure the succession, into which ethnic mobilization frequently entered. There was also the underlying fear that ethnic conflict might erupt at the conclusion of Kenyatta's presidency. Yet, whatever the portents, for the decade following independence Kenya had discovered a degree of national solidarity which no one could have foreseen.

Nigeria provided the contrary example. Here stability was anticipated. Nigeria was expected to justify the basic principles of Britain's decolonization policy. The Nigerians seemed to adopt readily the trappings of the parliamentary system, British legal niceties and the traditions of the civil service. Africa's most populous country, with 50–60 million inhabitants, seemed set fair to become an African "little England".

It may be that the optimism which was expressed in the West over Nigerian prospects was based rather on her commercial and social life than on political realities. The conventional view in the West was that Nigeria could be relied on to welcome and defend foreign investment, that she had a well-established middle class, little trouble from her trade unions and few radical voices. The combination of a gentlemanly feudal north, a landowning and voraciously capitalist west, and the clever, Christian-educated east seemed to offer even rosier prospects to London than those established between Paris and France's client Africans. Almost all the politicians were not only Western-orientated, but engaged in some form of commercial or professional relationship with their Western counterparts. The parliamentary and governmental system could therefore be relied on to maintain the colonial institutions they had inherited.

Two factors were obscured or ignored. This political-commercial system provided ample opportunity for personal accumulation of wealth in a country where the vast mass of the population was extremely poor. West Africa has been steeped in the market economy for many centuries. Many of its people have been reared on the doctrines of commercial morality. It was therefore accepted that leading personalities were entitled to greater rewards than ordinary people – but on one condition. To earn their prizes they had to show successful leadership, and success was measured by the benefits they brought to their people. Much, if not all, the ostentation and high living displayed by Nigerian politicians would have been excused if there had been distinct signs of improvement in the lives of a large section of the inhabitants. As poverty remained unrelieved, in some cases deepening, the flaunting of opulence by intemperate politicians became insufferable. The hostility they provoked extended beyond the individuals to the system they had used for their personal gain. The political institutions themselves became identified with the activities of those who had misused them; parliamentary democracy itself became tainted in the eyes of many Nigerians.

Because the Nigerian state had been constructed on federal foundations, with four regional parliaments and governments in addition to those at the centre, and because the regional institutions had been abused in the same way as the national organs, this disillusion was felt across the nation. When the first military coup occurred in January 1966, there was scant regret for the demise of the whole system.

Yet a coup of this kind invokes a sense of insecurity, especially in a country which had believed itself to be modelled on British traditions. It was out of the welter of uncertainty following the coup that emerged the second neglected factor.

It had long been evident that Nigeria was not composed of one nation, but rather of a number of societies, each of which could claim the attributes of nationality. The Hausa-Fulani of the north, the Ibo from the east and the Yoruba in the west formed the largest ethnic groupings. But there were many others, like the Tiv, the Ibibio, the Nupe, the Ijaw, the Edo, the Kanuri, smaller, but also with a distinct history. European colonialism probably served these societies more scurvily than any in the continent. By bringing them together under the same administration in 1914, the British government compelled communities with different cultures, religions, languages, often with a history of mutual conflict, to live within an unnatural straitjacket. In the absence of alien interference there might have been some chance for these societies to evolve into their own forms of statehood. Their leaders could then have decided to what extent they should co-operate, and what kind of inter-state relations would best serve their respective interests. The British system, which imposed separate regional administrations within a single state, yet never encouraged a common national consciousness, ensured the worst of both worlds. Ethnic separatism was often stimulated by colonial rule, but was always forced to express itself within a structure of a fictitious common nationality.

Inevitably, the state system itself was subjected to intolerable pressures. A man like Nnamdi Azikiwe illustrated the impossible dilemma. On the one hand he was trying to build genuine national organs, such as the Youth Movement and then his National Council of Nigeria and the Cameroons; on the other he could assert, "The God of Africa has created the Ibo nation to lead the children of Africa from the bondage of the ages." The natural continuity of this dichotomy was witnessed in the civil war when Azikiwe first supported Ojukwu in his attempt to create a separate Ibo state and then changed sides to help Gowon in his "One Nigeria" campaign.

If the British had created a situation in which neither ethnic nationalism nor a common Nigerian nationalism could grow, Nigerian leaders themselves played their parts in ensuring that the dilemma should be resolved in tragedy. Before World War II had concluded, contending ethnic associations were being formed. The Pan-Ibo Federal Union and the Ibibio State Union were followed by the Yoruba organization, Egbe Omo Oduduwa; some northerners had formed a Bauchi Improvement Association as early as 1943. Cultural interests were intertwined with political ambition in these ethnic bodies. From the end of the war until independence in 1960, political decisions were increasingly coloured by rival ethnic considerations. And the regional constitution under which independence was achieved, which enshrined ethnicity in its federal structure, had as many Nigerian as British parents.

After independence the federation was governed by a coalition between northerners and easterners, with the westerners as an official opposition. But there were constant strains within the federal coalition and inside the regions themselves. It became increasingly clear that the fruits of office were so rich that political life was dominated by ruthless ambition to gain the power to harvest them. This was particularly so in the wealthy west; rivalry for office in Ibadan became so bitter that violence, fraud and bribery had come to be the normal practices of public life in the mid-sixties. The gangsterism which resulted finally disillusioned most Nigerians with parliamentary democracy and paved the way for acceptance of the military coup of 1966. Attempts by the politicians to use sections of the army to aid their personal ambitions hastened the soldiers' intervention.

So when the army struck there was little public respect left for the political system which they destroyed. Yet without it, Nigerians who had been brought up in British customs felt threatened and helpless. They had never abandoned their traditional ethnic relationships for the larger nationalism. Now they quickly turned back to the communities in which they had always found the greater part of their security. Ethnic allegiance suddenly grew stronger than ever before.

The conflict which ensued hardly qualified for the term "civil war". It was fought between contending societies sufficiently homogeneous to be considered as nations. There was little of the dissension within families, villages or other communities normal to civil wars, although some Ibo remained aloof, continuing to live virtually unmolested within the federation. But the war itself represented a specific attempt by the vast majority of the Ibo people to break from the rest of Nigeria and form their own nation-state. During the course of the preliminary quarrels which finally erupted into warfare, the same secessionist policy was seriously considered by the north; and even after the fighting had started, there was a possibility that the west would follow the Ibo example.

For the fact was that after the initial military coup ethnic suspicions rapidly intensified. It came to be believed in the north that the coup represented an Ibo attempt to seize control of the central government. Many of the leading northern personalities had been assassinated; most of the rebel officers were Ibo; the new head of state, General Ironsi, was an Ibo. These suspicions, whether true or false, bred rumours. In turn, these led to brutal massacres of Ibo living in the north. The Ibo were convinced that only separate statehood could protect their society. The ethnic crisis, latent since the shotgun wedding of 1914, had burst into nationalistic fury.

Yet although the Nigerian war arose from ethnic conflict it is remarkable that its course and its aftermath never degenerated into genocide. There may have been individuals who felt an urge to exterminate the societies of their opponents, but they never gained control on either side. Some sense of a common Nigerian relationship persisted. Although there were atrocities on both sides, there was also a considerable amount of fraternization amongst the soldiers, who had after all lived together as members of the same army. The federal government's willingness to allow its opponents to be supplied with food and medical aid during the conflict also provided most unusual testimony to this spirit. It became increasingly evident that the quarrel was between cousins, if not brothers. As each of the communities proved its resilience by preserving its identity under these extreme pressures, mutual respect grew, until by the end of the war it had become clear to most that they would have to try again to live together.

The Nigerian tragedy brought into the sharpest relief the cohesive strength of ethnic communities within newly independent African states. It demonstrated their mutual suspicions, their potential centrifugal instincts, their debilitating influence on the process of nation-building. It also illustrated other, often contrary, factors. It revealed that the smaller ethnic groups could also play an important unifying rôle when the opportunity arose. In Nigeria, the Tiv, the Ibibio, Ijaw and Efik, along with a variety of smaller communities, took leading rôles during the war. They demonstrated their conviction that the interests of their people would be best protected by preserving the unity of Nigeria. They showed a resolve to abolish the domination of the great communal groupings. And they proved that they could supply personalities with a distinct contribution to make to Nigeria's leadership. (Gowon, for instance, comes from a minority community in the north; many of his colleagues from other small groups.)

The Nigerian war also revealed that the experience of the ethnic groups in living within the same polity had not been entirely negative. Trading contacts, relations within religions, life in the military forces, service in the administration, even common political experiences, all to some degree cut across ethnic separatism. It may have needed a war to reveal to Nigerians themselves the extent to which such influences had affected them; if so, they left the country with a positive legacy, however bitter the experience required to uncover it.

In widely varying degrees Nigeria's experiences were repeated across the continent. In Uganda, the dominance of the Baganda delayed independence; it was only reduced by Obote's military action against the Kabaka after independence had been achieved. Obote's deposition was followed by Amin's persecution of the Acholi and Langi. Zanzibar was the scene of bitter strife between African and Afro-Arab communities. The Arabs and Berbers of Algeria co-operated to secure French withdrawal but then resumed their traditional hostility. In Chad and the Sudan, warfare between northern Muslims and southern pagan-Christians was waged for several years, in the former case with participation by French troops. The Eritreans fought against over-rule by Ethiopians, Ndebele and Shona refused to forge a united opposition to white Rhodesians, the Hutu and Tutsi killed each other in Rwanda and Burundi. But perhaps the most subtle case history was that of Zambia. The anti-colonial movement here had split before independence. Although its division was caused mainly by policy and personality factors, it had been followed by ethnic rivalry. The Tonga of the south usually supported Harry Nkumbula, the older nationalist, and his African National Congress. Many of the Bemba-speaking groups of the north followed Kenneth Kaunda and Simon Kapwepwe and their United National Independence Party, which had hived off from the Congress.

Yet the Tonga were a comparatively pacific, hard-working, agricultural community. Although the ANC leaders often seemed irresponsible, particularly in their alliance with the white settler party and their flirtation with Tshombe and his Katanga secessionists in the Congo, there was little violence between the two Zambian parties. The greater danger arose from ethnic rivalry within UNIP itself. After independence this factor often threatened the stability of Kaunda's government and party. On one occasion, in 1968, sickened by its intensity at his party conference, he actually resigned and had to be persuaded to resume leadership of party, government and state. (For a fuller discussion of this see Chapter 9.)

It is clear, therefore, that ethnicity, or "tribalism", has presented very grave problems to those African leaders attempting to stimulate national consciousness, build nation-states and search for the means of development. Yet it would be false to regard ethnic loyalties as wholly negative for these purposes. The cohesion natural to ethnic groups can enable them to take experimental risks insured by a sense of collective security. This can be a valuable asset in the modernizing process. Membership of ethnic groups has also been important in linking city and countryside. Even though there have often been jealousies as urban inhabitants seemed to be gaining increased advantages at the expense of the rural population, the conflict between the two societies was never as sharply defined as appeared from statistics. Every countryman has a kinsman in the town, every townsman retains a stake in the countryside. The urban workers and the peasants were members of the same community, accustomed to helping each other, observing mutual responsibilities.

It was perhaps in mainland Tanzania that these positive aspects of ethnicity were utilized most deliberately. It has often been said that Nyerere was fortunate in never being assailed by the menace of tribalism. The common reason given is that Tanzania has no large, potentially dominant tribes. This is inaccurate. The Sukuma, for example, are almost as numerous as the Kikuyu of Kenya. But Nyerere succeeded during the anti-colonial campaigns in associating each communal discontent or ambition with the single cause of "uhuru" or "freedom". Once independence was attained, he and his colleagues, instead of regarding ethnic communities as a threat to the state, enlisted their special qualities in the practical tasks of nation-building, in communal responsibilities and efforts. It is true that regional imbalance has always proved a problem: but Nyerere demonstrated that, in certain circumstances, ethnicity can play a uniquely constructive rôle in the creation of nationhood.

4

Social Dilemmas

Anti-colonial nationalists taught their compatriots to expect new worlds once independence was achieved. The 1951 election manifesto of Nkrumah's Convention Peoples' Party (CPP) called for "A unified system of free compulsory elementary, secondary and technical education up to 16 years of age. A free national health service. A high standard housing programme. A piped-water supply in all parts of the country. A national insurance scheme." Tom Mboya of Kenya asserted that "Under colonial rule, little attention has been paid to the need to invest in education, health, technical training, and general community development for Africans ... Self-government and independence open great possibilities for economic and social development." Senghor wrote of his intention to develop "co-operation, not collectivist but communal"; Nasser enthused the masses with the slogan "Unity, Order, Work"; Nyerere used the moment of independence to assure his citizens that "we ourselves can lift from our own shoulders the burdens of poverty, ignorance and disease."

Thus most Africans expected the substitution of indigenous for colonial rule to bring improved living conditions, accompanied by a reduction of privilege, a greater sense of equality and communal welfare. There is every reason to believe that the nationalist leaders were entirely sincere in their propaganda. Most of them exhibited a high degree of idealism, often of martyrdom, in their efforts to remove colonialism and replace it with a new society not only self-governing but imbued with the spirit of social justice and communal co-operation.

Yet, only four years after independence, Nkrumah was attacking "a new ruling class of self-seekers and careerists", Sékou Touré had to warn his followers against "aventures personnelles", a Nigerian writer asserted that in his country "a small privileged group lives in comfort and even luxury. They enjoy the fruits of office and make fortunes through their association with foreign business and other interests ... This small group of privileged men employ every method – from imprisonment through blackmail to bribery – in defence of the present system because their wealth and fortunes are tied up with the status quo."

The growth of a wealthy, privileged African élite following independence was more ostentatious in west Africa than in the eastern countries of the continent. Yet even in Tanzania, one of Africa's poorest nations, where idealism reached its highest point, Nyerere had to issue a code of conduct for his leaders less than six years after independence. This code was embodied in legislation which forbade any leading public figure from holding directorships or shares in a private company, owning houses for rent, or receiving more than one salary. The President himself set an example when he sold an old house he owned in Dar es Salaam and his wife gave her poultry farm to a co-operative village. His dictum was "If we say we have to develop, it must be clear to the people that the benefits are going to the people themselves." Yet, even in Tanzania, the fact that a privileged élite had established itself was demonstrated by the necessity for such legislation.

During the first decade of independence a small coterie of comparatively wealthy Africans established itself in every new state. Its life-style was that of the former European rulers. Sometimes an American element was introduced by those who had been to universities in the United States. Cadillacs were to be seen parked outside American-style hotels. In French-speaking Africa the influence of Paris was all-pervading, even to the perfumes, jewellery and clothes worn by women, and the cafés and bistros along African boulevards. In the English-speaking states similar imitations were apparent, the most extreme being the spectacle of top hats and morning coats in certain west African countries.

Most Africans might have been ruled by Europeans for no more than about 70 years; but the impact of that rule had been more profound than any earlier external influence. Europeans brought with them a mechanical technology which fundamentally changed African life, at least in the towns and cities. It made possible an accumulation of wealth on hitherto unknown scales, and it offered opportunities for the expenditure of such wealth in previously unexplored directions.

This imported technology was accompanied by new social customs. Large stores like Kingsway in west Africa, Woolworths, O.K. Bazaars, invited customers to purchase goods from Europe which cost valuable foreign exchange to import. Garages sold expensive foreign cars. Hotels offered exotic European or American dishes. I quote the example of the Edinburgh Hotel in Kitwe, Zambia, where, on each occasion I have visited its dining-room, caviar, specially flown from Iran, has been on the menu! Banks not only encouraged customers to keep accounts, but provided for overdrafts or loans, foreign companies appointed agents, civil servants and academics were given loans for houses or cars, granted expenses for overseas leave and guaranteed pensions.

This way of life was based on the demands made by Europeans who came formerly to serve colonial governments. In his report to the government of Zambia in the year of independence, Dudley Seers, the international economist, noted that "In every town there are Europeans enjoying in plain view vastly superior standards of living, housing, education and medical care. This very small minority have the best-paid jobs in the mines and railways, work the most prosperous farms and own nearly all the financial wealth. They also hold almost every senior position in the civil service." But, as he added, "the Government is no longer in European hands ... Economic and social power has been abruptly divorced from political power."

European colonial policy during the period after the end of World War II, when decolonization gradually became inevitable, was to recruit the collaboration of those Africans with sufficient education to form something resembling a European middle class. The French pursued this policy most vigorously by bringing a selection of Africans into French political and cultural society. Houphouet-Boigny, once feared in Paris as a dangerous radical, was guided into the rôle of a minister in the French government. Léopold Senghor, of Senegal, became an honoured poet in French literary circles. Even Sékou Touré was sedulously courted by French trade unions, although he maintained sufficient African roots to reject the temptations offered by de Gaulle.

The Anglo-Saxons of Britain were not prepared to take their policy to the logical lengths of their Latin fellow-colonialists. The idea of African MPs sitting on Westminster benches would have shocked Labour and Conservative members alike. Yet in the colonies themselves similar tactics to those of the French were followed. In west Africa and in the Central African Federation especially, the future was held to depend on success in fostering a middle class of Africans accepting standards which would guarantee a continuation of British institutions after independence. Schools and universities and City firms vied with each other to inculcate British customs into the young colonial élite. And when constitutions were revised in order to assuage the rising demand for elected representation in colonial legislatures, franchise qualifications always included a wealth test.

So, on the morrow of independence, African leaders found their states already largely in the hands of those who had been trained socially as well as technically by their former colonial masters. Many of the leaders themselves had been similarly indoctrinated, although some of them recognized that the declared aims of independence could not be achieved until many of the European social mores had been discarded.

Yet this was easier to declare than to achieve. In the circumstances described above by Dudley Seers, how could African leaders resist the

E

demands of their own people to enjoy the privileges which they had been accustomed to witness as the prerogatives of Europeans?

The dilemma can be illustrated by a personal example. When I was on the staff of Fourah Bay University College in Sierra Leone shortly after the independence of that country, every staff member was entitled to take "home leave" for themselves and their families every year. "Home leave" for the British staff members meant returning to Britain for about three months every summer, the fares of the whole family being paid by the university, as well as a normal salary. Yet "home leave" was interpreted in exactly the same manner by the African staff members. In order that there should be no discrimination, they also travelled with their families to Britain at the expense of the university. So one could discuss London, Oxford, Cambridge or Durham with African fellow-staff members, but few of them had ever visited neighbouring Liberia or Guinea. Some, indeed, had never been into the interior of their own country, having lived their lives around Freetown or in another particular district.

Or the point can be demonstrated in a more general manner. I knew several of Nkrumah's close associates in Britain long before independence. They generally lived simple, humble lives in bed-sitters or as students in hostels. They all expressed egalitarian, socialist beliefs. Yet when I visited them in Accra after independence they had built huge mansions, often resembling palaces. Nkrumah was well aware of the dangers inherent in such ostentation. He inveighed against it in his dawn broadcasts from 1961 onwards, castigating those amongst his own colleagues who were "practising imperialism in their own land". He dismissed his two major lieutenants, Botsio and Gbedemah, on this count. Yet he was never able to eradicate such displays of privilege. The meagre effect of his strictures was witnessed in the notorious affair of the golden bed ordered by another minister, Krobo Edusei, not long afterwards.

There were Africans who foresaw the dangers which could arise from such situations. Writing several years before his own Malawi became independent, Dunduzu Chisiza displayed a remarkable perspicacity in warning against those very social pitfalls which were to trap many African régimes. He had, in fact, spent much of his time when imprisoned at Gwelo in Southern Rhodesia envisaging the difficulties which would have to be faced after independence. He was engrossed in this task when I visited him there in 1959. As we sat on a rough bench in the prison courtyard he was much more concerned to discuss these issues of the future than his own personal plight. Tragically, Chisiza was killed in an accident before he could realize his full potential as one of Africa's most courageous thinkers. I have no doubt that he would either have exercised a restraining influence on his leader, Hastings Banda, who shared our conversation that afternoon in Gwelo, or have gone into exile like his brother and other comrades who had no sympathy with the personality cult developed by the Malawian president.

Chisiza's analysis of the social dangers facing Africans after the conclusion of colonial rule is worth studying in some detail. It presents the outlook of many younger-generation Africans against what has sometimes become a ritual acceptance of European values in most African states during the years immediately following independence. This outlook forms an essential element for an understanding of the execution and the acceptance of most of the coups and revolutions which have overthrown so many African régimes during the past decade.

Chisiza began his social analysis by examining Western experts' theories that basic African social customs would have to be changed if economic development were to succeed. Although he admitted the logic of such recommendations, he shrewdly pointed out that some of them "would greatly endanger the psychological welfare of the indigenous masses". Among the illustrations which he gave of these difficulties, the most pertinent is that "the encouragement of individualism among people who derive their sense of security from 'mutual aid' would result in a terrible sense of insecurity". This dichotomy between traditional African communal culture and the individualistic demands of modern urban economic activity has been one of the most socially disruptive elements in post-independence Africa.

But it is when he deals with the creation of new social mores that Chisiza demonstrates most clearly his foresight of the central issue which was to plague independent nations. Having pointed out that almost all societies possess a group of people who set social values, who initiate changes and preserve the best traditions, he describes how the Europeans taught Africans to despise their own customs and measure all aspects of culture according to European standards. Yet independence destroys European social leadership as well as political power. And as the influence of indigenous traditional leaders has been undermined by the Europeans, a social vacuum is created. Chisiza recognized the dangers inherent in this vacuum and made specific proposals for filling it in a manner calculated to avert them:

> The African élite who are masters of the new situation must provide the social leadership required to fill the vacuum . . . The task of the new social leaders should be to steer the new countries away from the tragedy of wholesale imitation of foreign ways and from the blunder of returning to the traditional ways. Obviously, this calls for men of conviction who know their African as well as their European ways thoroughly and who are at once patriotic, progressive, and balanced.

He then proceeded to underline the danger of social conformity, with its inevitable product, intellectual conformity, which digs the grave of creativity, innovation and social change, the life-blood of the new nationhood. Again he proposed specific safeguards. To counteract the tendency towards social conformity in the new states, Chisiza advised that:

Political leaders must refrain from playing the double rôle of political as well as social leaders. Social leadership should be the responsibility of different people who should be given due recognition and encouragement by the political leaders. But the base of social leadership should be so broadened as to accommodate a variety of tastes and ideas, thereby preventing the popularization of a few pet ideas originated by a handful of people. Lastly, it should be made clear to social leaders that their job is not to throw overboard everything African, not merely to process foreign ways, but to uphold African ways of life where necessary, to adopt foreign ways where possible, and to strike practicable compromises where need be.

Perhaps this was a somewhat idealistic prescription for newly independent countries under such heavy and immediate pressures, with only a tiny experienced cadre to undertake so many duties. Nevertheless, it presented a set of ideals at which to aim. In fact, few new African states ever attempted to achieve such objectives. "The base of social leadership" was never broadened; leadership in social values remained almost solely the prerogative of political leaders, together with their civil-servant and academic friends; the élite in the main despised African customs, adopting the habits of their European predecessors.

It could be argued that this trend was more pronounced in west than east Africa. Certainly Africans in Lagos, Accra, Freetown, Abidjan, and Dakar revealed strong tendencies to imitate European life earlier than those in Nairobi, Kampala, Dar es Salaam, Lusaka or Kinshasa. In the north there had always been a mixture of Arab and European, yet Algiers, Rabat and Tunis displayed growing rather than diminishing French influence, whilst Alexandria and Cairo maintained the strong cosmopolitan character which had been traditional to them.

It is true that the west had a longer and deeper relationship with Europe than the east. It is equally true that from the earliest days of the slave trade in the fifteenth century a market economy had been deeply rooted in the west, extending far into the hinterland from the coastal markets. This had enabled European traders to continue their economic relations with African merchants when the slave trade was prohibited early in the nineteenth century. Material commodities, especially palm oil, were substituted for human cargoes, often between the same businessmen. Slave-raiding, slave purchases, state organization, military mobilization, and the taste for consumer goods, all common features of the slave trade, had prepared the ground for much of west Africa to adopt the capitalist ethic of the nineteenth century.

This has never been lost. One of the most obvious contrasts between west and east Africa today is the hundreds of petty traders on the pavements in the west, selling everything from oranges to watches, whereas in the east strenuous efforts have still to be made to forge any kind of marketing channels, there being little historical tradition of petty trading. Not surprisingly, therefore, during the colonial period and since, the growth of a petty bourgeoisie was more rapid in the west than in the east. This was accompanied by an expanding élite of professionals, civil servants, politicians and entrepreneurs. The traders and merchants took advantage of the increased economic activity encouraged by colonial rule, but increased their numbers rather than accumulating substantial individual wealth. The professionals and politicians integrated themselves as far as possible into European society and, at independence, stepped into European shoes.

Yet this feature of independent Africa was not solely confined to the societies of the west. Nairobi grew from early twentieth-century infancy as a European city. It might be surrounded by suburbs inhabited by thousands of Africans, whilst Kikuyu lands bordered its perimeter; many of its stores might be owned by Asians; yet city life itself was dominated by the European settler community and those who came to serve it. When Africans took over political control social life changed little. On the surface, at least, the only noticeable new feature was the appearance in hotels, night-clubs and restaurants of more black faces than previously. But their activities, attitudes and tastes seemed identical to those of their new European or Asian friends. Much the same was true, though to a lesser extent, of Kampala and Dar es Salaam.

The principal difference from west Africa was the domination of commerce in the east by Asians. This had little effect on social habits, for most Asians maintained a closed culture. But it meant that the business entrance into élite society commonly used in the west was open to only a tiny minority of east Africans.

In Lusaka, the Copper Belt towns and Kinshasa, Africans superseded Europeans in social activities much more quickly than in Nairobi. Although these had also been dominated by white settlers under colonial rule, their social as well as their political pretensions suddenly collapsed once independence came. Nevertheless, their influence on their successors lingered on. One had only to walk round a town like Kitwe at night to hear the same raucous singing, dancing, shouting, quarrelling in the bars;

the only difference was that now it was African miners who were expressing themselves as they had seen their white colleagues do in the past. In Kinshasa (formely Leopoldville) or Lumumbashi (formerly Elisabethville) the Belgian influence was just as pervasive.

Further south, of course, the whites maintained their social along with their political domination. Salisbury, Bulawayo, Cape Town, Johannesburg, Durban and Port Elizabeth remained white cities. Yet those few Africans who managed to attain a privileged status within their own societies revealed similar tendencies to those exhibited by their cousins in independent Africa. Imitation of white tastes and values dominated the African social outlook, whether it be in music, entertainment, materialistic ambitions or education.

Thus, all over the African continent, independence was followed not by the social equality which had been preached as an objective of anti-colonial agitation, but by the consolidation and expansion of a small, privileged faction. A section of this élite was already entrenched at the moment of independence. Colonial governments had collaborated with chiefs, new politicians, civil servants and professionals in the process of decolonization. Foreign firms, shrewdly foreseeing the end of colonial rule, had promoted and trained indigenous staff and made bargains with prospective leaders. Educational programmes had produced African teachers, doctors, engineers, lawyers, and civil servants. These policies had already laid the foundation of an élite, privileged community before independence. It was to use the opportunities of independence to increase its privileges.

This was not a "class" in the conventional sense. It did not represent ownership of property, although some of its members succeeded in accumulating wealth of one form or another. Nor was it monolithic. It was partly composed of those chiefs favoured by the colonialists, partly of the old-established commercial fraternity along the west coast, partly of the few who had gained entry to the professions. These comprised the older sector, especially in the west. But during the period between the end of World War II and independence they were joined by a growing body of the newly educated, the more successful traders, army officers trained in Britain or France, those who had gained prominence in politics.

One important feature of the new élite was the opportunity it offered for social mobility. Few of its members inherited élite status. Most of them came from humble homes, often gaining their opportunity through being selected by their family as the favoured son to be given an education. For educational qualifications, the gamble of commercial success or political good fortune opened the door to social acceptance, no matter how humble one's origins.

Independence, however, gave the politicians a paramount power within the élite. Not only did they inherit the positions of command vacated by colonial rulers; the fact that the state was the chief employer, that it dispensed the greater part of economic patronage, gave the politician economic power to add to his political domination. He was beseiged by relatives, age-group comrades, ethnic affiliates, who all laid claim to rewards, either from their affinity to him or as for rewards for assisting in his success.

Few African politicians heeded Chisiza's warning and refrained from playing "the double rôle of political as well as social leaders". Most of them took their opportunity to form the upper crust of the élite, pursuing and even exaggerating the pattern of life previously followed by their colonial predecessors.

This domination of social standards by the élite group proved to be one of Africa's most virulent cancers during the post-independence decade. In the first place it inevitably widened the gulf separating the privileged minority of Africans from the vast majority in rural areas and from the poor of the towns. In Gabon, for instance, in 1969 the average income per head was $400 a year, one of the highest in the continent. Yet for the majority, who lived in the countryside, it was only $70, whereas the average for civil servants was $2400.

This gross contrast in life-styles presented only one aspect of the conflict which increasingly embittered relations between the inheritors of colonial power and the masses. Rural revolt had played an important rôle in many anti-colonial struggles. Tax riots, conflict with chiefs, attacks on white farmers, resistance to husbandry or agricultural laws, had contributed vitally to a rejection of colonial authority in Algeria, Kenya, Uganda, Nigeria, Chad and elsewhere. These revolts were spasmodic and unco-ordinated, local reactions against grievances arising from the policies of colonial governments or their agents, which continued from the 1930s through the period of decolonization. They provided valuable ammunition for the anti-colonial nationalists. The FLN in Algeria, for instance, promised that "the land reform of tomorrow will be necessarily and ineluctably an *agrarian revolution* or it will be nothing".

Yet independence brought little agrarian reform, still less an agrarian revolution, in most new African states. Ben Bella tried to fulfil wartime promises in Algeria, but the military régime which deposed him showed itself much more concerned with building new industries, helped by Russia and Western Europeans. Parts of the Kenyan White Highlands were distributed to African farmers, but largely to the benefit of a few of the more prosperous. Some efforts at mass mobilization were made in Ghana, Guinea, Mali, Zambia and Tanzania; but, with the exception of the latter country, little success was achieved during the 1960s. Meanwhile, over almost the whole continent the vast majority of rural

inhabitants, four-fifths of the total population, continued life largely as
before independence. Some were even worse off as migration to the towns
left old men, women and children with heavier farming burdens, whilst
the fact that the population was often increasing faster than food supplies
left many people with less to eat.

In the towns as well as in the country the majority of inhabitants lived
in poverty. Rapid urbanization overtook the pace at which social provisions could be made for the migrants. The slums of Lagos, Kinshasa,
Cairo and a score of other towns spread rapidly as relatives and friends
joined those already resident, and an increasing number of young people
forsook the drudgery of country life for the largely imaginary "bright
lights" of urban life. The expectations of at least half of the new migrants
were dashed. There were not sufficient jobs and 50 per cent unemployment became common. Those who had any form of education expected
better posts than they were offered. All the time thousands of new school
leavers, educated to fill non-existent jobs, were coming on to the labour-
market. The pressure of competition continually rose, as did the frustration of expectations. Not surprisingly the incidence of crime, violence and
drug-taking followed the same upward curve.

The formula of stagnation in the countryside, discontent in the towns,
combined with ostentatious displays of luxury by the small élite, provided
a sure prescription for revolt. As the élite was constantly divided within
itself through contention for the seats of power, these resentments were
frequently exploited by rival groups. During the chaos which marked
much of western Nigeria's history throughout the 1960s, for example,
Obafemi Awolowo and Samuel Akintola were fighting for control of the
region, each exploiting the social conflicts between poor and rich farmers.

The social inequalities, which appeared aggravated when independence provided a minority of Africans with the opportunity to inherit the
privileges of colonial whites, certainly played a major rôle in creating
conditions in which coups against ruling régimes could succeed. They
might not have had the same effect if those régimes had produced better
results in improving the lives of their people. For most Africans were
prepared to see their leaders prosper provided that they felt they were
working genuinely on behalf of the ordinary people. When, five years
before independence, Azikiwe was exposed as having used his political
position to further his financial interests through the African Continental
Bank, he still retained the support of the Ibo in the Eastern Region; for
they believed that he was working for them and so entitled to become
wealthy. It was only when it became clear in Nigeria that politics had
become primarily a means to personal gain whilst the mass of people were
being left in poverty that the dry tinder of social inequality burst into
flames which engulfed the whole system.

Yet, even if the inheritors of the colonial estate had been honest, austere, dedicated men, they would have had to overcome enormous difficulties in satisfying the expectations they had raised in their people. For although the African élite had acquired political office, control over economic power lay in other hands. Unilever, SCOA and CFAO throughout British and French West Africa had adjusted their policies during the 1950s to anticipate independence. Nkrumah's magnum opus, the Volta scheme, was really dominated by Kaiser's, with its smelter using Jamaican bauxite processed in America, plus the cheap electricity provided by Ghana. In Zambia, Anglo-American and the Selection Trust maintained a firm control over copper production which provided the government with 65 per cent of its revenues. Zaire remained similarly dependent on Union Minière.

More will be said about the economic issues in the next chapter. Its significance here is that the political leaders soon realized that they possessed only partial power over their newly independent states. They therefore never felt the self-confidence to challenge the basic structures they had inherited, to forge their own social systems based on their own social values. It was easier to follow the accepted pattern, to step into the white man's shoes and act as he had, often taking the opportunities to accept the bribes proffered by foreign companies to maintain the status quo. And as premonitions of approaching disaster multiplied, with neighbouring régimes constantly crashing, the search for quick security through the accumulation of personal wealth became frantic. After his deposition, Albert Margai of Sierra Leone was ordered by an enquiry into corruption to repay over £770,000 which he was alleged to have misappropriated. Maurice Yameogo was charged with having embezzled more than £1 million when president of Upper Volta. According to the Coker Commission, over £16 million were misused by the ruling party of the Western Region in Nigeria. Even Nkrumah was accused of accumulating vast personal wealth, though as the charges were made by the military régime which deposed him and was trying to blacken his character, the truth of this will have to wait for a more objective examination.

The worst example of the collapse of all social values as public men fought for the personal fruits of office was certainly in Nigeria. There Africa's most populous nation, with over 50 million inhabitants, was almost destroyed by the venality of its leaders. With the federal and four regional governments controlling massive patronage, individuals, groups and parties fought without inhibition to secure those positions in politics, civil service and public boards which would guarantee their personal fortunes, varying from modest gains to the £32 million which Chief Festus, the Federal Finance Minister, was believed to have deposited in a Swiss bank. It is scarcely surprising that the military coup of 1966 which destroyed this political system was widely welcomed by the masses still living on under £1 a week. Yet the military coup did not purge the poison; the tensions which had built up under the corrupt system were to subject Nigeria to the horrors of two-and-a-half years of internal war, with thousands of the common people losing their lives, their children or their homes.

Of course it can be argued that the scale of corruption in the public life of Africa has been much lower than that of other continents, notably of America. According to the United States Attorney-General, more than 170 public office-holders or former officials were indicted or convicted on corruption charges during the 32 months to October 1971. He commented, "Corruption of public officials must sicken every American who honours his birth-right." For every public official charged or convicted there are many more who use office for personal gain. That is in affluent North America; it is well known that the situation has always been even worse in the south. And there are few public men or women living modestly in Europe.

Yet few Africans would be willing to judge their standards of public morality by the values of America or of Europe. Nor is comparison either a valid justification or an excuse for the consequences of corruption. Of course it is understandable that men who had been brought up in humble circumstances, surrounded by scores of demanding dependants, succumbed to the temptations offered when they attained office, often after dangerous struggles, sometimes entailing personal suffering.

It was the effect of corruption rather than the issue of personal morality which was crucial to the African people. The social atmosphere was polluted by the frenetic search for personal gain from public office. The traditions of co-operation, communal service, and personal generosity, were largely overlaid by the application of the alien principles of capitalist acquisition. Whether those African values can ever be recovered, or whether new generations, particularly those born in the towns, are doomed to be reared as slaves to the venal mores arising from such corruption, remains to be seen.

Nor were the effects confined to personal and social morality. They had a severe impact on national development. When public men succumb to bribery their decisions come to be taken on grounds other than those of the national interest. One particular example offers economic as well as social significance. Agronomists who sympathize with Third World aspirations have for some years been imploring developing countries to move slowly and gradually towards mechanized agriculture. They have pointed to the disastrous effects on the land produced by sudden mechanization, to the waste of resources as machines break down, cannot be repaired, and are crippled from lack of spare parts. They have shown, too, that agricultural progress depends on farmers learning new techniques step by step, that machinery often unnecessarily replaces labour where unemployment is rife, that the machine usually makes the rich farmer richer, whilst doing nothing to assuage the poverty of the poor.

Yet anyone who has travelled in the rural areas of Africa cannot fail to have observed the number of tractors lying idle and rusting, to have come across farmers or co-operatives with more than half their tractors out of service, to have seen the erosion of land caused by unskilled mechanical farming.

How is it that so many African governments and agricultural organizations have ignored the advice of the agronomists they commission, men like René Dumont, who has advised developing countries throughout the Third World, and poured scarce foreign currency into tractor-buying? The reason is simple. The tractor manufacturers, particularly those of the Western world, fell on hard times during the late 1960s. They therefore encouraged ministers, civil servants and representatives of public corporations to visit them. Having fêted such men, offered delivery for a small deposit, and promised a personal gift, they secured large orders. The firms provided the loans for purchase at high interest rates over short periods. The fact that the tractors might actually handicap the agricultural development of such countries was no concern of the firms. It was good business for them, and they stood to lose nothing as their export credits were guaranteed by their own governments.

Then, at least anywhere in west Africa, such firms added a minimum of ten per cent to their bills to pay for the bribe to the African representative, his party or business concern. This is the economic cost, the impact on national policy, the loss to the African citizen, of the corruption of social life.

If the élite which gained political and social power at independence was the product of social mobility, the further each nation moved from independence the less grew such mobility. For after they had discovered their opportunities in the new states, the élite began to consolidate itself.

In the first place, it greatly expanded after independence. The politicians entered the élite community through their positions in state and local government. In Nigeria, for instance, there were 80 members of the federal government and 160 members of regional governments, as well as the army of backbench members in all five parliaments. But if the politicians used their political position to gain entry to the élite, the foundation sectors of that community, the civil servants, businessmen and professionals, insisted that their numbers also be increased. In Nigeria, even before the civil war, the creation of twelve states in place of the four regions, and the massive wartime expansion of the army, over three-fifths of those employed outside agriculture held government posts. The civil service alone increased by a half during the first five years of independence. According to the 1963 census in Ghana there were over 100,000 commercial enterprises, although only about one per cent employed more than ten people. The Finance Minister of the Ivory Coast revealed in 1972 that public-sector personnel increased between 1967 and 1971 from 22,097 to 37,913.

There were frequent tensions between the bureaucratic and business sections of the élite and the new politicians. In 1965 civil-service discontent in both Upper Volta and the Central African Republic contributed significantly to military coups in both countries. And after a military coup, it was the bureaucrats who actually ran national affairs.

But on one issue the whole élite was agreed. They had the right, either through position or from their wealth, to ensure that their children and the children of their relatives secured a privileged education and preference in employment. This attitude greatly diminished the social mobility which had previously prevailed, resulting in an élite consolidation which approached the character of class formation. An inevitable consequence was that competition for entry to the élite became fiercer, the battle for position and its fruits still more bloody.

The new generation of the élite, the students from privileged homes, might contest the assumptions of their parents. In particular, they often rejected the European-based standards of culture, calling for an African way of life. Yet they still expected privilege : the students in Dar es Salaam publicly protested to President Nyerere against being included in his national service scheme – they were sent back to their villages for their pains; it has been known for students to protest against self-service cafeterias, having to clear their own plates, being asked to double up in rooms. Moreover, this new generation of student élite, whatever it may say about returning to African values, generally shows by its actions that it follows the European pattern of expecting privileged employment from its educational opportunity. African students oppose low entry qualifications to universities, functional curricula and compulsory community service; degrees in political science or civil engineering are much sought after, in the expectation that they will lead to careers in the foreign service, politics or lucrative engineering businesses. Agricultural and mining engineering are amongst the least popular courses.

As the élite consolidated itself into a closed community, so the social dangers foreseen by Chisiza began to appear. Conformity began to dominate the social scene. Not only were European customs encouraged; a kind of Victorian morality was adopted. Various campaigns were mounted against petty examples of modern European fashion, like miniskirts, the use of lipstick, popular music and dancing, usually by youths claiming to defend African culture.

But much more important was the attitude towards women. In Algeria, for instance, the veil was sufficiently lifted during the anti-colonial war for women to take an active part, to suffer and die like the men. But after independence was won the veil descended again, with women segregated and kept out of public life, in traditional Muslim manner. In northern Nigeria, too, an exception to the central principle of British decolonization was made. Instead of adult suffrage, a prerequisite of independence constitutions elsewhere, only male suffrage was demanded in the northern region. This was by local request, the northern Muslims having always kept their women out of public affairs. In few parts of Africa were women encouraged to participate in the life of the new nations, nor did the women themselves show much inclination to rebel against this subordination. In the west, of course, women traditionally played a crucial rôle in commerce, which gave them some considerable local political influence. It is also noteworthy that Julius Nyerere always stressed when speaking of traditional African forms of democracy that this usually excluded women; that in modern Africa the rights and responsibilities of adults must extend to female as well as male. But these were exceptions to the general pattern of male dominance, which was strengthened by conformity to the standards of Victorian Europeanism as the élite closed its circle.

There is a deeper sense in which African social life was undermined after independence. One does not need to accept the romanticism of a Richard Burton to recognize in traditional African life a tranquillity which disappeared from most parts of the world several centuries ago. Burton's famous description of life in east Africa as he saw it in the mid-nineteenth century paid no attention to the malnutrition, infant mortality, diseases, hard labour, and the monotony of African village life. Yet what he does convey is the peace of mind which was and still is achieved behind the multiple ills of traditional peasant society. In *First Footsteps in East Africa* he wrote:

> The African rises with the dawn from his couch of cowhide ... The hour before sunrise being the coldest time, he usually kindles a fire, addresses himself to his constant companion, the pipe ... About 7 a.m., when the dew has partially disappeared from the grass, the elder boys drive the flocks and herds to pasture with loud shouts and sound applications of the quarter-staff. They return only when the sun is sinking behind the western horizon. At 8 a.m. those who have provisions at home enter the hut for refection with ugali or holcus-porridge;

those who have not, join a friend. Pombe [beer], when procurable, is drunk from the earliest dawn. After breaking his fast the African repairs, pipe in hand, to the iwanza, the village "public", previously described. Here, in the society of his own sex, he will spend the greater part of the day talking and laughing, smoking or torpid with sleep. Occasionally he sits down to play ... Towards sunset all issue forth to enjoy the coolness: the men sit outside the iwanza, whilst the women and girls, after fetching water for household wants from the well, collecting in a group upon their little stools, indulge in the pleasures of gossip and the pipe. This hour in the most favoured parts of the country is replete with enjoyment, which even the barbarian feels, though not yet indoctrinated into aesthetics. As the hours of darkness draw nigh, the village doors are carefully closed, and, after milking his cows, each peasant retires to his hut, or passes his time in the iwanza.

Burton may have been using William-Morris-type spectacles, and he certainly did not venture below the surface of African village life. Yet what he saw with his poetic senses had some validity. Traditional African society evolved a set of profound spiritual values from which the African peasant gained self-confidence, self-reliance and a secure identity. It may be that these qualities were partially drawn from a form of fatalism, common to the very poor amongst whom death and suffering are commonplace. But they also stemmed from the holism which Jan Smuts tried to enunciate as a philosophy on a more complex but less profound level. African spirituality derived from a sense of identity in a natural order which includes living, dead and unborn human beings, animals, plants, flowers, trees, the land, and all that grows on it. This was a total, a "global" society, which provided all wants, spiritual, material and social. Its elements were expressed in various rituals, but its content was most clearly displayed in human relationships. Within each community these were considerate, co-operative and affectionate. No destitute widows, orphans or old people were to be found in African society, no maltreated children or assaulted women. There were times, of course, when restraints broke down, but always between rather than within communities, and usually under the pressure of fear rather than greed.

The effects of sudden change always tend to be destructive of social and personal security. Africans have been subjected to more catastrophic changes than most of mankind. Many African societies were uprooted or dislocated by three centuries of the slave trade. Then virtually the whole continent found itself under European rule. But it was the impact of European technology and social manners rather than of alien government which had the most catastrophic effect on the way of life of the majority of Africans. They could absorb the effects of seeing new rulers giving them orders; they could adapt alien religions to their own environment; but the technical demands of modern scientific economies and the social philosophy which went with them struck at the deepest roots of African mores.

European education created generation gaps of unbridgeable width between parents and children, between educated and uneducated brothers and sisters. Understanding within marriage became strained as few women were educated to equal heights with men. A significant number of students returned from abroad with European or American wives. New opportunities for employment took many young people into the towns where they had to learn mechanical skills, to divide their days according to new criteria, to associate with their fellows in novel relationships, to honour the new gods of wages, taxes, rents, shop goods, individual achievement, material success. The hallmarks of modern urban life, in Africa as in the rest of the world, are uni-culture and anonymity; they represent the exact antithesis of traditional African values. Although in all African towns certain elements of traditional communal customs were preserved, and although links between towns and country were never completely severed, the signs of disorientation caused by the conflict between urban and traditional values became common in every African urban area. The antipathy between African spirituality and technical materialism tore African social values asunder.

Some Africans recognized the dangers facing their people from this schism. Writers such as Camara Laye, Wole Soyinka, Cyprian Ekwensi, Amos Tuttola, Chinua Achebe and many others portrayed the dichotomy suffered by their compatriots. Their predecessors, men like Africanus Horton and Edward Blyden, had warned of the same dangers in the nineteenth century.

A few political leaders also were sufficiently perceptive to foresee the threat to social life which independence could project if it simply resulted in a black élite adopting the whites' materialistic, competitive values. Léopold Senghor always maintained that the village is the focal point of African society, that its institutions must be preserved in any social transformation; but Senghor's theory had little influence on the policies of his government. Nkrumah, Touré and Keita tried to curb the individualism which could stimulate the growth of a privileged class; but they had little success. Nasser attempted to redistribute land and wealth, to break the power of an élite which had flourished under the monarchy; but his conflicts with Israel and the uncontrollable population expansion thwarted most of his ambitions. Even in the Ivory Coast, the chief bastion of bourgeois privilege, an attempt had to be made by 1972 to curb the excesses which had been allowed to develop since independence. Finance Minister Konan Bedie had to announce a programme of austerity forced on him by financial difficulties. Senior civil servants and members of the government were to be deprived of car allowances when official cars were available; henceforth they would have to pay for their water and gas; their official furniture would have to last for five years; they would have to pay their own travel costs for holidays abroad; no more loans would be granted for buying cars or for weddings or funerals. Even service allowances to French technical assistance staff were cut by 50 per cent, whilst the minister revealed that free housing for public servants was costing the state nearly £1½ million a year. This belated austerity effort, though, did more to expose the material privileges gained by the élite than to hold out much promise of social justice; it had come about ten years too late.

Amidst this scene of continental social disintegration the slight figure of Nyerere stood out as a beacon of hope. Nyerere was one of the very few Africans to see the social dangers with complete clarity. Even before independence he had recognized the dangers which power could raise. At his party's annual conference in 1960 he declared to delegates: "I have seen some TANU officers getting drunk with power and scheming to undermine one another ... many of our leaders are working for responsible government to provide themselves with high positions." By 1962, the year after independence, he was writing a pamphlet proclaiming the virtues of self-reliance, development through the people's work, and insisting that the benefits go to the people, not to their leaders. By 1967 he still felt that "the present trend is away from the extended-family production and social unity, and towards the development of a class system in the rural areas". He therefore argued for "economic and social communities where people live together and work together for the good of all, and which are interlocked so that all the different communities also work together in co-operation for the common good".

In order to achieve this type of society, Nyerere told his people that they would have to combat the values inculcated by the British during their period of colonial rule. Their educational system, he believed, "emphasized and encouraged the individualistic instincts of mankind, instead of his co-operative instincts. It led to the possession of individual material wealth being the major criterion of social merit and worth. This meant that colonial education induced attitudes of human inequality, and in practice underpinned the domination of the weak by the strong, especially in the economic field."

But Nyerere was not content to preach social philosophy to his people;

he supported his idealistic words with action. Thus the Arusha Declaration of 1967 not only brought under government control major economic activities in the nation and encouraged the establishment of ujamaa villages based on co-operative organization; it also included a code of conduct for national leaders. This was deliberately aimed to halt the growing tendency towards the creation of an élite. Henceforth, aspiring leaders had to choose between a public career and their pockets. If they wished to enter or continue in politics they would have to live on the salary allocated to their post and forswear any second income. Later in the same year Nyerere was able to claim that "there are only ten people in our whole country who have an income of Shs.300,000 or more a year (£15,000 or more), and these people each pay more than two-thirds of that amount to the government in direct taxation." How many other African states could make a similar claim?

Beneath the political and economic storms of the post-independence decade lay this confusion of social principles and objectives. Outside Tanzania, the goals for which the anti-colonial struggles had been waged had in the main disappeared, although the leaders of Zambia were desperately trying to establish the same principles as the Tanzanians, faced with far greater difficulties. But for the vast majority of Africans not only had independence produced no social justice, but the visible power of the élite under military and civilian régimes seemed to have driven the concept itself beyond the horizon.

At the same time, the security of their traditional way of life, which had begun to be undermined during colonial days, was now seriously crumbling. Pressures for modernization, the lure of towns, the adoption of European culture, the attraction of material goods for the young and, overall, the venal example set by the élites, directly assaulted all traditional African values. Already the resultant social disorientation had played a major part in a loss of faith in the new nationalism demanded for building independent nation-states, in the active overthrow of régimes and the passive acceptance of coups. A reversion to the nostalgic security of ethnicity became common.

Whether the confusion so widely experienced would degenerate into social disintegration and subsequent chaos would depend on how seriously the lessons of the first independence decade were learnt and remedies applied. Whether African values would be submerged in the individualistic, competitive materialism which had attended economic development elsewhere remained an open question. All African leaders had repeatedly declared that the future mores of their continent must be based on an amalgam of the most valuable African customs with the best from other continents. But such a synthesis would have to be purposefully created;

F

few in any sector of public life had yet seemed prepared to sacrifice their personal interests to undertake the task. It might have to be achieved by people lower down the social ladder, in which case the élite would find it a very uncomfortable experience.

5

Economic Quandaries

The African continent produces about a tenth of the world's mineral production. It contains nearly a third of the world's hydro-electric power potential. Of the 18 major mineral ores it possesses substantial quantities of ten, varying between one-fifth and 95 per cent of world output. In a continent which occupies a quarter of the earth's land surface, three times the size of the United States, six times that of Europe, the area of land under cultivation per head of the population is about three times as high as that of western Europe, livestock population about double, and grazing areas for stock nearly seven times greater. Such resources, divided by a population of some 330 million, are sufficient to provide a per capita income much higher than the world's average.

Yet in 1970 the average per capita income of the African was only a little over $100, slightly more than southern Asia, but a third of that in the Middle East, a quarter of the Latin American figure, a fifth of the southern European. According to the United Nations study of the same year, by standards drawn from the number of school-children, doctor-patient ratio, and consumption of energy, 16 of the 19 least developed countries of the world were in Africa.

There are many reasons for the poverty of the vast majority of Africans amidst the riches of their continent: several thousand years of isolation for most of them from contact with the rest of mankind; the handicap of tropical climate and poor soils; the slave trade and alien rule which succeeded it; the lack of interest displayed by European imperialists in the development of their subjects; a consequent absence of modern technical equipment, skills, organization, social institutions and capital for investment.

Yet the peoples of the new countries had been promised improvement from self-government. Nkrumah assured listeners that "If we get s.g. [self-government] we'll transform the Gold Coast into a paradise in ten years." His fellow nationalist leaders had all made similar promises – though the more thoughtful, like Nyerere, had warned that hard work was the second prescription for reform after uhuru (freedom). And the people believed their leaders. Support for anti-colonialism contained a greater weight of economic and social expectation than simply a desire to gain indigenous rulers.

The economic progress of Africa since independence has therefore to be judged according to the improvements made in the life of its 330 million peoples, and the preparations made for future generations. For the vast majority of Africans may experience minor vicarious thrills from photographs of massive new stadia, airports or triumphal arches; they may share some sense of pride from seeing pictures of their national representatives sitting at the United Nations, being received at Buckingham Palace, the Kremlin, the White House or in Peking; but they are much more personally concerned to know that there is the first school or clinic in their village, that their children need no longer suffer from yaws, bilharzia or kwashiorkor, that they obtain sufficient money for their maize, rice, cocoa, coffee, cotton, sisal, groundnuts or cattle to enable them to buy a few goods at the market for their families.

It is difficult to know how much daily life has changed for the majority of Africans since independence. Statistics reveal that some general progress has been made; a growth rate of about four per cent a year in real gross domestic product was achieved in the 1960s, though this was no higher than during the last colonial decade. Yet such an overall figure conceals many disparities. High mineral prices and the advent of rapidly increasing oil exports could account for most of the growth. It also tended to concentrate growth in certain countries, leaving others stagnant. Population increase at well over two per cent drastically reduced the resources available per person. The servicing of heavy debt accumulation had already begun to reduce the proportion of national income which could be allocated to the needs of the people.

As one travels in Africa the evidence may appear contradictory. On the one hand there are certainly many more cars, large houses and hotels in the towns. There are also many more people living in the towns and cities, for African urbanization was one of the highest in the world during this period, reaching a rate of 5.5 per cent. So that the appearance of the main streets, with their large cars, modern stores, restaurants and hotel lounges is deceptive. Behind them are always to be found narrow alleyways lined with mud walls, tin roofs, wood stoves; around the perimeter of most towns sprawling shanty towns proliferated during the 1960s, often without running water, sewers or even discernible roads. And the street corners are increasingly inhabited by groups of youths, unemployed, or semi-employed.

The contrasts may not be as sharp in the countryside, but they are there. Here are wealthy farmers, especially where cash crops have become established. Often it will be found that the prosperous farms are owned by a civil servant, politician, or businessman from the town. Then there are still many large farms owned by foreigners, some by foreign companies, like the Anglo-American Company estate outside Lusaka. One will also see prosperity increasing on a smaller scale where a farm institute or experimental project has been started. Small-holdings, pig units, vegetable plots, and fruit farms have begun to appear, new cattle graze on the veld; occasional new high-yielding strains of plants have been introduced; terracing and trees on a hillside contrast with the bare eroded soil of neighbouring slopes.

Some of these advances are new since independence, others continue from beginnings made under colonial rule. In some districts improvements begun during the colonial period have been abandoned or neglected under independent governments. Usually little or no change is visible. The more common sight is the traditional maize patch of the subsistence peasant outside a ring of thatched mud huts, a few scrawny hens, a group of goats, a bony, dry-uddered cow. Frequently, too, beside the path leading to the unchanging hamlet will be seen a rusty tractor, unused for years since a spare part was needed and has never arrived. Most rural Africans say that nothing has changed since independence, except that most of the young people have gone to the town, leaving old men, women and children to tend the village and grow the food.

It cannot be expected that the peasant who finds so few changes in the life of his community will be persuaded that the nation is progressing by evidence of more cars, office buildings, hotels in the towns, or by seeing that the minister who visits the district with his large entourage is an African instead of a European. Nor are the unemployed in the towns compensated for the squalor in which they live by the sight of blacks replacing whites in the mansions, cocktail lounges or night-clubs. This contrast in living standards within the African communities, which has sharpened since independence, has been a major cause of a general acceptance that the coup or revolution might bring reform. Even the coercion of military rule has often appeared little different to the mass of people from the exploitation practised by civilian politicians and bureaucrats. It is judged according to the same criteria – does it produce a fairer deal?

Nor was it simply an absence of improvement in material standards which disillusioned so many African communities with the initial results of economic policies under independence. Colonial rulers had found that most Africans were deeply integrated into their local communities. When honest attempts were made to introduce improved methods of agriculture or husbandry, they were usually rejected unless local leaders were first persuaded of their benefits. Twenty years ago, in the midst of Mau Mau, driving from Nairobi towards Machakos, one could see on the one side red, bare eroded hills, on the other the silhouette of an infant forest. In

Machakos itself an intelligent district officer had gained the confidence of a group of Kamba chiefs. They had led their people in throwing their witchcraft implements into a communal pit, collectively terracing their hill slopes, planting trees as wind and rain breakers. The secret of this success in the midst of violence, antagonism and obstruction was the enlistment of leadership from the chiefs.

Most African leaders failed to learn this lesson, despite their own experience of the importance of local allegiance. Independence to the vast majority of Africans signified much more the right to make local decisions than the substitution of black for white national rulers. Thus many well-intentioned national schemes based on decisions taken at the centre foundered through local disinterest caused by non-involvement. Pride in Africa tends to be rooted much deeper in the local community than in the nation. And every community has its own customs, many of which do not conform to national plans. Some leaders learnt this lesson from early failures, gave authority to local leaders and tried to mobilize village and district energies so as to build national policies from the base. Nyerere with his ujamaa villages and Kaunda with his village development committees provided the outstanding examples of learning from experience; but they represented only a tiny minority.

The first decade of independence has thus witnessed a widespread failure by Africa's new governments to fulfil many of their citizens' expectations. Per capita monetary increase was only about 1.6 per cent a year. When South Africa with its self-sustaining but white-dominated economy is deducted, together with the extravagant consumption of the tiny black élites, little or nothing remained for the majority of African populations. Many actually suffered declining living standards. Considering that South Africa, the United Arab Republic (UAR) and Nigeria accounted for half the continent's national income, whilst only a few countries gained the windfalls bestowed on oil and copper producers – Libya and Nigeria, Zambia and Zaire – the plight of the vast majority of Africans is clear.

To understand this failure to achieve one of the main objectives of the anti-colonial struggle we must first examine the economic legacy bequeathed by the colonial powers.

It is almost a platitude to repeat that the colonial economic relationship consisted of Africa contributing raw materials and unskilled labour, Europe capital and skilled personnel, with Europe using the cheap materials, exporting manufactured goods to Africa and thus securing the profits. However platitudinous it may have become, this circuit dominated the economies of colonial territories. Nor did the process of decolonization alter it. After 1945, European colonial governments became more active in the economies of their colonies, contributing aid, investment, technical skills, educational opportunities, health and agricultural science, and devising development plans. This was considered to be preparing colonial subjects for eventual independence.

What is crucial about this process is that it never envisaged altering the economic structure. Even Arthur Creech Jones, Colonial Secretary in the Labour government from 1946 to 1950, and a renowned British socialist, told his own Fabian Colonial Bureau when they pressed him to nationalize the copper mines of Northern Rhodesia (Zambia) that economic policies must be determined not by the British government but by local inhabitants. As the only local inhabitants of Northern Rhodesia with any influence were white miners and settlers, the chances of removing the mines from the grip of foreign capitalists by this process were not very great.

Indeed, almost all the development expenditure of the colonial powers was concentrated on improving the physical and human infrastructure of their colonies. Roads, railways, dams, office buildings, better educated and healthier workers, consumed most of the effort. And the purpose was to improve facilities for private business to expand and prosper. A few indigenous and more Asian entrepreneurs reaped minor benefits; but all important productive enterprise, together with banking, insurance, shipping and most trade was in foreign hands. In any case, apart from petty trading in consumer goods, the pattern of economic activity remained the same – export to Europe, import from Europe with control and profits remaining in European hands.

This policy might moderately increase the gross domestic product of the colonial countries and slightly expand employment, but how could it solve the central issue of improving the standard of life of the African masses? The answer of European colonialists was that economic activity would be stimulated, albeit from the operations of foreign capital; that this would produce indigenous owning and middle classes; that in their turn African workers would be drawn into the money economy, paid wages and acquire skills. In short, that Africa would follow the same pattern that had created wealthy Europe and America in the nineteenth century. It is significant to note that this Euro-American egocentricity had become so total that it was even accepted by the British Labour Party, which, in 1951–53, accepted the received argument that a federation of central African colonial territories would attract overseas capital and consequently improve the living-standards of African inhabitants. Indeed, this same argument ran right through Labour's attempted negotiations with the Smith régime in Rhodesia, where continued political impotence was considered a reasonable price to pay for the material benefits it was assumed would follow from an injection of British capital.

Whether the Africans ever had any desire to create the kind of societies developed in Europe and America or not, they were never to be offered the opportunity. For the world economic situation had changed radically since the nineteenth century. Private investors always primarily seek rapidly developing markets, preferably where an industrial base has already been established. In the nineteenth century major investment was attracted not to the tropical colonies but to the areas of European settlement, the United States, Australia, Canada, and, of course, to Europe itself. In Africa the only major recent investment occurred in mining (in South Africa, Zambia, and Zaire), and more recently in oil found in north Africa and Nigeria. In the first five years following World War II more private capital was invested in South Africa than in all the colonies combined. By 1964 Shell alone had invested more in Nigerian oil than the total manufacturing capital of that country.

Post-war investment policies did not substantially deviate from former patterns. Europe, North America, Japan, Australia and South Africa remained the main foci. Yet what little capital found its way to black Africa (or to Latin America) made a specific impact on the countries involved. What it never did was to encourage significantly the growth of a class of indigenous entrepreneurs. Nor did it establish capital goods industries. Control over its operations was retained in foreign hands; it assisted in the rise of small élites and of tiny labour aristocracies; it divided the surplus it created between expatriated profits and reinvestment in supplying the extravagant demands of the élites, either by local enterprise or by imports. It therefore stimulated quasi class formation, but at such a low level that there was never any chance that European promises to create a genuine African bourgeoisie would be fulfilled. It did little to meet the mounting crisis of unemployment, for it applied capital-intensive techniques. It did nothing to solve rural needs for, apart from some interest in plantations, it was only concerned with urban locations; and as it did not raise an industrial labour-force, the demand for rural production remained almost static. Indeed, to the extent that fiscal measures were applied to the countryside, the rural dwellers were taxed in order to provide the revenues for building a largely urban infrastructure, providing substantial wages and salaries and supplying the luxuries demanded by the élite.

A major weakness suffered by African leaders when they took political control of their states was the loose thinking, disguised as economic analysis, which they inherited. Colonial administrators had led them to believe that increased educational opportunities – within the European structure and often employing European curricula – better health facilities, more roads, railways, harbours, irrigation and hydro-electric dams, plus a few improvements in agriculture and cattle-tending, would bring the economic improvements their people demanded. Foreign capital, assisted by overseas aid, could be relied on to increase production. In other words, the conventional formula accepted in Europe, by which governments provided facilities for private enterprise but remained as far as possible outside the productive processes, would best serve African needs.

Nor, was it only official colonial advisers who retained their blinkers. Most of the independent advisers who had the ears of African leaders failed to analyse seriously the economic situation bequeathed to Africa at independence. There were notable exceptions, like Thomas Balogh, who warned Nkrumah about the dangers of his Volta Dam obsession; Dudley Seers, who wrote a perceptive report for Kaunda; René Dumont, who, after spending much of his life in pointing out the menace of élitism and premature mechanization to francophone colonial leaders, then found time to advise Nyerere, Kaunda and Siaka Stevens of Sierra Leone.

Yet usually the advice given was taken from text-book blue-prints written for stereotyped situations which ignored Africa's specific problems. To cut the bonds of dependence and mono-production, industrialization was the received remedy. Even Arthur Lewis, the noted West Indian economist, who was accepted as a first authority by Nkrumah and other early African leaders, basically accepted this theory. It ignored the fact that industrialization could only be achieved quickly through foreign capital, which would dictate its own terms.

This theory was offered without much study of Africa's needs by social democrats and Marxists alike. A refinement of it was that new industries should concentrate on import substitution, that such infant industries would have to be given protection against competition until they had become established. This suited perfectly the interests of foreign investors and the emotions of new nationalist leaders. But it ignored the paramount needs of rural inhabitants and urban poor, the deepened dependence in which it left African economies, its exacerbation of unemployment, and its preservation of unskilled status for the majority of Africans.

Africa had been left by her European masters as a set of disparate, artificial units, almost wholly dependent for the livelihood of its inhabitants on the export of primary products. About three-quarters of these exports were concentrated on some 20 commodities. The continent had been bequeathed a rudimentary infrastructure, consisting largely of roads and railways running to ports where exports could be dispatched and imports received. A skeleton bureaucracy had been created, usually officered by Europeans. A growth in educational opportunities was accompanied by European curricula, standards and ambitions. The working class was very small, for what industry had been built was confined to import substitution, the use of locally available materials, the assembly of imported components, and the operation of machines manufactured abroad. There was no serious capital goods industries, and neither plans nor training for building them.

It was broadly assumed by most of those sympathetic with African ambitions that industrialization to the pinnacle of self-sufficiency in capital goods production was essential if Africans were to become independent economically as well as politically. It was also recognized that this would require some form of association between the new states; despite some genuine efforts, political suspicions after independence soon revealed that this was unlikely to be achieved for some years.

Nevertheless, most economic advisers and observers still expected African development to follow the pattern which during the past century had transformed Europe, America and the white-settled colonies from agricultural into industrial societies. Yet few nations had achieved this transformation solely through their own efforts. Britain had been able to use the massive treasure of India; North and South America had originally relied on European capital and experienced settlers; Germany and France had their colonies as well as infusions of British capital; Japan was the industrial product of the USA; perhaps Russia came nearest to self-reliant achievement, but the horrors of her experience hardly made her a model to attract imitation.

If it was supposed that Africa would become a twentieth-century Mecca for development capital the expectation was stillborn; the experience of Asia should have destroyed that illusion. Capital had always been attracted to development potential, of which there were few signs in Africa. It would go to South Africa, where the basis of a modern economy had already been built through the needs of gold-mining; but nowhere else was the prospect tempting for heavy investment.

In any case, capital policies had changed as the character of capital investing institutions were transformed. Gone were the days in which competitive industrialists and financiers were seeking new opportunities to gamble on investment in underdeveloped lands stimulating industrialization. In the second half of the twentieth century the large investment needed for capital goods industry lay largely in the hands of the new multi-national corporations. They were concerned with careful calculation of assured profits, apportioning the market between themselves, economies of scale, the advantages of operating in an established industrial environment. They might seek to lower costs by producing some equipment in a semi-developing country like India, but they were not interested in the grass-roots development which would be needed in Africa north of the Limpopo.

So Africans had scant hope of basing an industrialization programme on the conventional foundations of a capital goods industry. This implied that any industrialization which took place would leave them even more dependent on those foreigners who would sell them the machines they needed.

Moreover, where the multi-national corporations were interested in investment – Kaiser's, for instance, in Ghana's aluminium – capital-intensive methods would be used. The corporations were geared through their management, machinery and finance to one pattern of technique. They applied it regardless of local needs.

Nor did the post-independence wage policies of African states encourage experiments in other forms of technology more suitable for their development needs. As they accepted the colonial wage structure they had inherited, much of their tiny labour-force became a labour aristocracy. They therefore forfeited the potential advantage of cheap labour and encouraged foreign companies to use capital-intensive methods which lowered the labour content of their costs. As a result, although wages rose considerably during the post-independence decade, the labour-force itself remained almost static.

My first qualms over Nkrumah's pet Volta scheme were raised when I visited the site of the new harbour and industrial complex at Tema which was to depend on the power resources mobilized by the dam. This was as early as 1955, two years before independence. I was taken there by an African girl, a member of the socialist students' organization. The contractors, a British firm, were very considerate, showing me over the whole site and explaining the plans for development. But when they invited the girl and me to lunch there was a moment's hesitation. Later it was explained to me that this was the first time that an African had eaten in their dining-room! Yet it was Nkrumah who had asked me to make the visit. He considered the project crucial to the future of Ghana. He had already been Prime Minister for three years; two years later he was to take his country into independence.

If this is an example of how hard colonial social practices died amongst foreign firms, the economic significance of the Volta scheme was much more important and provides an illustration of a major economic dilemma faced throughout the continent.

Nkrumah and his colleagues recognized, at least intellectually, that the Ghana they were to inherit in 1957 would be profoundly dependent on external economic control. They also knew that their country's economy relied heavily on cocoa production, the price of which was controlled abroad. Their remedy seemed to lie in building their own industrial complex so as to control the means by which they could diversify Ghana's production. It is true that Nkrumah had often insisted that only a wider west African unit than a single state was essential for economic development. He accepted the arguments of those who maintained that the areas designated by the colonialists as states were artificial, that they promoted economic balkanization, and that wider associations were essential if development plans were to be given any chance of success. But Nkrumah was also an intense Ghanaian nationalist, he was more affected by the political than the economic attractions of African unity, and he put immediate thoughts of west Africa federation aside when considering his special Volta project.

Nkrumah believed himself faced with the choice of building his dam on the Volta to create a Ghanaian industrial base which would allow his country to escape from the grip of foreign economic control, or leaving Ghana as an agricultural country, dependent on exporting cocoa, the price of which would be outside his fiat. He therefore gambled on the first alternative. Yet he found that by doing so he had placed his country still deeper in pawn to foreign interests. He had to use a large proportion of his foreign reserves, accept capital-intensive techniques, and agree to the consortium which operated the aluminium smelter importing bauxite from America or the West Indies. In other words, his own dam supplied cheap electricity which was used by an international company to lower its costs and increase its profits. Ghana's unemployment problem was ignored in the construction of the dam, its associated public works and the production of the smelter. Meanwhile, all other development projects were expected to follow the same methods in order to avoid increasing the costs of the dam project, whilst the comparatively high wages paid to the few workers in capital-intensive construction set a dangerously inflated standard for other Ghanaian workers.

The Volta scheme certainly engendered some economic activity in Ghana, not only providing cheap electricity, a new town and harbour, and industrial opportunities, but also easy transport for cattle to be brought to the market by ship instead of on the hoof. Yet it contributed importantly to Nkrumah's economic troubles. It used up her reserves, forced her to repay heavy loans at high interest rates, prevented her from increasing company taxes and compelled her to allow profits to be repatriated for 30 years. At the end, Ghana was saddled with a heavy debt burden, her own bauxite deposits were left idle, few of her labour-force were employed or being trained, and she found that only a proportion of the electricity potential could be utilized as her national market was too small. Above all, the effort had cost her a distortion of economic development, substantially contributing to the economic failure which led to Nkrumah's downfall.

Such were the consequences of an attempt to apply the theory that only rapid industrialization could free Africa from foreign economic domination and the weakness of monoculture. The fact that this experiment had taken place in one of Africa's strongest economies reinforced the lesson. State capitalism had produced results which brought chaos to the state and increased domination by the foreigners. Yet both Marxists and capitalists agreed that quick industrialization was the answer to underdevelopment. Africans were still poor; they did not possess the machines or capital to build their own modern economies. How, then, could they break the circle of remaining poor because of lack of resources, and inability to mobilize resources because of their poverty?

Africans were left with an apparent choice of evils. Should they encourage those international companies which would invest in their countries to promote what industrial growth they chose, or should they resign themselves to remaining without industrial development until they could afford it themselves? If they chose the former course, they would place themselves at the mercy of international capitalism, aggravate their unemployment problems and see most of the surplus created either sent overseas or absorbed by an extravagant élite, involving political dangers from social resentment. If they took the latter, economic progress could only be slow, they would still depend on overseas prices and markets, and they could expect domestic opposition from those who envied the opportunities of élites in neighbouring states. In this dilemma there seemed little hope of succour from external sources. The Western world expected that any help given would facilitate the operations of their capitalist institutions; Eastern Europeans drove similar hard bargains, as concerned as the West with the interests of their own economies.

The post-independence decade provided two contrasting examples of states which tried to adopt each of these alternatives. The Ivory Coast attempted to follow the capitalist road to economic growth; Tanzania tried to apply the principles of socialist self-reliance. Between these two opposite poles many varied and mixed experiments were made, usually pragmatically rather than ideologically. Following the decease of Nkrumah's policies, accompanied by lack of success in Guinea's and Mali's similar efforts, it seemed to much of Africa that the basic choice lay between Houphouet-Boigny's approach and that of Nyerere. The relative successes and failures of each will significantly affect the outlook of Africans during the 1970s. It is therefore relevant to examine in some detail the policies of both countries in order to understand what has become the central issue in Africa's economic arguments.

It has often been claimed that the Ivory Coast has achieved Africa's "economic miracle", like those of Japan in Asia and West Germany in Europe. The figures are impressive. For the first ten years of independence her average annual rate of growth was 10.5 per cent. Discounting a 2.5 per cent rise in prices and three per cent population expansion, this still represented a five per cent annual growth rate per capita. The average income per head of some $286 was one of the highest in the continent.

This feat of continuous economic growth has been achieved by an open-door policy towards foreign investment, attracted by the right to repatriate profits overseas. Under French colonial rule the main economic activity was the export of agricultural produce, especially cocoa, coffee and timber. After independence agriculture was diversified – pineapples, bananas, palm oil and rubber supplementing the traditional crops. Some agricultural production was undertaken by the peasants – usually cocoa, coffee and bananas – but this represented only a tiny percentage of national output. By far the greatest proportion was produced on plantations, mostly owned by foreigners, some by a small African plantocracy (of whom President Houphouet-Boigny was one outstanding example). Much of the post-independence economic growth was achieved through increasing exports of these agricultural products, which provided favourable balances of trade and thus a small surplus with which to finance investment.

Although agriculture remained predominant in the economy, the expansion of industry took place at a far higher rate. During these ten years, whilst agriculture was growing at five per cent, industrial growth exceeded 18 per cent a year. Much of this was concerned with the processing of local crops, rice-shelling, palm oil pressing, fruit-canning, wood-mills, paper-factories and the like. Most of this industrial activity was designed to provide alternatives for imported goods. No major industrial plant was installed, though a few factories for the assembly of cars and radios were built. Virtually the whole of the industrial sector – 95 per cent – was constructed and owned by foreigners.

The visual evidence of this prosperity was spectacular, Abidjan was transformed from a small colonial town of 125,000 in 1955 into a modern city of about 500,000. It displayed skyscraper offices, large hotels, fashionable shops, swimming-pools, a casino and luxury villas. Hotels were being expanded, a convention centre built, a Riviera-style marina constructed, the object being to attract at least 500,000 tourists a year. In the south-west a huge new deep-water port was being built at San Pedro; in the centre a vast artificial lake at Kossou, three times the size of Lake Geneva, was being created to provide new facilities for fishing, irrigation and a fresh source of electricity.

The Ivory Coast was, of course, a French colony. Its president after independence, Félix Houphouet-Boigny, had been transformed during French rule from a radical enfant terrible into the favourite son of Paris.

He held ministerial office in French governments and became a close confidant of General de Gaulle. He was a reluctant convert to the separation from France that national independence implied, but was supported by the French when he insisted, against Senghor's wishes, on breaking up the West African Federation into individual nation-states.

It was natural, therefore, that the Ivory Coast would receive specially favoured treatment from the French when it became independent. Capital, technical assistance and French advisers were lavishly available during the 1960s. For his part, Houphouet-Boigny offered rich opportunities to French investors, maintained the privileged position of French trade and became Africa's most reliable supporter of French foreign policy – even in her cynical commercial relations with South Africa.

Moreover, as a former French colony, the Ivory Coast was given the opportunity to negotiate associated status with the European Economic Community. As a result, she could draw on European development funds, could attract capital from other European states and gained advantages over her Ghanaian and Nigerian competitors in the markets of the Six.

It would appear, then, that the independence story of the Ivory Coast justified the appellation "miracle". This, however, depends on what criteria are chosen as the basis of judgement. If the test is an increase in production, the erection of new buildings, a more diversified economy, and an expansion in goods available, Houphouet-Boigny can justly claim to have led his country during the 1960s to one of Africa's highest pinnacles of success. But if the objective of independent African governments is to improve the lot of the majority of its citizens, we have then to examine below the figures to reach any assessment. For, as has been indicated earlier, growth in domestic product or higher average incomes calculated by dividing the national product by the number of inhabitants does not necessarily portray improvements in the lives of the majority of people. It depends on how such increased resources are allocated.

The first fact which shadows this picture of apparently growing prosperity is that a much larger number of Europeans – almost all French – were to be found in the country after independence than in colonial times. Much French "aid" or technical assistance was accounted for by the number of teachers who preferred service in Africa to military service. They, of course, perpetuated French teaching in the schools, whether or not it was appropriate to African conditions. Many others came to the Ivory Coast as "advisers" to government departments, businessmen or planters. Altogether, the European community amounted to 35,000, nine out of ten French. They monopolized the leading rôles in banking, industry, commerce, technical skills and plantation agriculture. Some conception of their activities in the country can be gained from the fact that by 1965 private funds sent overseas reached more than twice the total of all foreign aid and private capital entering the Ivory Coast.

How were the African inhabitants affected by the country's economic growth? Was the expansion of the national economy accompanied by genuine development of living-standards?

In the first place, the Ivory Coast shared with other developing countries a wide gap between urban and rural life. According to the state's official figures, differentials in earnings varied by as much as 1:12. A townsman bought eight times as many consumer goods as a country-man, an urban worker earned between two and three times the wage of a similar worker in the rural areas. Town or country should not be thought of as monolithic communities. One has only to explore behind the glitter-ing façade of Abidjan to realize that most urban inhabitants do not enjoy the high wage shown as the national average. Most of the modern quarters of the towns are occupied by Europeans; most of the Africans still live in squalor, many of them unable to find employment. Flourishing capitalism in the Ivory Coast is very largely the capitalism of Europeans, although the government did raise a fund to enable local inhabitants to acquire shares in foreign companies. Even if it were to succeed, though, control of capital and its use would remain in European hands.

Nor is rural society monolithic. For one thing, tens of thousands of the Mossi from Upper Volta come to the Ivory Coast every year to work on the plantations, which does not help the employment opportunities or bargaining power of Ivoreans. But there were also wide regional varia-tions. In 1970, the average wages of a peasant employed in the south was 50,800 CFA francs, compared with only 20,900 CFA francs in the north. Most of the rural inhabitants remained subsistence farmers. Those who supplemented their domestic food production by growing cash crops received insignificant payment for them. In 1964, for instance, of the 46 *milliard* CFA francs earned by the country's coffee and cocoa exports, only 29 *million* went to the peasants. The profits of agricultural boom were largely confined to plantation-owners, mostly European, and a few African planters.

If we look at the picture of the entire population, a statistical break-down presents some interesting features. From a total population of some four-and-a-half million by the late 1960s, it was estimated that 2,340,000 were actively engaged in some form of work. Of these, about a quarter of a million were in paid employment, one eighth in public or administra-tive services, three-eighths in urban private enterprise, one half in the rural private sector. Perhaps another 50,000 were self-employed in some way, mostly in running buses or lorries, in petty trading or as craftsmen. Of the quarter million in paid employment, only about 12,000 held any position of authority, whilst 160,000 were unskilled labourers. The rest were divided between skilled workers and those with subordinate positions in factories or offices.

The most significant feature which emerges from this analysis, though, is that over two million of the active inhabitants, or 85 per cent, remained subsistence peasants. The "economic miracle" had hardly affected them. One specific example of deliberate choosing to perpetuate this situation may be given. It was planned to expand oil-palm production over a five-year period, 1966–70. The alternative was either to concentrate on developing village plantations, run by peasant farmers, or on the block plantations of European owners. The state corporation responsible allocated 35,000 hectares to the Europeans and 9,200 to the villages.

The central argument of the Ivorean élite and their French supporters was that the economic activity engendered by foreign capitalists would provide the country with a self-sustaining economy which could then be inherited by the Africans. Little evidence of such a trend was visible during the first decade. Despite the accent on expanding agricultural production, the country remained a net importer of food. The machines which equipped the new factories were bought from abroad. The fourfold increase in timber exports was dangerously deforesting the land – in 1956 9.8 million hectares were covered by forest; in 1970, 6.3 million. Despite diversification, in 1970 over three-quarters of exports were still confined to coffee, cocoa and timber. The government had to admit that fluctuating cocoa prices still governed its revenues. A 50 per cent drop in the world price in 1971 caused a financial crisis. Few Ivorean capitalists had emerged, whilst profits repatriated to Europe continued to increase and the debt burden rose. Association with the EEC seemed to have brought more benefits to European exporters than to those of the Ivory Coast.

It is true that the élite class had prospered and expanded. During the second half of the decade administrative expenditure was increasing at 12.3 per cent annually, and the number of civil servants by 7.5 per cent a year. It is also true that a little of the prosperity had rubbed off in certain rural areas, with improved housing, new cash crops and opportunities to produce materials for processing industries. Even here, though, the main beneficiaries had been the European planters and their wage-paid labourers; the subsistence farmers had seen little or no improvement. In fact, with food production increasing at only a slightly higher rate than population growth, many must have suffered a declining standard of living.

It was feared, too, that the new projects at Kossou and San Pedro would overstrain the economy by adding another massive debt burden. The International Monetary Fund (IMF), which sent American advisers to report on the schemes, revealed that in order to finance them the Ivory Coast government had agreed to borrow overseas funds on such severe terms that it was doubtful whether the country could afford repayment. The building of the Kossou Dam required the displacement of 100,000 people. It was hoped by the government that they would agree to move to San Pedro, but less than ten per cent of the first batch were willing to do so. If this pattern continued, not only would grave social problems be raised, but the San Pedro area itself would suffer a labour shortage which would prevent it from developing into the rich agricultural district envisaged. In this case, the vast state investment in the scheme would benefit only the forestry companies using the new port.

The most revealing figures emanating from the IMF report concerned the relation of savings to investment. It asserted that "Whereas from 1960 to 1966, 75 per cent of the financing of public investments was guaranteed from internal resources, this percentage fell to 60 per cent from 1965 to 1970." And this was during a period of high export prices. In short, the government was increasingly gambling with future prospects by accumulating a rising foreign debt, whilst the rate of domestic savings was progressively belying its expectations in the health of the country's economy.

Small wonder, then, that as the weight of all these burdens began to be felt, the government in 1971–2 had to call for austerity. Its new 1971–5 development plan lowered the target growth to 7.7 per cent annually, its 1972 budget reduced expenditure increases and cut perquisites. It was revealed that during 1971 the foreign debt had increased by 30 per cent; yet the government still claimed that it could raise itself five-sixths of the finance needed for its development plan. No doubt it hoped for a substantial supplement from foreign private investment, though whether the declared policy of state participation in such ventures would materialize remained a moot point.

The capitalist experiment in the Ivory Coast had neither proved nor disproved itself by the early 1970s. Its successes and failures during the first independence decade depended on the criteria adopted for judgement. The national product had grown progressively at a spectacular rate; yet the majority of inhabitants appeared to be living in much the same circumstances as formerly. New industries and agricultural exports flourished; yet they were almost entirely owned by foreigners. If one sought early improvements in general standards of living, greater social equality and increased indigenous control over economic activity, they were not to be found in the Ivory Coast. If one believed it necessary to increase economic growth at any cost to provide a base from which the indigenous inhabitants could eventually participate, the Ivory Coast could claim to provide a model. Only the future would supply objective proof of the ultimate consequences; it would be for the peoples of the

Ivory Coast themselves to judge whether the policy of their leaders represented success or failure.

The policies adopted by Tanzania over the closing years of the decade represent the opposite pole from the Ivory Coast. Foreign investment was strictly confined to defined areas of activity; discrimination was exercised in favour of citizen entrepreneurs; the land, certain categories of buildings, banks, insurance and many businesses were nationalized; social and economic development was based on a communal structure of village life; leaders were prohibited from retaining more than one source of income. The focal principle of Tanzanian national life became "self-reliance".

The two countries were not vastly different in fundamentals at the time of independence. Both had to rely almost entirely on agricultural production and the export revenues it provided; neither seemed likely to discover the mineral wealth enjoyed by some African states; although there were differences between French and British tutelage, both were bequeathed colonial bureaucracies, educational systems, economic and social infrastructures; each possessed a sea coast, with harbours used by colonial rulers to import manufactured goods and foodstuffs, and to export agricultural produce.

Perhaps the most important similarity was that both the Ivory Coast and Tanzania possessed leaders of strong personality, dominating their fellows, both having proved themselves superior in intelligence to colonial administrators. Yet perhaps the most crucial single factor guiding the two countries along opposite roads was the differences between the two men, Houphouet-Boigny and Nyerere. The Ivory Coast leader, of course, had taken full advantage of that element of French policy which allowed some Africans to participate in the political life of France. Most of his eminence was due to the success he had made of his career in French politics. He was therefore able to exploit this position to obtain specially favoured treatment from Paris after independence. Nyerere never had the opportunity to gain similar favours from London. It seems certain that he would have rejected them if they had been offered; on one occasion he deliberately forfeited British aid over a matter of principle.

The strategy which came to be associated with Nyerere and Tanzania at the end of the 1960s had not yet been formulated at the time of independence. Indeed, Tanzanian policies can be seen to have evolved as the product of Nyerere's own experiences. He began as a conventional anti-colonial nationalist, though never as strident as others of his and the previous generation. At Edinburgh University, for instance, during the immediate post-war period when anti-colonial agitation was in vogue, Nyerere spent his time listening, reading, thinking. He was a quiet observer at the frequent discussions on the future of empires which attracted Scottish, Indian, West Indian and African students; but he attended to learn, not to preach.

On his return to Tanganyika he was concerned to see a movement formed which would represent the inarticulate ambitions of his fellow-countrymen, rather than any particular ideology. He believed that their basic desire was to build their own society on the foundation of their traditions, whilst abolishing the scourges of disease, poverty and illiteracy which had always handicapped them. The only path to this goal was that which led via independence. So his Tanganyika African National Union was formed as an alliance of those who desired various local reforms, based upon one common factor: they could only be achieved through self-government.

Independence, freedom, uhuru – all aspects of the same concept – thus dominated Nyerere's thought and that of his colleagues until it was achieved in 1961. But this was no more than the replacement of alien by indigenous government. It might produce remedies for the various grievances complained of by different groups of his movement; but it could not constitute an ideology, nor even a strategy for government.

Nyerere, although a practising Roman Catholic in a largely Muslim society, had been fortunate in uniting the many communities which reside in Tanganyika into a single entity determined to secure national sovereignty. He knew better than anyone that this was an unsure foundation for nation-building. On the morrow of independence he said to me, "I must now find out what to do with independence." Characteristically, to discover the answer, he again turned to listening. He resigned as Prime Minister and spent nine months in touring his vast country to hear what people really sought.

On his return his answer was still sentient rather than political. He felt that the people wanted to maintain the traditional communalism of their society which was based on concentric groups revolving around the hub of the family. He found that they felt a deep antipathy towards either the individualistic competitive mores of the Western world, or the divisive class struggle concept of the communists. From these observations, Nyerere intellectualized an egalitarian spirit in African traditional society not entirely borne out by historical empiricism. He admitted that the social equality with which he endowed traditional African society extended only to the male half of its members, excluding women from equal rights. This flaw, he believed, should be rectified in the new African communities he suggested should be built on the foundations of the old.

So when Nyerere became Tanganyika's first president at the end of 1962, he had acquired a philosophical framework to offer his colleagues and fellow-citizens. The focal objective was a society based on collective responsibility, co-operation, self-help, social justice and hard work. The policies of his government for the next five years were to be geared to achieving this objective; but there was still little frank analysis of economic cause and effect, of political tools, of social, national or international threats.

It was through trial and error, especially through his failures, that Nyerere reached his particular form of Tanzanian socialism. He had been left with a typical colonial development plan, providing for an expanded infrastructure to facilitate increased agricultural exports which, in their turn, would stimulate the tiny market economy to allow light industries – owned, financed and managed by foreigners – to be established. Yet already it was evident that this would lead to the creation of a small labour aristocracy and increased unemployment. In 1962–3 wages rose by nine per cent, cash earnings by 35 per cent. At the same time employment was falling – by 15 per cent between 1958 and 1963. Nyerere, with his emotional roots in the countryside, recognized the danger of widening the urban–rural gap.

Yet Tanganyika's first self-prepared plan, 1964–69, still retained many of the received ideas current in Europe, communist as well as capitalist. Its three main objectives were to increase per capita income, supply trained Tanganyikans to all sectors of national life, and raise life-expectancy. There was the conventional heavy emphasis on industrialization, whilst 78 per cent of public investment was to be sought abroad, in addition to that attracted to the private sector. In short, there was an assumption that "more" was equivalent to "better".

In general the plan failed, although notable progress was made in post-primary education. Only just over half of the anticipated foreign aid materialized, the short-fall could not be bridged by domestic savings, insufficient skilled personnel were available and projects scantily prepared. Above all, priorities had not been determined, with consequent muddle, inefficiency and lack of co-ordination. Inevitably, the targets set in the plan were found to be completely out of reach after only two-years' effort.

One particular failure not only caused Nyerere special grief, but taught him a significant lesson. He had high hopes that his Village Settlement Agency, begun in 1963, would help to resuscitate rural life to the extent of at least halting the widening gap between town and country. In the event, run by expatriates and inefficiently managed, it exposed the dangers of over-capitalization. Farmers were saddled with heavy debts and showed little enthusiasm for making the efforts essential to success. A lesson was taught that the provision of too much public money before social responsibility had been demonstrated could retard progress. Nyerere's hopes of building from the village to the nation by this method were dashed.

By 1966, the government's efforts to plan a socially progressive

economy had relapsed into crisis. The dangers inherent in the structure of
its plan had been exacerbated by external pressures from the white-
dominated south, an influx of refugees from the Congo and Rwanda,
quarrels with Britain and West Germany, the revolution in Zanzibar (a
nettle which Nyerere grasped by arranging the Tanzania Union), and by
coolness from the Americans. Drought and catastrophic falls in world
prices for certain primary products, especially for sisal, had exposed the
weakness inherent in relying on agricultural export revenues. Difficulties
were also experienced in the East African Community, where the privileged position of Kenya led to grave imbalance in trade between
Tanzania and her wealthy neighbour.

Despite these serious, weighty extraneous factors, the operation of the
plan itself had revealed the flaws of its strategy. Industrial production rose
by 11 per cent a year; wages increased by 16.7 per cent in 1965, 15 per
cent in 1966 in private employment, only slightly less in the public sector.
The cost of living rose rapidly, and employment in agriculture fell as
young men and women went in search of new opportunities in town.
Inevitably, the rural–urban gap widened steadily. There were signs of
élitist ambitions in the capital. Nyerere's social philosophy, the raison
d'être for independent government, was brusquely affronted.

The President reacted characteristically to this open threat to his objectives. At the beginning of 1967 he again went to his people. For a month
he travelled amongst the inhabitants of eight of the 17 regions, his longest
tour since 1961. At the end of his journey he attended a three-day meeting in Arusha of his party's National Executive Committee and met his
regional commissioners. To both groups he re-affirmed the party's commitment to democratic socialism, based on self-reliance. He warned them
that Tanzania could not depend for her development on foreign aid
which, even if it were offered in sufficient quantities, would only make the
country more dependent than ever. He attacked the trend towards the
formation of an élite, insisting that anyone with ambitions for public office
must be content to live an austere personal life. Henceforth the party was
to be composed of peasants and workers, from the leadership to the
humblest member.

From Arusha Nyerere travelled to the capital, Dar es Salaam, where he
addressed a mass meeting for two-and-a-half hours. He followed this by
announcing the nationalization programme mentioned above. He had set
the country alight with new enthusiasm, particularly amongst the young.
Marches were held all over the country demonstrating support for the
newly formulated policies. The message was heard far outside Tanzania,
inspiring many young Africans to envisage goals vastly different from the
foreign-dominated, élitist-ridden régimes under which they were living.
It is scarcely an exaggeration to suggest that the Arusha Declaration came

to hold an equal significance for Africans with that of the *Communist Manifesto* to nineteenth-century Europeans.

Yet it was one thing to proclaim principles and enunciate policies; it was quite another to apply them. There were those in high places who resented the curtailment of their opportunities to become wealthy and comfortable. In the towns, politicians, civil servants and public officials had become accustomed to living as the Europeans had done before them; in the countryside, some farmers had grown comparatively wealthy and were antagonistic to the new spirit of communal co-operation. Dissidents could expect to receive material and moral encouragement from the overseas enemies of Tanzania.

Moreover, the new, more sharply defined policies could only be put into practice through leadership at every level. Neither the party nor the civil service was equipped for this task. After the Arusha meetings two interpretative papers were published. The first proposed changes in school-teaching to give greater emphasis to the skills which would be needed in farming, where the vast majority of children would earn their living. The second re-emphasized the importance of the ujamaa village, first suggested by the President in 1962. It proposed that people should be persuaded to move to a village, establish communal plots, sharing the proceeds and labour, and then create a community farm. Here were the real roots of Arusha practice. Could the nation's children be brought up in a co-operative rather than a competitive ethos; could a communal spirit replace competition and individualism at the heart of the country's economic system? This would crucially depend on what kind of leadership could be mobilized before the spirit of competition, transplanted from Europe through the towns, permanently infected the roots of national life.

By the time that the 1960s had ended, Tanzania's socio-economic philosophy had become a beacon carried by young African militants wherever they might live. They saw it as their answer to those who were trying to imitate Euro-American life-styles, who tried to impose authoritarianism or who preached that only foreign capitalists could secure advances in national wealth. Moreover, the Tanzanian experiment had begun to represent a cult amongst overseas liberals, many of whom had little knowledge of African conditions.

Both these symptoms ignored Nyerere's actual objectives in compiling the Arusha Declaration and the discussive pamphlets which succeeded it. The President only intended the Declaration to form a set of guidelines. Detailed policy decisions would have to be argued out by party and parliament. It was also essential for the people of the country to take part in this national discussion, to use the principles enunciated to devise plans of action suitable to their particular needs. The adulation of both young

Africans and foreign liberals displayed an uncritical attitude directly contrary to the practical, analytical spirit which Nyerere hoped to inspire.

It was too early by the end of the decade to judge the extent of success and failure attained by the Arusha policies. At least another ten years would be needed to determine whether a balance could be established between party, government, civil service and parliament enabling initiative to be allied to agreed principles, efficiency be achieved without creating a stifling, autocratic bureaucracy, originality to became associated with discipline. It had still to be proved whether leaders would accept austerity without attempting to overthrow the régime, if urban workers could be restrained sufficiently from using their power of organization for a genuine spirit of national social justice to be created, what cost would be incurred in undermining the ambitions of substantial farmers. It had yet to be seen whether Nyerere's concept of rural socialism could satisfy those Tanzanians accustomed to hear about or see for themselves the style of life adopted by the élites of Nairobi, Lusaka, Lagos or Abidjan, London, Paris, Moscow or New York

Above all, the Tanzanians had still to show whether their form of rural socialism could provide an increase in national wealth sufficient to open the way to progressively rising standards, and whether this could be achieved without class formation. For Tanzania still remained heavily dependent on export revenues; her increasing import costs reflected the inflationary trend of the industrialized world; in order to develop the policy many extra officials were needed; and ujamaa villages had so far only shown their ability to socialize low-level production. Meanwhile, rapid population increase hindered social welfare provision and productive investment. The Chinese had pioneered some labour-intensive, intermediate technology factories. They were also supplying the excitingly significant Tan-Zam railway between Zambia and Dar es Salaam. But where were the capital goods on which a modern economy depends to be produced and how were they to be financed? Could the ujamaa method increase productivity to supply Tanzanians with more goods and services?

Yet there were already practical signs that Arusha had inspired certain basic changes in Tanzanian national life. The insistence on austerity caught the imagination of a large section of the nation. Ostentation of any kind became unfashionable, the subject of angry criticism supported by public opinion. Ujamaa villages, based on co-operative labour and shared products, were established all over the country and shown to be practical, at least at the current low level of productivity. The second five-year plan, published in 1969, seemed to have absorbed some of the lessons of the first. It had to correct some errors of prediction. Hopes of expanding the sisal industry, for instance, had been completely dashed. In 1964 sisal was selling at about $204 a ton; in 1968 it was a mere $91.8 a ton. Employment in the industry had fallen from 96,400 to 41,668, foreign exchange earned from $52.8 million to under $22.44 million. Such are the hazards of planning in a developing country.

Another significant mis-estimate was that of population growth. It had been anticipated that the growth would be about 2.2 per cent; in fact it was discovered to be 2.7 per cent, or an additional 350,000 people a year. Hardly surprisingly, therefore, the proportion of primary school entrants (about 50 per cent of school age) had remained static over the plan period.

Having found by experience the difficulties of securing foreign investment and, at the same time, realizing the degree of dependence entailed in relying on foreign capital, the planners this time determined to seek 60 per cent of government funds and over 60 per cent of parastatal revenue from inside the country. The priorities lesson had also been learnt. Not content with declaring that "rural development receives top priority", the plan then laid down the products which were to be expanded first – meat, dairy products, fish, rice, wheat, flue-cured tobacco, cotton, pulses, oil seeds, vegetables and fruit. Meanwhile, the growth of a class system in the rural areas was to be combated not simply by exhortation to use the ujamaa principle, but by explicit provision for government help to ujamaa groups: by training, education and demonstration schemes.

It was clear from the second plan, too, that the earlier emphasis on industry had been abandoned. Provision for industrial expansion took second place to rural investment, the new parastate bodies were to absorb most of what was provided and the increase in industrial employment was restricted to the modest target of 50 per cent – 40,000 to 60,000. The hope was expressed that foundations for a capital goods industry could be laid in the next plan; in the meantime, efforts were to be made by the government to use industrial allocations to decentralize urban growth from the capital and link new industrial projects with agricultural resources and needs.

Thus, by the beginning of the 1970s, Tanzania was showing a distinctive style of government based on an approach to economic problems which stressed the need for self-reliance, an accumulation of domestic savings with their investment primarily in rural development, the retention of productive surplus, its use through national control to foster social justice, egalitarianism and co-operative living. It offered a direct contrast to the policies of the Ivory Coast. During the 1970s it seemed probable that other African states would observe the two experiments as alternative poles, their respective successes and failures as evidence of which offered the greater attraction as a model.

No other African government had taken such a decisive attitude to its economic policies as the two examples discussed above. Most tended to be pragmatic, meeting immediate demands with short-term solutions. The francophone states generally accepted French aid and guidance, Gabon rivalling the Ivory Coast as an attraction for French capital. Guinea and Mali tried to remain outside this pattern, both leaving the franc zone itself. Financial, economic and technical difficulties beset both countries however, and before the end of the 1960s Mali had returned to the French orbit whilst Guinea was drawing closer.

Amongst anglophone states a greater variety of economic experiments was attempted. Malawi openly accepted her dependence on British and South African assistance, Swaziland and Lesotho remained almost South African satellites due to their geographic situation, but Botswana courageously attempted a more independent policy. Despite the fact that her economy had been virtually integrated into that of South Africa by the British, under her president, Seretse Khama, she tried to formulate her own policies, to establish friendly relations with Zambia whilst avoiding openly antagonizing the South Africans. The fact that important minerals were discovered within her borders gave her a potential strength on which independent policies might be founded, although increasing her attractions as a future victim of the southern whites.

Kenya provided the greatest surprise in the east. During the 1950s she had taken the most militant anti-colonial line, the struggle between her white settlers and the Kikuyu-led Africans highlighting the white–black conflict throughout the continent. After independence, however, despite Tom Mboya's document, "African Socialism", she became a Mecca for foreign capital deliberately attracted by her government. It was used both to expand her industry and to settle African farmers on those areas of the White Highlands vacated by Europeans. Her economic policies thus tended to create boom conditions in cities like Nairobi and Mombasa, as well as enclaves of comparatively affluent farmers. In both, European or American capitalists operated in harness with a small African élite.

Whilst Ghana, Uganda and Sierra Leone wallowed in economic difficulties compounded by military coups, Nigeria in many ways provided the most fascinating contradictions in the continent. In the first place, her size, with a population of well over 50 million, gave her the status of Africa's giant. In the early sixties she became a byword for élitism, financial and political corruption, culminating in two military coups in 1966. The following year saw the beginning of her tragic civil war which was to last two-and-a-half years and almost tear her national fabric to pieces.

Yet, as the 1970s opened, the giant, instead of subsiding into a bloody grave, revealed renewed virility. Trade boomed, foreign investors fought with each other to supply capital, the growth rate exceeded all the expectations of the new development plan and overseas reserves reached new pinnacles. This was made possible partly by the opportunities offered by rehabilitation and reconstruction, partly by the spectacular expansion of oil production. By 1971–2 Nigeria was exporting £580 million in oil; the planned figure was £329.5 million.

At first sight this might appear as a return to the brash, turbulent days of immediate post-independence. This would be a distorted picture. The military government of General Gowon had certainly not been able to banish corruption, exorcize ostentation nor bar private fortune-hunters from public life. But the laissez-faire of the first federal republic had been modified. The government took a greater responsibility for economic direction, and in the crucial case of oil was participating with other members of OPEC in controlling the activities of the major oil companies.

There were many danger signals in the Nigerian economy. The plan made provision for half a million new jobs over the four years; yet it was estimated that the labour-force would increase by over 2.5 million during that period; and at least two million were already unemployed. Agriculture was stagnating, showing a decline in the output of export commodities, whilst food prices continued to soar. This poor performance was also handicapping agro-industries by denying them the necessary materials. The plan had expected private investment of £165m in 1971–2; in fact investment had exceeded £250m. Very little of this came from ordinary citizens. What price was the country paying in repatriated profits, in foreign control?

Because of the effects of the Adebo wage and salary awards, costs were being substantially increased; yet the increases would apply to only a small proportion of the population and might retard employment. Imports were increasing well beyond plan estimates and balance of payments problems were only avoided because of the rapid growth of oil exports. But oil was a wasting asset; how would such imports be paid for in the future unless they were concentrated on productive rather than consumer goods? Perhaps most menacing of all: in the first year of the plan there had been 50 per cent over-expenditure on the armed forces; no one had offered any proposal as to how this was to be reduced in the future. Was Nigeria, therefore, to be permanently burdened with a defence expenditure out of all proportion to her budget? If so, development was certain to be curtailed.

Despite all these doubts, the African colossus was certainly stretching its legs, generously lubricated by its newly found oil wealth. The direction of its march remained somewhat hazy, but that it would vitally affect the continent's economy, and indeed economic affairs outside Africa, there seemed no doubt.

Algeria, another oil state, also remained somewhat of an enigma although the national direction here was less uncertain. Left by the French almost devoid of professionals, technicians or artisans, the Algerians brought in foreigners to help them. They seemed to accept conventional economic wisdom, seeking heavy industry, centrally controlled government, nationalization and a massive education programme. National affairs became largely controlled by young technocrats, more concerned with the growth of the national economy than with people's shortages, unemployment, high prices or the welfare of the rural population. Yet with her oil revenues and the prospect of vast resources of natural gas, the foundations of a capital goods industry might be laid. Moreover, agrarian reform was not entirely neglected, a state scheme of supporting co-operatives on undeveloped land indicating the pattern.

In the rest of the continent the two most influential examples were probably in central Africa, where Zaire and Zambia went their separate ways. General Mobutu Sese Seko had brought the former Congo through many vicissitudes to something like political calm. He was not content to continue to depend on the Belgians, as Houphouet-Boigny had done with the French. Yet he did believe that some form of capitalist system remained essential, although under constant government supervision. He favoured an open-door policy of trading directly with any interested country, rather than through the intermediary of his former colonial masters. He did not even adopt the preference system to which he was entitled as an associate of the EEC. Nor was internal development neglected. The Inga Dam on the Zaire river had a potential of a third of the world's total hydro-electric resources. With the vast mineral wealth of Zaire, the country could become one of Africa's huge industrial complexes – along with Nigeria and Algeria The immediate question for the 1970s seemed to be whether Mobutu would recognize the connection between rural needs, ethnic vagaries, the operations of foreign capital and political peace.

Meanwhile, Zaire's neighbour, Zambia, although closely linked through exploitation of the Copper Belt which runs through both countries, was proceeding along vastly different paths. Kaunda's Zambia provided the only example of another African state attempting to achieve the same goals as Tanzania. Not only were Kaunda and Nyerere close personal friends, holding related philosophies, but the principles which guided each country showed close similarities. Social justice, based on the interests of the majority of citizens, formed the core of national policies in both countries. The major difference was that whereas Tanzanian wealth was almost entirely agricultural, Zambia possessed rich copper mines providing her with revenues unknown to her neighbour, but also with many social problems from which Tanzania had escaped. Both governments, though, based their policies on state control of the main economic institutions, combined with an emphasis on building national prosperity from the village upwards. Both had yet to discover how to share national resources equitably between town and country without provoking conflict.

The unique exception to this broad, varied pattern of African economic life was, of course, South Africa. It could be argued that Portuguese policies in the three territories they ruled, and Rhodesian attitudes, should be linked to the South African perspective. But neither were of crucial importance, nor did they have the impact on the continent projected by the Republic. South Africa possessed the only self-sustaining economy in the continent. It had grown from a backward, inefficient rural collection of peoples in the nineteenth century, to a modern industrial complex, where vast foreign capital was invested, but which in the post-war years reached a point of technical self-sufficiency. In other words, although foreign capital remained essential, management and control no longer rested entirely in foreign hands.

The effects of South African economic power began to be felt in other parts of the continent during the 1960s. As the political policy of apartheid artificially restricted the domestic market, so South Africans began to look to black Africa for potential new markets. This demanded political and diplomatic initiatives, which brought a new direction into South African foreign policy. Traditionally, South African ministers had defended their segregation policies from international attack by insisting that they did not interfere in the domestic affairs of other countries. This changed during the sixties as Mr Vorster's government sought either to seduce black Africans into an entente by economic bribes or subvert those régimes which refused the bait. The initial line of attack was the red route of Cecil Rhodes, through Botswana, Rhodesia and Zambia, to Zaire and Kenya. Zambia would have been the greatest of these prizes, but in the more distant future Nigeria offered an even more tempting target. Hence the covert South African intervention in the Nigerian civil war and the scarcely veiled efforts to get rid of Kaunda.

The fact was that, although multi-national corporations might swell their profits by using the cheap labour provided by an apartheid policy which restricted Africans to unskilled jobs, this inhibited expansion of South African domestic production. If, therefore, black African countries could be added to white South Africa's empire, the surplus could be profitably invested and white supremacy escape from the laws of capitalist production.

The power of the South African economy had already been revealed by the necessity for the Portuguese territories, Rhodesia and certain black states, especially Zambia, to trade extensively with the Republic, whether they wished to do so or not. Much of the political and economic future of the whole continent would depend on the success or failure of South Africa's new verligte foreign policy, with its barely hidden economic motives.

In facing this economic offensive, with its powerful political and military supports, black Africa suffered from debilitating schisms. In the euphoria of attaining national sovereignty, African leaders seemed to have forgotten their earlier assertions of the essential need to unite in order to secure greater economic strength than any nation could achieve in isolation. Despite the constant exhortations of the Economic Commission for Africa, national governments insisted on devising their own economic policies, even if they duplicated or contradicted those of their neighbours. The attempts at co-operation which were tried, like the East African Community or the Afro-Malagasy Common Organization, tended to be used for national rather than international interests. Yet probably no African state other than Nigeria had a large enough population to develop its own self-sustaining economy. Each national policy was doomed to frustration unless it could be integrated into a wider association.

The opening of the 1970s, then, saw African economies still in an indecisive state, usually living from hand to mouth, at the mercy of powerful external economic forces and disruptive internal political elements. Africa remained largely the economic playground of Europeans and Americans, few of her governments having the strength or the clarity of mind to resist the manipulations of international powers In no state had mobilization of any mass group reached the point where it could dictate to its government or offer serious resistance to external interference. The choice of domestic policies still lay between the philosophies of Tanzania and the Ivory Coast; but serious modern economic development and genuine African self-reliance still awaited the recognition that national economic sovereignty in the African context inevitably entailed continued dependence.

6

Political Perplexities

I was visiting the late Sir Charles Arden-Clarke in his sea-girt Christiansborg Castle in 1955. He was then Governor of the Gold Coast, which was to become Ghana two years hence. The Governor had come to terms with Kwame Nkrumah some fours years earlier, and the two men were working in harness to bring the country to independence. Yet my discussion with Sir Charles centred on the political difficulties which Nkrumah was experiencing at that time. In Ashanti violence roamed the streets; few ministers dared show themselves in the city of Kumasi.

At one point in our conversation the Governor waved his hand at the portraits hanging on the walls of his office. They were all of his predecessors in office. "These are the men I blame for our present troubles," he declared. Here was one colonial servant – one of the few – who recognized that the official justification for colonialism, its function in preparing colonial subjects for self-government, was a myth.

Ten years later I met Arden-Clarke in London. Nkrumah, now President of Ghana, was in serious political trouble. I had recently discussed his problems with him at his request. Sir Charles asked me whether I thought he could be of any service to his old friends if he made a personal visit to Accra. I had to tell him that I did not think he could help. For by now the political problems of Ghana had moved far away from the Westminster-type parliamentary system which the former governor had helped to create. Indeed, many of them were caused by the artificial grafting of that system on to a society with a totally different historical experience from that of Britain. The graft had been performed by an alliance between British governments and the small, largely professional élite of Ghana. Not only was the system alien to Ghanaian traditions, but much of Britain's colonial practice had been antithetical to it. Even when the British Colonial Office hesitantly projected a representative system as the goal of political development, little time remained for it to be experienced. It took Britain several hundred years to evolve a representative parliamentary structure. Ghana's first fully representative elections were held just three years before independence.

This is but one instance of the political inheritance bequeathed to

Africans by the European colonial powers during the short independence decade. Between 1956 and 1966 over 30 sovereign states were created in the continent, all of them out of the residue of nearly a century's European rule. And the central feature of colonial government was that it was authoritarian. No colonial subjects had asked an imperial nation to govern them. Colonial rule was imposed by a state commanding greater power than the society which it colonized. The power factor remained focal to the colonial relationship throughout its existence. The exercise of alien power represents the exact antithesis of representative government.

The theory that the purpose of colonial rule was to prepare subjects for self-government was only heard after World War II. It became particularly common in Britain, the French and Belgians being more frank in admitting that their empires formed elements of national economic, military and psychological power. The Germans and Italians had never professed otherwise.

British imperial apologists only offered this justification when decolonization was seen to be inevitable. There had never been any question of granting representative government before the war. The constant conflict with Indian nationalists, led by Mahatma Gandhi, epitomized the attitude of successive governments. With the victory of Indian nationalism, however, accompanied by a reduction in British international power and a loss of much of her former wealth, Britain was no longer prepared to face major colonial wars. Moreover, it became increasingly apparent that to cede political authority did not necessitate a loss of profitability.

Even so, the British were slow to face the political facts of the post-war world, although never so tardy as the French. Reluctantly, they began to glimpse the inevitable in west Africa. As they did so, new constitutions were introduced into the Gold Coast, Nigeria and Sierra Leone. Each of them provided for greater representation of local people in legislatures and executives. But the concept of full adult representation was still strongly resisted. Colonial officials remained antagonistic to "agitators", or "trousered blacks", as Lugard had termed Africans who adopted European ways. Many of those so contemptuously described were to become leaders of the new nations.

If colonial servants showed antagonism to African political spokesmen in the towns, they resisted even more strongly any pretensions to representation from the rural peasants. The attitude of colonial administrators to the rural inhabitants betrayed a sharp dichotomy. During the 1930s revolts had broken out in the countrysides of many colonies. Usually they were caused by resentment against the actions of collaborating chiefs, and were suppressed by colonial force, often with the assistance of sections of the African urban élites. These revolts occurred in such dissimilar colonies as

Nigeria, Sierra Leone, Kenya, Uganda and Chad. They nevertheless had challenged colonial authority. Instead of regarding rural communities as permanent antagonists, however, colonial administrators subsequently tried to protect them from the influence of urban politicians, constantly holding them up as examples of loyal colonial subjects who had no desire to see colonial rule replaced by indigenous government. For many colonial servants, rural Africa seemed a haven of rightminded values, with due respect for the hierarchy of authority, inhabited by "natural African gentlemen". They appeared to have forgotten that only a few years earlier they were describing the same people as "barbarians" and "savages".

This new attitude persisted down to the midnight of colonialism. Although African nationalists made what use they could of rural resentments, to a large extent they were prevented from organizing or educating in the countryside. The most blatant example was in northern Nigeria, where half the total population of the colony was effectively insulated against the dangerous doctrines of nationalism as British administrators lent their authority to authoritarian emirs and the hierarchical structure which they crowned. As a result, the north delayed independence and when it came found itself alienated from the south.

If there was reluctance to provide genuine national representation in the west, where the British connection had lasted for several centuries, in the east, centre and south much higher barriers were erected. In 1910 the British parliament had handed over its authority to a small minority of white residents in South Africa with no provision for future representation of the vast majority of inhabitants. Henceforth the white community, one-fifth of the population, was accorded the power to impose its will on Africans, Coloureds and Indians.

From that time onward behind British colonial policy there always lurked the assumption that most of the centre and east would follow the example of the south. It is true that in 1923 the Devonshire Declaration, re-affirmed by Lord Passmore seven years later, asserted the prior interests of Africans over white settlers in Kenya. But the crucial word in the Declaration was "interests". This implied a completely different concept from "rights". For every British government subsequently asserted that it knew best what was in the interest of Africans. Thus, throughout east and central Africa, British governments claimed that some form of multi-racialism or racial partnership would bring the maximum benefit to the vast African majorities. Non-racialism, or full adult representation irrespective of race, was condemned as "the counting of heads". As many of those in powerful positions in British governments had never really accepted adult suffrage as a right of the British people, they found no paradox in condemning it as a prescription for "anarchy" in Africa.

H

Many and devious means were employed to bar adult suffrage from east and central Africa. The Baganda were given special privileges in Uganda so that the nationialists were forced to accept a form of federal structure to obtain independence. In Kenya, national parties were forbidden until shortly before independence, when a regional system was thrust on the new nation. In Tanganyika, the colonial administration scarcely concealed its support for a multi-racial party as a rival to Nyerere's TANU. In Zanzibar, a constitution was devised which allowed the Arab-dominated party to hold office with a minority of votes.

The most blatant attempt to block full adult representation was made in central Africa. The Central African Federation, for which both major political parties in Britain must share responsibility, represented an effort to create a quasi-South African situation. Only the comparatively small proportion of whites to Africans made it impossible to adopt a complete replica of apartheid. African objections to the scheme were rejected "in their own interest". The gentlemen of Westminster believed that Africans would come to value more highly the economic advantages which were supposed to accrue from the white-dominated Federation than the right to govern themselves. Only the determination of the Africans themselves to secure governments which represented the people regardless of race prevented the British/white-settler plan from becoming permanently established.

Even when forced by joint African and British opposition pressures to grant and then to extend voting rights, British governments demonstrated their outlook by instituting complicated constitutions, devising "fancy franchises", and curtailing political activities. They also placed a premium on granting political privilege to those Africans possessing comparative wealth. All these measures were designed to prevent Africans from electing their own governments and avoid transferring political power to the elected representatives of the whole people.

Not until well after 1960 were the British forced to recognize that their objective of white leadership, or its later alternative, strong white influence in the new governments, could not be achieved. They tried to maintain their general policy of sustaining minority white leadership even when it had patently failed in certain countries. The first of these was Tanganyika, where Nyerere had so comprehensively organized all sections of his people that multi-racialism had been decisively defeated as early as 1959. It was obvious even to the British government by that year that Africans must soon be given control of their own country. Yet when I arrived in Dar es Salaam in the July, I was assailed by angry queries as to why the British government appeared to be delaying independence. My answer was that I suspected the British were fearful that if independence under full adult suffrage were accorded to the Tanganyikans it might spell disaster for the white-minority régime of Welensky in the Central African Federation. Sir Roy later confirmed this suspicion when he reported that in March of the same year Lord Perth, a Colonial minister, had told him that "so far as our general colonial policy is concerned, a halt is being called to the rapid advance of colonial territories to independence. For Tanganyika, for example, we are proposing a long-term programme."

The policy of creating genuine self-governing instruments was thus always half-hearted; at its worst it was blatantly hypocritical. But the institutions themselves demand examination, for it was they which provided the base on which Africa had to build her political future.

It is only fair to assume that the European ministers, civil servants and parliamentarians who forged institutions for the colonies believed that the structures within which they themselves worked could not be improved. The British parliament, for instance, demanded with justice that before independence was granted the whole population of a colony should be consulted on the constitution under which it was to exercise self-government. From their own experience its members considered that the best method of providing for this was by national elections contested on an adult franchise. This was the precondition laid down for every British African territory with the exception of northern Nigeria, where local custom limited the suffrage to male adults.

What British members of parliament failed to recognize was that the parliamentary system had worked successfully only in a very few environments even in Europe, that colonial Africans had been governed in such a manner that they had never been given the opportunity to adopt the rôles essential to parliamentary democracy, and that their traditions were vastly different (though no less democratic) from those of the British. Moreover, no members of parliament and few political critics seem to have made an elementary analysis of the British system.

The British constitution evolved out of centuries of conflict, bargaining and compromise. The precedents and traditions on which it rests are unique. The fact that it is unwritten demonstrates that its acceptability arises from circumstances which cannot be paralleled elsewhere. Moreover, parliament is only one element in the power-structure. The City, the trade unions, the Confederation of British Industry, the civil service, the educational system, the judiciary, the armed forces, Fleet Street, all wield powers which influence and sometimes surpass those of the legislature and executive. The whole structure is diffused through the country by a complex system of local government, also subject to a variety of external influences.

The parliamentary system exported to the African colonies had virtually none of these props to sustain it. Nor had the Africans developed that class or group formation which occasioned the creation of a party system in Britain or which led to the establishment of various pressure groups. It was these organizations which preserved some semblance of balance within the political establishment. They were able to seek social redress, initiate policies, represent special interests, provide at least an appearance of popular influence.

In African experience authority was based almost entirely in the traditional structure of local communities. The advent of an imported national parliament thus led to confusion. Little attempt was made to connect the traditional power-structure with the new institutions. The novel national parliament might compete with customary authority, or local power-structures might exercise their influence in parliamentary elections. In either case, the function of parliament in reflecting the will of the people would be impaired, whilst the institution itself could be seriously undermined. In fact, with the parties which were formed representing no group interests of a national character, no classes, and scarcely any ideology, elections tended to become haphazard affairs, usually determined by which party had first found the resources for mass organization, made most promises or offered the highest bribes. Yet the localized factor remained paramount. Whoever would govern the country would have to find the means of attaching to themselves those with authority in local, ethnic communities.

The French and Belgians, the two other European peoples engaged in the process of decolonization during the two decades after the war, never emulated British hypocrisy by claiming to have prepared their colonial subjects for self-government. The French did not even claim that independence was the goal of colonial policy, but were forced to accept it in 1959–60 in circumstances outside their control The Belgians held out some vague ultimate concept of self-government for their Congo, Rwanda and Burundi, but it was always in such a distant future as to be purely academic. In the Congo no preparation for running the state and no representative institutions existed until a few months before independence was suddenly decreed in June 1960.

French colonial policy took a vastly different path from that of Britain and has had a more profound impact on African politics than that of Belgium. Theoretically it was based on the philosophy of assimilation, on the creation of a Greater France in which all citizens would have equal rights, regardless of race, colour or origin. In practice the theory proved largely mythical, but with sufficient substance to affect significantly the political development of French colonial subjects after, as well as before, they became independent.

The old communes of Senegal had been accustomed to participate in a minor way in Parisian politics from before World War I. After World War II they were joined by the rest of the colonies. Representation was granted to Africans in the French National Assembly, the Council of the Republic and the Assembly of the French Union, though never in numbers approaching the proportion of their populations.

The French, of course, did not possess the British facility of recruiting troops from India. They therefore reinforced their national armies with forces from their African colonies, who fought in colonial wars in Vietnam and Algeria. Moreover, France pursued a mercantilist economic policy towards her colonies. Without the world-wide trading network of Britain, she openly employed the franc zone as an area of comparatively closed trade. French manufactures, more costly until the end of the 1950s than world prices, were given a preference often amounting to monopoly in her colonies. Colonial exports, usually controlled by private French interests, were provided with price supports to help to pay for them. Considerable aid was given from Paris; French trade depended on it. Tariffs and exchange controls protected this commercial domination, whilst the free transfer of money between France and her colonies ensured the constant interest of private capital in colonial investment.

These features of French colonial rule had a significance far beyond military and economic fields. They tied French colonial subjects much closer to Paris than was ever the case between their British neighbours and London. When African soldiers who had fought in the French army returned home they swelled the ranks of the unemployed. President Olympio of Togo was only one African leader who found that they were determined to make vigorous demands on the newly independent governments. It cost him his life. Moreover, France had no intention of sacrificing her defence framework as a result of colonial independence. General de Gaulle and his Secretary-General for African Affairs, Jacques Foccart, ensured that, with the exceptions of Guinea and Mali, the ex-French colonies remained closely bound by French policy after they had gained sovereignty. Defence agreements were signed, French forces continued to occupy African bases, and French troops were prepared to protect by force favoured régimes such as the Ivory Coast, Gabon, and Chad against attempted rebellions.

From the economic sphere, too, there were political repercussions. In employing their mercantilist system the French did not feel the need to use economic constraint in the manner of the British. French administrators were not expected to raise sufficient revenues in the colonies to balance their budgets. They were able to draw on Paris and the giant African federations as well as on territorial revenues. Thus, when colonial leaders came to take control themselves, no habit of financial discipline had been formed. The inflated administrative salaries, paid foreign vacations, high wages and extravagant educational systems continued; indeed, education was often prodigally expanded.

The profound dependence on France which resulted from these policies continued into the period of independence. It had been assumed in both Africa and France that the concept of Greater France would survive indefinitely. Political parties, trade unions, the educational system, the trading pattern, were all geared to the French connection. The deuxième loi Lamine Gueye of 1950 admitted African higher officials into the French state service, with equal salaries and conditions. The Code du Travail promised African workers similar rights to those in France. These were hailed by Africans as outstanding victories for the policy of assimilation.

By 1956 the loi cadre allowed the colonial territorial assemblies to assume powers hitherto held in Paris. Two years later came the transformation of the French Union into a Franco-African Community which seemed to seal the combination of local domestic autonomy and Greater French responsibility for joint Community affairs.

It was there that the integration process ended. France turned towards Europe, devaluing the franc and thus becoming more competitive in the world markets. Later the European Common Market accepted many French imperial responsibilities, whilst France herself encouraged her colonies to trade outside the franc zone in order to gain the foreign exchange to strengthen it. The ex-French colonies were forced to associate with the EEC, preventing them from free collaboration with English-speaking African states and other members of the Third World.

Meanwhile, pressurized by the example of British West Africa, former refusal to contemplate national sovereignty gave way to an acceptance that the French territories too must become independent states. De Gaulle's government, having reversed its policy in Algeria, and now pre-occupied with Europe, agreed. Unfortunately, both the African and the French leaders chose separate national independence for the colonies, thus breaking up the massive federations of west and central Africa which could have become more viable units. Despite the pleas of Léopold Senghor, who recognized the mistake, the two federations were divided into 12 sovereign states.

This left francophone Africa even more dependent on France. To Senegal, French price supports for her groundnuts became still more vital. De Gaulle felt an obligation towards Houphouet-Boigny who had supported him in the Community concept and had been forced only reluctantly to accept independence. The Ivory Coast was accorded special favours. The rest of French Africa, except Guinea, already punished for rejecting de Gaulle's Community, and Mali for a time, became equally dependent on French aid and whims throughout the first independence decade.

Although the French might have veered away from blatant mercantilism and sought new riches in Europe, they did not consider it to be in their interests to sever their links with the Africans. De Gaulle's declared belief was that there remained great benefits for France in a continued association with Africa, particularly so long as her balance of trade with former colonies remained favourable. Aid, however, was to be increasingly concentrated on facilitating trade and development. So thousands of French teachers, technical assistants, advisers and investors continued to dominate francophone states, cushioning their leaders from the necessity of meeting the real needs of the new countries. Although many French troops were withdrawn during the 1960s, a strategic reserve was left, ensuring that independent French-speaking states continued to be ruled by leaders who accepted the policies of Paris.

Thus French Africa entered the period of independence inheriting a residue of political institutions from the demise of the assimilation policy; Belgian Africa was bequeathed a confusion of new, untried institutions without the personnel or experience to allow more than a perfunctory attempt to operate them; whilst British Africans had to try and employ institutions evolved in a totally different environment, in the absence of those elements which had made them practical in Britain.

Ignorant of these handicaps, the advent of independence raised the enthusiasm of Africans to fever pitch. They anticipated the advent of a new era. What, exactly, did they expect in the realm of political innovation as they saw the imperial flags being lowered?

Various answers to this question were given by different sections of African society. The mass of the people, who lived in the countryside and remained members of subsistence communities, had been told that the district commissioner was the enemy, that when he had been driven out a new era would open. They expected to become again masters of their own villages and districts under their own local leaders. In addition, they expected more help from central governments, now composed of those whom they had supported against the colonial power.

In the towns, unemployed demobilized soldiers and new migrants from the country wanted jobs. Many of them expected that this would be their reward for service to anti-colonial movements or from their relation to members of the new governing group.

There was little ideology in these expectations, except a general desire for fairer shares, for greater social justice. Few of the hopes placed on independence seemed to bear directly on the character of political institutions.

Indeed, is was almost entirely the small élites in each state who visualized personal opportunities for wielding political power, for shaping political careers. It is not generally recognized that, with few exceptions, independence had been negotiated between the colonial bureaucracy and a small African élite. With certain notable exceptions, of which Algeria, Tunisia, Morocco and Kenya are examples, there had been no mass grass-roots revolt against colonial government. The various stages leading to independence had been negotiated by delegations of political leaders who had become acceptable to the metropole, even when they had previously been persecuted. They were aided by appropriate lawyers and constitu-tional experts. In almost every case the members of these delegations had accepted the assumptions of the colonial government. They aimed at nothing higher than replacing the officials of the colonial power in the seats of the institutions already created. As President M'ba of Gabon declared, "Gabon is independent, but between Gabon and France nothing has changed; everything goes on as before." Men like Jomo Kenyatta, Félix Houphouet-Boigny, Milton Margai, Fulbert Youlou, Abubakar Balewa, Hastings Banda, some of whom had earlier been thorns in the flesh of colonial governments, considered that they had succeeded in political revolution when control over national institutions was handed over to them. They even agreed to limitations on the power of such institutions, through the insertion of entrenched clauses, judicial reviews, regional powers or Bills of Rights into their constitutions.

A substantial part of the decolonization process in Africa was thus accomplished through co-operation between the bureaucracy of the metropolitan power and the colonial élite. Sometimes the two parties had collaborated in eliminating more radical leaders, like Nyobe of Cameroun or Morocco's Ben Barka; with others, colonial policy had divided the nationalist movement. The members of the negotiating delegations and their colleagues stepped into the offices formerly occupied by their colonial masters and began to administer the same institutions. But these could not satisfy the expectations of their people in country or town; nor would the younger generation which had not experienced the process of decolonization recognize the substitution of black for white faces as an ultimate fulfilment of the anti-colonial revolution.

By the time that independence had been achieved, the ambitions and demands aroused amongst the ordinary people had reached something like national dimensions. Anti-colonial campaigns had attempted to reach out to all sections of society. Even where there was obstruction from colonial administrators, the effort to restrict the spread of nationalism itself had often provoked those who were being "protected" into anti-colonial consciousness.

The most successful nationalist campaigns were those waged by parties which recognized the importance of mass mobilization. Among them may be numbered Bourguiba's Neo-Destour in Tunisia, Nyerere's TANU in Tanganyika, Banda's Congress Party in Malawi, and Nkrumah's CPP in Ghana. Even where rival parties contested dominance in the anti-colonial movements, their various activities aroused new interests and stimulated new aspirations amongst large sections of society.

To this extent, then, politics had become nationalized before independence. The more farsighted political leaders had realized from contact with their peoples in countryside and town that ethnic consciousness need not produce conflict, but could, in fact, contribute positively to the concept of a national loyalty; that there was a widespread latent desire for better standards of life, more educational opportunities, greater health facilities, improved agriculture, and higher industrial skills. The people were willing to listen to prescriptions for reform, even to the facile argument that colonial rule alone stood between them and Utopia.

Having listened, the inhabitants of the new states now expected practical results from African government. Yet it was through the parties that concern had been aroused, hopes raised, ethnic, religious, regional variations identified with a national direction. These had been the means of communication between capitals and countryside. And it was precisely at the moment of independence that the parties began to atrophy.

Independence produced a paramount need for government ministers, civil service permanent secretaries, army officers, businessmen, bank chairmen, directors of information or broadcasting, professors and vice-chancellors. Pressures, at least from élites, forced new governments to proceed rapidly in the direction of Africanizing the top jobs, even if this led to a deterioration in efficiency or a fall in the morale of subordinates.

In this urgency to appoint Africans to the commanding heights of national employment, the party was often neglected. Many of those who had played crucial rôles in party organization and mobilization for its support were now transferred to office in one of the many branches of national life needing an African executive. As a result the party languished, with the consequence that the most vital communication channel between central government and people fell into decay. Alienation of the people from government, frustrated expectations, hostility or apathy towards policies and a reversion to preference for ethnic, district or regional over national interests inevitably followed.

Two men to see this danger were Habib Bourguiba of Tunisia and Julius Nyerere of Tanganyika. Bourguiba was fortunate in that his country balanced an established middle class and prosperous agriculture at the time of independence. The width of the gap between town and country never extended so far as in most African states, whilst the countryside did not feel as remote from the central government as elsewhere.

Bourguiba may have been even more fortunate in that his national struggle had called for martyrdom, had often been bitter, and concluded in a brief military conflict. He, his colleagues and many of his people had therefore been tried and proved at the bar of personal sacrifice in the cause of nationalism. Nevertheless, soon after independence in 1956 he recognized that his Neo-Destour party represented the only national instrument capable of sustaining a constant dialogue between leaders and people. He therefore concentrated on strengthening party organization and setting it to the task of mobilizing the whole people, from the village level upward, in the responsibilities of nation-building. The comparatively peaceful experience of Tunisia during the post-independence period was significantly due to the importance given to the party's organization and to the functions it performed.

The value placed by Nyerere on his TANU party was demonstrated when he resigned as Prime Minister a few weeks after independence in order to spend most of the next year in party organization. Like Bourguiba, he recognized TANU as his only countrywide agent in nation-building. He saw that the mobilization of Tanganyikans had succeeded in a universal acceptance of only one objective, the attainment of independence. This was now achieved. There was therefore a danger that rivalries, quarrels, conflicts, would break out between so many different communities; or the even greater menace of popular apathy. If the people of Tanganyika were to build a new nation based on any social concepts, their needs, desires, aspirations had to be identified, integrated and moulded into a national policy. Nyerere was under no illusion that independence was the climax of the revolution; he considered it to be the beginning.

At the same time, Nyerere knew that TANU, whilst a successful organization in the anti-colonial campaign, had never been more than a loose association of groups with the one common aim of self-government. Tanganyika was a much larger country than Tunisia, its communications more primitive, its peoples less homogeneous. Nyerere had used the strategy of associating together all with complaints against colonial rule, even though some of their demands appeared self-contradictory. This would not suffice for the tasks of building a new, united nation.

Yet the legacy of colonial administration was equally inadequate. In comparison with neighbouring Kenya, Tanganyika had been lightly administered. The colonial officers had been thinly spread, communications between them and the capital extended and weak. This had led to a lack of cohesive administration and little sense of national community. In any case, colonial local government had been essentially autocratic, entirely unsuitable for the purpose of national participation.

Nyerere seems to have wavered in his conception of the character which his party should develop. In its earliest days it had been considered as a vanguard party, its purpose to co-ordinate other organizations. Then it gained a mass membership, though still through somewhat scattered local branches. Nyerere was personally disinclined to accept the theory that the party should be highly disciplined, with cadres of leaders in each district. He distrusted the concept of a leadership group, fearing that it might become a bureaucratic class giving orders rather than reflecting the wishes of the ordinary people. It was only some time after the Arusha Declaration, when he saw that informed, dedicated leadership was essential if the principles of the Declaration were to be put into practice, that he accepted the cadre notion.

Nevertheless, although the party passed through various phases during the 1960s, from his first national tour of 1962 Nyerere was convinced that TANU must be his chief instrument in the mobilization of national consciousness. It steadily gained in significance, until it became the first organ of the land, superseding government, parliament and civil service. For the party had its roots amongst the people, represented them and was composed of them. It came to be considered as the embodiment of the nation's vision, responsible for guiding all other political organs along the path dictated by the people's ambition.

Later in the sixties, Kenneth Kaunda of Zambia was to come to the same conclusion. His difficulty was that his UNIP was never able to command the same degree of national allegiance as his neighbour's TANU. Whereas Nyerere would have had to create an artificial opposition party once the elections of 1959 were completed, for no other party could attract sufficient votes to gain a single seat in the Assembly, Kaunda's old friend Harry Nkumbula kept his opposition Congress alive throughout the immediate post-independence period. Moreover, there were bitter conflicts within UNIP, whilst, whenever Kaunda tried to discipline refractory members of his party, he found himself faced with another opposition body. Despite these handicaps, Kaunda always recognized the supreme importance which the party represented in his attempts to build a united, progressive nation. He tried continually to create a party organization capable of acting as the agent of dialogue between the masses in village and town and his government in Lusaka.

Both Nyerere and Kaunda demonstrated their appreciation of the crucial nature of the contact between people and policy decisions by appointing a variety of representatives to live and operate in the regions. Not content with departments in the capital responsible for regional affairs, ministers of their governments were sent into the provinces. In a like manner, civil servants were allocated to the regions, whilst both parties also followed the principle of devolution, local, district and regional sections all emphasizing the desire that every community within the nation should participate in the formulation of policy.

These, however, were the exceptions. Even in Tunisia, Tanzania and Zambia, the extra attention given to party organization demonstrated the degree to which parties came under debilitating pressures following independence. In most of Africa they simply ceased to perform the function of communicating between the masses and the leaders which had been their unique rôle during the anti-colonial period. They tended either to wither organizationally or to become little more than means for securing office and preference – or both.

The worst examples were seen in Nigeria. Here the prizes of office were so munificent, the opportunities for patronage so wide, the competition so fierce, that fratricidal wars were fought both between parties and within each one, eventually reducing the system itself to such a shambles that a breath of relief sighed through the country when it was abolished in the 1966 military coup. The parties, which had been formed in each region to represent the people's opposition to colonial rule and their aspirations within an independent state, had deteriorated into little more than cabals providing their leaders with the forces to deploy in their ferocious battles for power.

If this was the extreme case – though no more extreme than that of the Congo – it only illustrated more graphically than the average the almost universal malaise which sapped party activity after independence. It was merely one indication that the party-parliamentary system instituted by the alliance of colonial governments and African élites was incapable of meeting the needs of newly sovereign states. The parliaments themselves showed increasingly little desire or capability to debate the crucial issues of the nation. The convention of government and opposition was alien to African tradition and, in any case, could only work successfully when broad agreement had been reached on the direction which basic national policy should take. Africans had had neither the time nor the opportunity to come to a common mind on such fundamental issues. They still had to be fought out with the various weapons to hand. Where multi-party systems existed they usually represented conflicting ethnic communities. So the politicians used their parliamentary positions to make demagogic appeals to the populace, to indulge in party manoeuvring, to organize electioneering in order to maintain their personal status.

Elections themselves often became giant auction sales, with promises and bribes from rival candidates substituting for political policies designed to meet the needs of the nation. In many francophone countries the method introduced by Guinea was adopted. The whole state formed one constituency, with the party winning a majority of votes gaining all the seats in the assembly. It was common, too, in anglophone as well as in francophone states, for the dominant party to absorb its opponents. The control over patronage exercised by governments gave the ruling party sufficient rewards to attract its critics, who knew that it was unlikely that they could attain office through an electoral system heavily weighted in favour of an existing government. In Ghana an election was cancelled to "save unnecessary expense"; Kenya disqualified almost all opposition candidates in her local government elections; Obote, in Uganda, indefinitely postponed his country's elections.

These various processes might be thought to have strengthened the dominant party. This only resulted, however, where a broad consensus had been established on the central principles of national policy, where the party was seen as a means of communication and organized as such. Battles between and within parties, as in Nigeria and the Congo, obviously weakened the party system itself. Control of all seats through bare majority votes caused resentment and invited violence as a means of gaining power. Absorption of oppositions tended to obscure important issues from public debate, leaving the people without channels for airing their grievances. Only where genuine debates were conducted within the party structure, truly reflecting differences of public opinion rather than merely factional efforts to secure control, was this danger averted.

When Nkrumah decreed his one-party state, those of us sympathetic to him justified his action on the grounds that it was a necessary, temporary measure to bring some kind of political order out of the chaos which had already been marked by violence and death. He told us that we were wrong. We were, in fact, still European-oriented. Nkrumah was quite frank. He explained that in his view the single-party state was much more suitable for African conditions that the multi-party system of Western Europe, which, he pointed out, had in any case hardly proved a lasting success outside Britain, the Netherlands and Scandinavia.

Nkrumah was eventually to provide evidence that the single-party state may also fail in Africa. It deteriorated into a set of warring factions each attempting to gain control of the rich fruits of office whilst the majority of Ghanaian people suffered deprivation. Yet much the same scene was enacted in Nigeria with her multi-party system. Nkrumah's fall was evidence of his failure to organize a single-party state on the principles which he himself laid down, rather than a condemnation of the concept itself.

It is no coincidence that in the first few years of independence there appeared to be greater stability in those states with a dominant party than in the pluralistic countries. Ghana, Guinea, Tunisia, Tanganyika, Mali (where party organization was probably stronger than anywhere else), Senegal, the Ivory Coast, Liberia, Kenya (de facto), all provided examples of single-party régimes which survived the first few years in comparative peace. The mutinies in east Africa may seem to contradict this judgement, but the soldiers never claimed to challenge the ruling régimes and the results were short-lived. The attempted coup of 1963 in the Ivory Coast was a more serious exception, but caused little disturbance in most of the country.

It was later that some of the single-party régimes shared political crises with those which had maintained multi-party systems. Nkrumah was deposed in 1966, Keita of Mali in 1968, Obote of Uganda in 1971. All had deliberately tried to build systems based on a single-party structure in which the party was accorded major responsibilities in the nation-building process.

Throughout the continent the constitutions bequeathed by colonial régimes disappeared within a few years of independence. Political crisis followed political crisis. They engulfed single-party systems, multi-party constitutions, military régimes alike. Is any common cause for this political collapse to be discerned? The answer must be tentative, for not only does it seem certain that the upheavals amongst African régimes have not yet concluded, but much of the evidence accounting for those which have already taken place is still obscured.

Certain aspects of the post-independence situation appeared common to virtually the whole of Africa outside the white-dominated south. The difference between those states in which ruling régimes were overthrown and those where continuity was maintained is to be sought in the narrow margin of varying approaches to these common problems. At the same time we cannot ignore what Ruth Schachter Morgenthau has termed the "random element", quirks of personality, chain reactions of apparently insignificant shifts of policy, sudden communal emotions, the impact of events in other countries.

The movements which had taken the leading rôle in anti-colonial campaigns proved themselves incapable of meeting the major challenges of independence. Agitation and nation-building call for entirely different attitudes and usually for different types of people. The mobilization which had been effected by these movements raised people's expectations, but did not long continue once independence was attained. As the need of politicians for mass electoral support disappeared, political leaders became remote from the electorate. Moreover, in the new independent states the interests of the people and of the élite, which had been mutual in opposing colonial rule, tended to diverge. Elites sought the pomp and prestige accorded by their new status; the people looked for changes in their standard of life. The posing, messianic pretensions and ostentatious lifestyle of political leaders and their followers affronted those who had given them power and who now looked in vain for past promises to be fulfilled.

One virtually universal feature of the nationalist movements was their focus on a single charismatic leader. Most traditional African societies had been based on some form of monarchical government. The king or chief had advisers and almost always a method of learning the people's will, which he was expected to carry out. But one man sat at the apex of the power pyramid. In colonial times this concept was maintained through metropolitan monarchs and their governors. Shortly after independence the former colonies adopted a presidential system, except in the few cases where an indigenous monarch inherited colonial authority. The presidents assumed the rôle of traditional monarch, but they had to rely on a balance of power amongst national institutions for their authority, the civil service, the party and the army. They, like their predecessors, were expected by the public to satisfy their expectations.

Many presidents were not content to play the traditional rôle. They believed that they could take absolutist powers. Frequently they found that they were wrong. When sections of the public grew angry over the coercion used against them they resisted, as witnessed in the peasant revolt of Mulele in the Congo, the rebellion of the southern Sudanese, the secessionist attempt of the Ibo. When members of institutions or sections of them became dissatisfied or ambitious they found little difficulty in deposing the leader. The series of military coups where particular groups of soldiers overthrew the régime and then enlisted the services of the civil service to run the country provided ample evidence of this.

The ethnic problem also played an almost universal part in the power-structure. From the leader down to the humblest official ethnic considerations had to be taken into account. Within the ruling group it was expected that fellow members of an ethnic community would be given preference in appointments. These could form an important power base, but they would also provoke rivalry from contending communities. Nevertheless, the practice was understood and generally accepted in African society. Even those leaders who recognized its dangers were compelled to accept it as an element to be reckoned with and therefore tried to balance their leadership groups accordingly.

Thus, in the immediate situation which followed independence, most of those who had led the country in anti-colonial campaigns became occupied in government and administration, nationalist parties became centred on the capital, their lines of communication with the people became progressively tenuous, élites were intriguing for positions of influence and affluence, and charismatic leaders became increasingly isolated. Here was the perfect prescription for fratricidal strife, a collapse of institutions and a spate of revolutions.

The major difference between those states where this apparently inevitable sequence of events occurred and those which avoided it was discernible in the character of the ruling régime and the measures taken to remedy these common weaknesses. Nor should the personality of the leader be ignored; the contrast between the personality cult of an Nkrumah and the modesty of a Nyerere held more than a personal significance; but one has to add that this factor must also take into account the survival of a messianic Hastings Banda.

The contrast between Ghana under Nkrumah and Nyerere's Tanzania is particularly apposite here. The presidents, parties and governments of both countries became committed to socialist ideals and policies. So, indeed, were many other African régimes, though more often in demagogy than in practical terms. But in both Ghana and Tanzania one saw evidence that the objective of social justice was genuinely held by the presidents and by a number of their closest colleagues. Yet the proclaimed socialist ideology of the former dissolved in political and economic chaos, whereas in the latter a socialist philosophy dominated politico-economic policies providing strong foundations for the régime.

The crucial difference between the two national experiences would seem to centre on the contrasting characters of their parties, strongly influenced by the type of leadership exercised. Of course, the socio-economic structures of the two countries also differed. The traditional competitive commercialism of the west has already been mentioned. It was absent in much of the east. Yet, although such factors played some part in creating special problems and influencing the character of parties, they would not seem to be crucial. Kenya, for instance, became as commercially minded as any west African state, whereas Guinea largely accepted the co-operative philosophy common in east Africa.

Nkrumah's CPP was widely considered to be the prototype of a mass nationalist party. In contrast to its predecessor, the United Gold Coast Convention, it was never based on the intelligentsia or professional class. It appealed to urban wage-workers, the unemployed and ex-servicemen. At the same time, it was also heavily weighted with small traders, especially the market mammies, petty bourgeoisie, clerks, new school-leavers, and some farmers. It was generally regarded with suspicion by the higher educated, many professionals and a section of traditionalists. Most of the subsistence peasants remained apathetic.

So, although more of a mass party than its predecessor, the CPP did not achieve such a national following as to be able to ignore its influential opponents. Moreover, Nkrumah himself was always conscious of the fact that he had never attracted the votes of a majority of his adult citizens. He constantly used to refer to this failure as though it continually caused him a sense of insecurity. It may even have been one of the factors which gradually gave him a persecution mania.

Nevertheless, the CPP was sufficient of a mass party for it to have laid foundations on which it would have been possible to pursue full national mobilization after independence. Instead, it became a body within which leaders and officials employed patronage to increase their status and wealth. State and party had to rely increasingly on coercion rather than persuasion; no real attempt was made to extend political education to the masses through party cadres; the party itself never developed a coherent ideology; factions disputed, but never debated serious issues; the party bureaucracy and its parliamentary members were constantly at odds; the life-style of its leaders progressively affronted the populace.

Nkrumah saw most of these weaknesses; yet he seemed unable to do much to rectify them. His vanity prevented him from facing unpalatable facts. He became increasingly impatient of criticism. Indeed, some of his actions aggravated his party's decline. The decision to establish a one-party state was made more in anger against opposition than in order to revive democratic discussion within the party structure. The CPP had been organized largely as a vote-gathering machine; once elections were abolished it lost most of its raison d'être, for it never became a forum for policy discussion or decision.

Nkrumah's major attempt to express criticism of the party's conduct illustrated his remoteness from the people and his inability to enforce discipline. His dawn broadcasts of 1961 castigated those who were using their political positions to live in ostentatious luxury. Yet he merely laid it down that party members should not own more than two houses with a combined value of £20,000 and more than two cars. This was hardly likely to appeal to the ordinary people as an austere standard. Moreover, most of those whom Nkrumah dismissed in 1961 for corruption, personal aggrandizement and accumulation of riches were back in office the following year.

At the other end of the spectrum, the tiny group of Marxists in the party became increasingly ineffectual as they became immersed in the minutiae of doctrinal debates. Some of their speeches and writings may have lent a specious veneer of socialist semantics to the party, but they had influence neither on decisions nor on identification of the issues. Their younger recruits, trained at the Winneba Ideological Institute, repeated the dogmas of European communism without ever making the effort to study or analyse their own Ghanaian society and its problems. Consequently, when Nkrumah turned to state corporations and controls in his effort to apply socialist doctrines to his deteriorating economic situation, these instruments were simply used as further opportunities for graft, patronage and bribery.

In short, Nkrumah's CPP, although starting its life with the objective of popular mobilization, failed to extend its communications to the mass

I

of the people after independence. It became a means of personal advancement, a hot-house of factionalism, a nihilistic machine. It was therefore incapable of facing the tasks of identifying the economic or social problems of the new nation, setting an example of living styles, educating the people in the responsibilities of national construction or leading the national effort essential for producing economic independence out of political sovereignty. As the people became increasingly conscious of this failure their disillusion mounted. The only manner in which the party could respond was to increase coercion. A régime based on force is always liable to encounter superior force, which fate befell Nkrumah's CPP régime in 1966.

Nyerere's TANU had grown as an amalgamation of various interests much in the same manner as the CPP. It had no more of an ideology than Nkrumah's party, concentrating solely on the issue of independence. Tanganyika could offer fewer prospects of personal gain to her leaders than Ghana, for she was much poorer, with a lower potential for development. Nevertheless, leading members of the party and their associates expected rewards from the new state. The life-style of Dar es Salaam might seem dowdy in comparison with that of Accra; but it was princely compared with that of the vast majority of inhabitants.

The major difference was that Nyerere recognized that his party would have to change its structure and purpose if political independence was to be applied to the building of a nation. He had the advantage that his party was national in the sense that it had no serious competitors and few coherent critics. Warnings of trouble appeared from some trade unionists who did not accept that their members' privileges must be curtailed for the sake of social justice; the danger was averted by the adherence of the leading trade unionist, Rashidi Kawawa, to the party and the firm alliance established between him and Nyerere. The ultra-leftists were even less effective than in Ghana, whilst the army, though briefly dangerous during the 1964 mutiny, was concerned with service conditions rather than politics. Perhaps the most serious menace to the unity of the party was the demand from many sections of the community for quick Africanization. This not only endangered efficiency, but projected a slight racialist cloud into the national horizon, for many influential positions were held by Asians, some of whom became Tanganyikan citizens.

Nyerere met each of these threats by discussion and persuasion instead of by coercion, although he was sufficiently aware of potential threats to his régime to take powers of detention. Yet his crucial approach was to concentrate on organizing his party as the central organ of the nation.

As mentioned above, within two months of independence Nyerere resigned as Prime Minister to devote all his efforts to the party. He thus demonstrated from the start his belief that the party represented the supreme instrument in the state, of greater importance than parliament or government, eventually a controlling influence over the state itself. Above all, Nyerere was determined that TANU should be completely representative of the people, in a more direct manner than was possible for legislature or executive.

It is difficult for those brought up in the European or American multi-party system to understand the profound democratic spirit which imbued Nyerere and other Africans who saw their parties as the embodiment of the people's will. It was not just that Tanzania evolved a single-party constitution which preserved elections by providing for two party members to contest each constituency every five years. This prevented the party from either becoming a vote-gathering machine or rusting away from inactivity as in Ghana. It also encouraged instead of inhibiting discussion and innovation. Yet the concept of democracy in the Tanzanian system was much deeper than this.

Essentially, Nyerere believed that genuine democracy was not sufficiently served by the electorate sending representatives to legislative bodies, whether local or national. The people could only fully express their wishes and ensure that they were carried out by active participation themselves. This not only ensured that their interests were kept firmly before the eyes of all with executive power; it also taught the people themselves that form of responsibility which comes only from trying in practice what is preached in theory.

The party was the only national organ which could provide the opportunity for this type of popular participation. Final decisions on policy might have to be taken by representatives, whether in party or government; but participation in the decision-making process and popular activity in implementing such decisions could only be organized through the party. It was the party, therefore, rather than legislature, executive or departments of state, which was given the responsibility of organizing discussion on plans and policies, initiating new projects, leading popular execution of programmes, educating the young and the peasants in national principles, providing leadership in social, political and economic development, helping the people to liberate themselves from ancient and modern chains.

It was not only Nyerere and TANU who recognized the supreme importance of developing a party which could perform these functions. One of the most remarkable achievements of an African party was that of Bourguiba's Neo-Destour in abolishing polygamy and emancipating the women of largely Muslim Tunisia. Kenyatta's KANU played a major rôle in reducing the ethnic tensions which had become traditional in Kenya. Kaunda, despite the persistence of his opposition and schisms within UNIP, nevertheless strove to make his party the central agent for involving the Zambian people in the pursuit of national consciousness. Even Senghor and Houphouet-Boigny, who had been accustomed to loosely structured organizations, began to realize at the beginning of the 1970s that the survival of their régimes might well depend on stronger party cohesion.

If the degree of popular participation in the dominant party generally marked the difference between stability and the risk of political crisis, Nyerere had one further advantage. Although he and TANU had neither developed nor enunciated any more coherent ideology than Nkrumah's CPP at the moment of independence, his socialist philosophy developed throughout the 1960s. It arose neither from books nor from visions: it grew out of his own and his people's experiences. We can see this philosophy developing throughout the post-independence decade. Self-government had to be achieved if the people of Tanganyika were to order their society according to their own wishes. Once that was attained, national effort had to be devoted to raising the living standards of the mass of people, most of whom remained at subsistence level. This required both co-operation amongst them to make the most of scarce resources and restraint on the part of the privileged few, whether élite, urban workers or wealthy farmers. Co-operation under state direction failed; so the alternative of self-help must be tried. Meanwhile, awareness of external influences, economic and political, grew both from domestic experience and from observation in the rest of the continent. So foreign aid or investment must be examined with much greater discrimination. The philosophy enunciated in the Arusha Declaration, based on popular participation, self-reliance, co-operation and the supremacy of the people's needs, evolved empirically.

With a party embracing all national elements, encouraging free discussion on the means of attaining accepted ends, and an ideology based on the aspirations of the common people, Nyerere was armed to resist those factional forces which destroyed other régimes. How long the stability thus achieved lasted would now depend on the success of the experiment in building economic prosperity, on the personality of party officers, the efforts forthcoming from the people themselves and, not least, on the ability to resist external intervention; but the framework of an instrument capable of building a socially just new state had been erected. It offered one model to those anxious to avoid the catastrophic crises suffered in other African states.

This variety of political experiments was conducted in a context wholly inimical to the success of any of them. The most disastrous inheritance bequeathed by Europeans to Africans was the concept of the nation-state. It had grown only in modern times in Europe, usually out of strife, and bringing Europeans immeasurable suffering. Idealistic Africans, and others from America and the Caribbean concerned with liberating Africa from colonial rule, had always believed that the African continent could escape from the havoc which the nation-state had wrought elsewhere. The Pan-African movement, from the beginning of this century, had aimed to produce a sense of African continental unity out of the demise of imperial rule. The famous Manchester Conference of 1945, for instance, had declared: "We demand for Africa autonomy and independence, so far, and no further, than it is possible in this One World for groups and peoples to rule themselves subject to inevitable world unity and federation." A west African federation had always formed an essential part of the vision held by early nationalists from this region. Pan-African unity was the gospel of every nationalist. Yet, not only were these hopes for "world unity and federation" disappointed: when decolonization swept through Africa during the 1960s, it perpetuated the balkanization of the continent initiated at the Berlin Conference of 1884–85. Sovereignty was accorded to new states delineated by the colonial boundaries originally drawn by the European imperial powers. Africa became a continent of 42 nation-states, together with a few residual territories still under some form of alien rule. The new states varied in size from the just over 300,000 of Gambia and Equatorial Guinea to the nearly 60 million of Nigeria. Only three African countries (Nigeria, UAR, and Ethiopia) had populations of over 20 million; 35 were inhabited by less than 10 million, 28 under 5 million.

If the nation-state is defined as a single ethnic community possessing sovereignty, there are virtually no societies in the world which could qualify. The conflicts of ethnic groups unwillingly bound together in states have kept Europe in a condition of tension for several centuries. Certainly the concept has had no place in African history. It was customary for Africans to travel throughout the continent in trade, warfare or migration without hindrance from frontiers. Many still do so, like the migrant workers from Upper Volta, Mali and Guinea who seek work each year in the Ivory Coast or Ghana, the Masai in Kenya and Tanzania or the Tuareg of the Sahara. But national sovereignty is being increasingly employed to expel foreigners and stiffen barriers against free movement. The acceptance of separate national sovereignty inevitably provoked a rash of ethnic troubles. The Congo, Rwanda and Burundi, Nigeria, Chad, the Sudan, all demonstrated in tragically spectacular ways the fact that the colonial boundaries had never enclosed homogeneous communities. Every African state suffered from similar, if less violent, resentments amongst communities unwilling to accept the supremacy of a national government which they felt might be alien to them.

Economically, of course, separate national sovereignty made nonsense.

Efforts to establish capital goods industries, to build iron and steel complexes, to rationalize and specialize in production, were entirely unviable so long as national sovereignty reigned supreme. As Nkrumah said on one occasion, "Many African states still impose customs duties and import restrictions originally designed to limit the trade of the colony in the interest of the manufacturing industries of the imperial power." Consequently, "the price of our manufactured goods is far higher than it need be if there was a larger market".

If the object of political independence was to effect an economic revolution capable of transforming the life of Africans, the maintenance of sovereignty was bound to frustrate it. Some African leaders saw this. Nkrumah tried to form a union with Guinea and Mali; Senegal and Soudan formed an abortive federation; the east Africans built a Community on the base of the common services they had inherited from colonial days. Nyerere even offered to postpone Tanganyikan independence so that the three eastern colonies could gain sovereignty simultaneously as a federation. Most of the francophone states attempted to associate economically in a common organization. The Economic Commission for Africa made continual efforts to promote supra-national co-operation.

The handicaps were too great. The economic operations of the ex-colonial economic forces encouraged separation, although whether this was in their own best interests is a moot point. The close control exercised by France over her former African territories after independence, followed by their association with the EEC, prevented francophone and anglophone states from forging a common economic policy. Even their monetary zones were separate and often competitive. In any case, there was constant fear of an economically dominant state securing a controlling power, or conversely, having to subsidize its weaker associates. Both fears led to the breakdown of the French federations at the time of independence; similarly, they continually weakened the east African association.

The need for some form of political co-ordination was as great as that for economic co-operation. Indeed, it is doubtful whether the degree of economic association demanded could be achieved without close political collaboration. Yet here again the difficulties were enormous. Africa was by no means a united continent at the time of independence. There were open quarrels between Morocco and Algeria, Somalia, Ethiopia and Kenya, Ghana and Togo. Many states, Ethiopia, Nigeria, Chad, Rwanda, Burundi, the Sudan, Cameroun, Congo, were torn by internal dissensions. Others were soon to experience the same trauma. There were constant suspicions that other African régimes were supporting one or other rebel group. Arab quarrels and the effects of the Arab-Israeli conflict constantly exacerbated inter-African relations. Alliances were formed, the Brazzaville, Monrovia, Casablanca blocs, each deeply suspicious of their rivals. Even when these seemed buried in the formation of the Organization of African Unity in 1963, suspicions and divisions did not disappear. Nyerere was once provoked to declare after an OAU summit that there seemed to be a devil abroad in Africa.

Perhaps the most inhibiting influence on African political development during this decade was the creation of the Central African Federation. Because this was imposed on the Africans of the three territories against their wishes, and because it seemed to consolidate white supremacy on a permanent basis, it discredited the institution of federation itself. It led to an outburst of anger when it was rumoured that a similar federation might be created in east Africa. Nyerere saw through these clouds of suspicion and realized that an east African federation could be formed under African leadership; but African hackles had been so raised by the experience of central Africa that his rationalism generally fell on deaf ears.

The effects of this disunity and the reactions to those who constantly appealed for African unity destroyed any hope that political development in the continent could be co-ordinated. It fed those who expected to gain status and rewards from national sovereignty, who were not prepared to forgo the enjoyment of controlling a national apparatus. Sir Abubakar Tafawa Balewa, Prime Minister of the Nigerian Federation, responded to Nkrumah's call for unity by declaring shortly before independence, "A United States of Africa? Oh, surely it is very premature to start talking about anything like that. Nigeria has not the slightest intention of surrendering her sovereignty, as soon as she gained her independence, to anyone else, including other Western African countries." Balewa's determination to maintain national sovereignty undiminished represented the almost unanimous attitude of African politicians. Even Nkrumah himself showed little practical evidence of willingness to modify Ghanaian sovereignty.

Yet it was obvious that the concept of the nation-state was unsuitable for Africa and destructive of her chances for stability or progress. Nigeria or the Congo were large enough and sufficiently wealthy to try to solve their political difficulties through domestic federal structures. Not only did these fail through the conflict between ethnic, regional and national interests, but they provoked further quarrels between other African states. The wastage of scarce manpower from the proliferation of administrators, politicians, diplomats and technicians entailed in separate national structures, the inability to forge common policies towards external forces, political and economic, the absence of any consensus on political institutions, all led to retarded economic development, international conflicts and internal instability. The fact was that few African societies had developed the attributes of a nation by the time of independence. Where there were comparatively homogeneous communities they usually lived across national boundaries, aggravating instability. This was certainly an unfortunate legacy of European imperialism; but it left independent Africa to suffer continual political unrest so long as the hypnosis of national sovereignty survived.

It is easier to indicate the weaknesses of the nation-state system than to suggest alternatives. All thoughtful African leaders recognize the handicaps the system brings them, yet they also know that national pride is now involved, along with a great many vested interests. Nevertheless, it has become obvious that Africans will never be able to solve their political problems, to develop institutions capable of sustaining ordered progress, nor to use their political authority to effect radical reforms in their economic relations until they find a relevant substitute for the nation-state and national sovereignty. The African political scientists who have spent so much of their time in arguing fine points of political alignments or the semantics of ideologies might, with better results, undertake the task of devising new institutions capable of serving the special needs of the African people for supra-national organs linked with smaller, communal veins of authority. For this would reflect the realities of African society, a common entity composed of hundreds of group personalities. Peaceful development through acceptable political institutions depends on representing this reality and discarding the alien structure left by Europe.

Racialism

Black Africans have little racial or colour consciousness. It is remarkable that after nearly a century's experience of suffering discrimination on account of their colour, they have shown so little inclination to retaliate when they gained the power to do so. There may have been a few exceptional cases of racial antagonism since independence. Even in Dar es Salaam, Africa's most tolerant capital, white people were made to feel uncomfortable in public for a few days after the 1964 mutiny. Whites were held hostage in the Congo wars and isolated incidents of anti-white terrorism have occurred elsewhere. But these scarce examples illustrated a resentment against people believed to be acting in the manner of former colonial masters; none of them has shown any evidence of animosity towards white skins or differences of race.

A sharp contrast is evident between the African and the American black's reaction to whites. One of the most highly intelligent, rational American blacks I know once told me how he had been held on his grandfather's knee as an infant and repeatedly taught that he must hate all whites. Emotionally he had been fixated ever since, although his reason rejected these emotional reactions. To the best of my knowledge this kind of attitude has never existed in Africa, even where discrimination was most severe. Indeed, one can quote the moving statement of Nelson Mandela, South Africa's "Black Pimpernel", at his trial before he was sentenced to incarceration on Robben Island. "I have fought against white domination," he declared, "and I have fought against black domination. I have cherished the ideal of a democratic and free society in which all persons live together in harmony and with equal opportunities. It is an ideal which I hope to live for and to see realized. But if needs be, my Lord, it is an ideal for which I am prepared to die." Mandela and his colleagues suffered more brutal racial discrimination than anyone in Africa; the ideal of a non-racial society which they sustained in their bitterest hour of trial is one which all respected African leaders share.

This is not to suggest that there is no racialism practised in the continent. In 1949 bloody racial conflicts broke out between Africans and

Indians outside Durban. Economic competition and rumours of sexual affronts fanned the flames. Yet the most remarkable feature of the affair was that it was subdued by African and Indian leaders, has never recurred and was quickly followed by the creation of a firm alliance between the Africans and Indians in common resistance to the discriminatory measures of apartheid.

In other parts of the continent, too, friction has been witnessed between African and Asian. In east Africa the Asians were accorded a superior status to Africans under colonial rule. They virtually controlled commerce and petty trading, many of the younger generation also taking a major share of professional, skilled and semi-skilled jobs. After independence there was inevitable resentment amongst Africans towards the superior socio-economic position which Asians retained. This was aggravated by African unemployment and disappointment when their expectations of economic improvement did not materialize from political independence.

Until General Amin's mindless outburst in 1972, however, this envy was never exploited by leaders or governments. Indeed, each east and central African government deliberately included both Asian and European ministers in its appointments. Far from reacting to the racial discrimination which had been universally practised by both colonial rulers and local white settlers by reversing discriminatory rôles, African leaders made strenuous efforts to subdue resentments amongst their citizens and build genuinely non-racial societies.

What they all agreed on, however, was that citizens and non-citizens should be treated differently. At the time of independence most inhabitants were given the opportunity of becoming citizens of the new states regardless of race. They were given two years in which to make up their minds what nationality they wished to assume. A few Europeans and a large number of Asians chose to become citizens of the new African states. In Kenya, for instance, of the 180,000 resident Asians 120,000 opted for Kenyan citizenship. It was those who chose to retain or take out citizenship of other countries, notably of Britain, who presented the main problem. Africans saw no reason to allow people who had rejected the offer of citizenship to remain in dominant economic positions. With unemployment high and Africans still suffering from the discrimination in education, training and employment imposed by colonial rulers, it seemed fair to give citizen applicants first choice, even if this entailed prohibiting non-citizens certain forms of employment. Discrimination was practised on grounds of nationality, not of race.

This statement must be modified in one respect. Immediately after independence there was widespread clamour in east Africa for governments to follow a policy of Africanization. Even Nyerere had to face the demand. Africanization, however, is different from localization. It carries a certain racial flavour. The rationalization was that because Africans had suffered the greatest discrimination under colonial rule, whilst Asians had been accorded privileges less than Europeans but higher than Africans, independent African governments must discriminate in favour of their African citizens in order to correct the balance.

This clamour was so insistent that Nyerere himself had to bow to it for a short time. Although ideally he would have liked to insist that all appointments were made according to merit, based on citizenship regardless of race, he recognized the frustrations under which ambitious Africans were suffering. Yet he allowed such discrimination to continue for only two years. Early in 1964 he issued a directive declaring that the period of Africanization must now end and appointments be made from amongst Tanganyikan citizens according to merit alone. This may well have played some part in provoking the mutiny of the same month. For one of the main demands of the soldiers was the removal of their European officers.

In all the east African countries Africanization was quickly superseded by localization, though there were frequent administrative difficulties and muddles in processing many Asian applications for citizenship. Nor could government edicts alone remove the resentments felt by Africans for the greater wealth, business acumen and professional skills shown by most of the Asian community. But this was economic or class envy, rather than racial antagonism. As we have seen, it was felt between Africans and Africans as well as towards Asians.

One factor, however, exacerbated the division between the races. Although Pandit Nehru, his Commissioner in east and central Africa, Apa Pant, and later Mrs Gandhi, all urged Asians to integrate themselves into their local societies, many of the Asian communities remained cultural hermits. Anyone who had the experience of being entertained by conventional Asian families in east Africa will have been aware of the persistence of Asian custom. Few, if any, Africans would be present. The men and women were segregated. The extended family would form a unit, private and often commercial, living a separate life from the African communities amongst which they lived.

This was not universal, but it was general. The Ismailis, under the guidance of the Aga Khan, probably assimilated to a greater extent than other Asians in east Africa. But they were the exception; and Africans resented this cultural segregation. One highly literate African told me in Uganda long before independence that the Africans found that, once they had broken down the colour bar, they could mix comfortably with Europeans; but never with Asians. This was a cultural barrier, not based on race or colour, but it tended to separate the two races, aggravating the economic tension which had been left by colonialism.

The main exceptions to the general rule that African leaders resolutely opposed every form of racialism were seen in Uganda and Zanzibar. The two cases were quite different. In the former, General Amin, having used his power in the army to depose President Obote in January 1971, proved quite incapable of governing the country. Fratricidal conflicts within the army, provoked largely through inter-ethnic hostility, resulted in large-scale massacres. Amin quarrelled with the Israelis, who had been training his army and air force. Although they had helped him to power, he expelled them all. He had little conception of how to run the economy, his greatly inflated military budget only increasing his economic difficulties. Despite the fact that Mr Heath, the British Conservative Prime Minister, had shown immense pleasure from Amin's coup, immediately following as it did Obote's trenchant contempt for Heath's policy of selling arms to South Africa, Amin did not hesitate to antagonize Britain. Through his manner of making speeches calculated to please his current audience, usually without any thought of consequence, he found himself pledged to expel all Asians from his country. The fact that at the very time he made this speech he was negotiating for additional Indian doctors reveals just how disorientated were his ideas.

It is significant that Nyerere immediately condemned Amin's policy as racialist. Whereupon Amin changed course again, as he had done several times during the preceding week, and decided that Asian citizens of Uganda would not be included amongst those to be expelled. He made it plain, however, that he hoped ultimately to get rid of all Asians from the country.

Even in this case the issue seemed to be less overt racialism than erratic behaviour on the part of Amin. He could lunch in a friendly manner with leaders of the Asian communities almost simultaneously with making speeches justifying the expulsion of their people. He seemed to have no conception of the damage he was doing to his country, even to his own position. Nor was he apparently conscious of the dangers he could produce for the whole of east Africa. For when people are living in the uncertain times of change such as those which followed independence, they do not need to be racialists to have their natural sense of insecurity turned into hostility towards privileged minorities. The fact is that Amin was essentially a soldier, with a soldier's personality, totally ignorant of political realities.

In Zanzibar the situation was different. The revolution of 1964 over-threw a system under which a mainly Arab party had been allowed by the British colonial government to take power with a bare majority of seats but a minority of votes. Sheikh Karume took control after the revolution and became first Vice-President after the formation of Tanzania from a union between Zanzibar and Tanganyika until his assassination in 1972. He was a strange man, sometimes kindly, sometimes cruel, always dour, intractable. He exploited the antagonism between the various African communities and the Arabs and many brutalities resulted. Yet, again, this was not sheer racialism. The Arabs dominated landowning and clove-growing. They were considered to have exploited their African workers. Once again, there was a strong current of economic antagonism sweeping the tide of what appeared to be racial discrimination. The myth of "racial purity" certainly did not appeal to Karume; he even made the bizarre suggestion that racial differences between African and Asian should be bridged by compulsory marriages between members of the two communities.

There have been suggestions that racialism was responsible for the civil wars in the Sudan, Chad, Nigeria and Algeria; that Arabs fought "Negroes" in the Sudan and Chad, Hausa the Ibo in Nigeria, Arabs the Berbers in Algeria. This is to misinterpret the meaning of "racialism". The term has been much abused over the past few years, just as wide misunderstanding has been created over the meaning of "race" itself.

Religious differences – between Christianity, Mohammedanism, Animism – ethnic variations, economic rivalries and political contests, all entered the conflicts mentioned above. But the contestants all considered themselves "Africans", even though their primary allegiance might be to different communities. Moreover, the leaders of each of these countries made strenuous efforts through economic, social and educational development to fuse the contentious ethnic communities into national societies. Indeed, in the educational field, the use of Swahili in east Africa and of Arabic in north Africa was gradually producing supra-national cohesion across existing state frontiers.

A word should be said here about the difference between the racial situation in French- and English-speaking African states. The French theory of assimilation was not entirely empty pretension. Colour consciousness and racial discrimination seems to be a largely Anglo-Saxon weakness. There was probably as much discrimination in French as in British colonies; but little of it was on grounds of colour or race. It was colonial domination rather than racial prejudice which occasioned discriminatory practices. The French accepted distinguished Africans into French society in a way which would have been unthinkable to the British, just as it would have outraged British parliamentarians and public to see Africans sitting on the benches at Westminster as they did in Paris. And if the number of Commonwealth coloured immigrants had ever reached the proportions of non-Europeans living and working in France, Enoch Powell would have had apoplexy.

The consequence of this different racial attitude of the French – partially shared by the Belgians – was that race relations in francophone Africa after independence were more relaxed than in the English-speaking states. Frenchmen, in business, the professions, the army, were welcomed in greater numbers than under colonial rule. They helped to make French-speaking African capitals into imitations of Paris, Lyons or Marseilles. If the younger generation began to complain that they were being deprived of opportunities by the competition of French citizens, the complaint was made on economic or social grounds, never on those of race.

In the two west coast states of Sierra Leone and Liberia, too, the tensions were caused by a mixture of political and economic resentments. In both territories released slaves had been settled on the coastlands in the late eighteenth and early nineteenth centuries. In Sierra Leone they had developed into a community known as Creoles. In Liberia they were called Americo-Liberians. In both cases these established, with the assistance of the British and Americans respectively, a privileged status for their community. In Sierra Leone they were accorded political rights before the peoples of the interior and had developed a comparatively sophisticated economic and social life in and around Freetown. In Liberia they remained the dominant political group, centred in the single party, the True Whig Party, monopolizing government and business employment.

In both countries resentment amongst the peoples originally native to the territories began to mount. In Sierra Leone it was reflected in the increasingly prominent rôle taken by the peoples of the interior in the political developments which led to independence in 1961. In Liberia, long since independent, it had less impact. The various leaders of Sierra Leone after independence, the Margai brothers and Siaka Stevens, all aimed to unite the various communities into a national whole. President William Tubman of Liberia and his successor, President William Tolbert, claimed to be pursuing the same objective. None of them entirely succeeded, although unification probably proceeded faster in Sierra Leone. But the significant feature of the tensions raised by these distinct divisions of national society was that consciousness of racial difference seemed to be completely absent. Both the Creoles and the Americo-Liberians had non-African blood in their ancestry. Yet when conflicts occurred between them and the indigenous peoples this factor never became an issue. Resentment was confined to political, economic and social privilege.

So far we have concentrated on the absence of racial consciousness in

Africa. But race is, nevertheless, a primary factor in the affairs of the continent. The whole of Africa is constantly aware of the racial issue, especially as it affects black-white relations.

This racial consciousness does not arise generally from domestic problems, however. Nor is it to be traced to the effects of the widespread discrimination under colonial rule. It is the shadow cast from the southern tip of the continent which generates this constant racial consciousness. All Africa is affected by it to some degree. For many states it is a determining factor in each major decision.

My first personal encounter with South African racialism epitomizes the crucial issue in that country. I was travelling to Cape Town in 1950. There was only one coloured man on the ship. He happened to be travelling first-class, whereas I was in the tourist section. But we met and talked, getting to know each other well. The journey took nearly 14 days and I noticed that for the first dozen my friend was treated as any other passenger. It was when we began to sense the impending arrival, when cases were being packed, preparations made for the last night on board, when people began to make arrangements to meet in Cape Town, that the atmosphere changed. As soon as the whiff of South African soil was scented amongst passengers, attitudes to the African visibly altered. Women who had made female cooing noises to his wife beside the swimming-pool over his two small children now studiously ignored them. Men who had politely talked to him turned away at his approach to speak in raised voices to their white companions. Words such as "nigger", "native", "kaffir", were heard for the first time in scarcely lowered tones.

When I saw my friend on the dockside beside Table Bay in the early morning he was being treated as a different being, he and his family segregated from the rest of disembarking passengers. No helpful policemen or customs officials assisted him and his family. At the railway station he had to queue separately for his tickets, occupy a dirty, uncomfortable compartment for the long journey to the Ciskei. No hotel would accommodate him in Cape Town, only one – Indian – café would allow him to share a meal with me.

This man was Gladstone Letele, a distinguished professor of African languages who had just been lecturing in London University for the past two years. If one were concerned with such concepts, he represented Western civilization to as high a degree as any South African – and much higher than all but a handfull. Yet in his own country he was a pariah, not because of anything he had done or omitted to do, but because he had a black skin.

Since then I have listened to many apologists for apartheid, in South Africa and outside. I have talked with Cabinet ministers, professors, trade unionists, mine-owners, journalists, farmers, clergymen. All have given their own justification for the racial segregation which is the foundation-stone on which apartheid rests. No argument I have heard explains the treatment I saw meted out to Gladstone Letele.

It is not necessary to repeat here all the details which have made up the policy of apartheid over the past quarter of a century. They are now well documented, available for all to study. Two aspects are relevant to this chapter: first, the light which apartheid throws on the phenomenon of racial or colour consciousness in human society; second, the effect which southern African racial policies are having on the rest of the continent.

In South Africa race has been equated with skin colour. This, of course, betrays ignorance of the realities of racial origins. South Africans of all colours, like most people in the world, are the products of racial mixture. In South Africa itself specific strains of the Negroid, Caucasoid and Mongoloid racial stocks have been present for many centuries. Those who boast about "racial purity" are talking nonsense. Similarly, those South Africans – including the government – who refer to the Africans living in the country as "Bantu" are equally displaying gaucherie. "Bantu" describes a set of languages, or sometimes a group of communities, not a racial type. Many of the Africans in South Africa do not even speak a Bantu language.

Yet with all their ignorance, obscurantism and irrationality, the white community of South Africa has created a pseudo philosophy which has had a more profound influence on international race relations than any other body of opinion. It is based simply on the dogma that the human race is divided into separate categories according to their skin colours. The fundamentalists of the Dutch Reformed Church, who have had a profound political and social influence, maintain that this division was ordained by God, that the whites are His "Chosen People", that it is the duty of God-fearing citizens to maintain separation of the categories, with the whites dominant over the rest. The more sophisticated base their faith on the presumed existence of such categories, maintaining that it is politic to keep them separate. A combination of the two related attitudes has produced the specific philosophy that it is right to keep racial groups – or more accurately colour groups – segregated from each other.

In practice, of course, in any society inhabited by two or more such groups, complete separation is impossible. Consequently, no proponent of apartheid has ever been able to devise even a theoretical plan under which the Africans, Coloureds, Asians and Europeans of South Africa could live in separate communities. Inevitably this has led even the most idealistic apartheid supporter to accept the power relation between European and non-European. Because the white man holds the power, his community has gained and defended privilege. Segregation in practice gives the white community, less than one-fifth of the total population, control of over 86 per cent of the land; Africans, two-thirds of the inhabitants, are left with less than 14 per cent. No provision is made for separate homelands for the Coloured or Asian communities.

The state of mind and emotions which has produced the apartheid philosophy is the product of a syndrome of experience unique in the world. The feelings which engender apartheid policies are to be found in many societies, notably in the southern states of America. But the actual complex of forces which created the apartheid policy is unique to South Africa.

It is false to assume, as many do, that apartheid was invented in 1948 when Dr Malan led his victorious National Party into office, forming South Africa's first all-Afrikaner Cabinet. The term only became current from that year; its connotation dated from the eighteenth century. From the decision of the Dutch East India Company in 1717, against the advice of their governor, to develop the colony on a basis of slave labour, relations between white, black and Coloured were rooted in the master-servant image.

Apartheid is to be seen as nothing more than an extension of previous white South African policies, continually seeking means to enforce segregation on Africans, Asians and Coloureds. The emotional obsession of the white community for removing all non-whites from its sight even overcame its own economic interests. For the past century, based on the original diamond and gold wealth, South Africa has been progressively industrializing. The need for labour, especially for semi-skilled and skilled workers, and for a large domestic market runs entirely counter to the policies of segregation. Yet social emotions have prevailed as they have come increasingly into conflict with economic interest. And this choice is approved by the vast majority of South African whites. Smuts's United Party, in government until 1948 and the official Opposition ever since, has never challenged the basic assumptions of apartheid. It could hardly do so, for it was its own governments under Smuts which had laid the foundations for the policies since followed by the Nationalists.

The first and primary constant element in the growth of apartheid is a sense of fear, exacerbated amongst the Afrikaner community in the twentieth century by their discovery of a new source of persecution. The process of industrialization brought the power of large capitalists into the political spectrum. Almost all of them were English-speaking South Africans or foreigners. Once again the Afrikaner believed that his birthright was under seige. He had defeated the assault during the Boer War, but again his community had to fight against English-speaking South Africans to safeguard what they considered South African values. Ultimately, this meant attaining such power as would enable them to

K

impose Afrikaner values on all South Africans. Malan's electoral victory of 1948 provided one milestone in the Afrikaner march; the declaration of a republic in 1961 another. But the most important factor in consolidating Afrikaner power was the steady incursion of Afrikaners into the world of business and finance. The English-speaking community had been defeated politically; it then accepted Afrikaner policies. Now its monopoly of economic power was seriously eroded as the Afrikaners deliberately moved into the modern business world.

Whether these domestic victories will eventually undermine the Afrikaner's inborn sense of insecurity, accumulated over three centuries, must be left for the future to determine. The Afrikaner, after all, is a "white African", with no other continent in which to seek refuge. But no sooner had his community appeared to gain complete power in his own country than it appeared seriously threatened from abroad.

The conventional idea that the Afrikaner community is so certain of its own rectitude that it is unconcerned about external criticism is only partially accurate. It applies to the stereotyped Afrikaner living in the heart of the veld with little contact outside his local market and church. It may also apply to those semi- and un-skilled Afrikaner town workers, who are the bitterest opponents of any advance amongst the non-Europeans they see as immediate competitors. But these types have become a steadily decreasing proportion of the Afrikaner community as economic modernization has progressed. Increasing numbers of Afrikaners are concerned that South Africa should be accepted as an integral part of international society. This applies politically, economically and, perhaps above all, in the world of sport, which is an obsession in South Africa.

So the international campaigns which have been waged against South Africa since the war, at the United Nations and in its subsidiary organs, in the Commonwealth, in business and finance, in the arts, and on the sporting scene, have deeply affected white South Africans, and particularly the more sophisticated Afrikaners. They have even forced South Africans to make some slight modifications in their traditional customs, like allowing certain foreign non-Europeans into the country to compete with white South Africans, and promising to send multi-racial teams abroad. They have not, of course, persuaded South Africa to alter the strict segregation of her own sportsmen.

But one of the main effects of these campaigns has been to reinforce the Afrikaner sense of persecution just at the moment when many Afrikaners had begun to feel that they had broken out of their state of domestic inferiority. Their reactions followed the same pattern as when they were fighting domestic battles. As they again sank into a defensive posture, they became even more aggressive towards those who opposed their philosophy, especially towards their own non-European inhabitants.

This sense of persecution, the underlying fears of a minority living in the midst of an oppressed majority, the constant feeling of being the only righteous amongst the world's wicked heathens, has been underpinned by short-term self-interest. The privileges maintained by the whites against all attacks may well damage their long-term economic interests; but, in the immediate terms which limit the horizons of most people, they have assured an affluent and comfortable life. Mining companies, manufacturers and farmers have all enjoyed the profits which accrue from cheap labour. Trade unionists have feather-bedded their weakest members by avoiding the competition latent in a free labour-market and open opportunities for apprenticeship; white households, however humble, have saved themselves unpleasant labour by the use of non-white domestic servants; and all whites, however illiterate, lazy or unintelligent, have been able to claim a superior social status from the accident of their birth. Particularly amongst the English-speaking section of the white community, cynical opportunism has led to a support for apartheid measures for which no ideological belief is held.

Deeper beneath the surface of racial prejudice there lies a psychological current which contains a strong element of sexuality. This is an aspect of racialism which calls for much more thorough analysis from psychologists than has yet been attempted. Maccrone's pre-war study blazed a trail which has not yet been adequately followed.

The sexual content of racial consciousness is patently evident to observers inside South Africa and accepted by many South Africans themselves. The heavy emphasis on sexual legislation in the apartheid programme, with its Mixed Marriages and Immorality Acts; the embarrassed confusion over treatment of Coloureds, whose existence bears living witness to the sexual attraction of non-whites for whites; the large number of prosecutions under the Immorality Act, with the startling number of policemen and clergymen involved; the character of stereotyped jokes, with their heavy overtones of white/non-white sexuality; the obsession with the same theme of a substantial section of South African literature – all these provide convincing evidence that many white South Africans feel strong sexual attraction towards non-whites, that apartheid is designed to restrict and punish the expression of these feelings.

In this respect a significant distinction is to be drawn between South Africans and Portuguese. Miscegenation was never frowned upon in the Portuguese African territories until emigration of poorer citizens from Portugal and settlement of Portuguese soldiers was encouraged from the 1950s onwards. Even then, although the white communities of Angola and Mozambique gradually became more colour conscious, more determined to assert their social superiority, the cardinal law of apartheid never applied; which explains why so many South Africans have made

Lourenço Marques their regular holiday centre. Portuguese domination is based on economic considerations and national prestige rather than racialism.

This does not profess to be a profound analysis of racial or colour prejudice. Yet an examination of the elements which have produced in South Africa the most virulent form of racialist disease the world has known may provide clues to the causes of infection elsewhere. To contemporary African leaders, however, it is the impact of South African racialism on the rest of the continent which is immediately important. For South Africa is the generator which provides the power for racialism throughout the continent and beyond, to Europe and America. If South Africa were to falter, Rhodesian and Portuguese racial domination would quickly collapse.

The South Africans were unable, even in association with Britain, to defend their bridgeheads in Kenya and the Central African Federation. Their ambitions were defeated there by a combination of African pressure and white weakness. The residual problem of Rhodesia, where self-indulgence rather than ideology sustained white intransigence, became an embarrassment. Yet the South Africans felt that they had to sustain both the Rhodesians and the Portuguese, if only as buffers against encroachments from the outside.

Faced with these serious defeats, South African governments, first under Dr Verwoerd and then under Mr Vorster, changed their tactics. Traditionally their efforts had been devoted to sustaining white supremacy wherever it aspired to power and to encouraging the maintenance of European colonial rule where there were insufficient white settlers. Now South Africa substituted for this strategy an international extension of her own domestic apartheid. The whole continent was to be considered as a set of Bantustans. Lesotho, Swaziland, Botswana, Namibia and Malawi were to be treated like the Transkei or Zululand. In Rhodesia, separate "homelands" would be created for the Mashona and Matabele. In each case, of course, the wealthy areas would remain under white control; even in areas designated black, economic power would rest in white hands, either those of the country concerned or of foreign capitalists. The rest of the continent would also be considered as Bantustans, and where ethnic separatism arose, as in Biafra or the Congo, the South Africans would promote its cause. As the only modernized economic power, South Africa would then be able to influence the whole continent along paths favourable to her own interests. This was the prospect faced by African governments as the sixties progressed.

The 1960s saw a remarkable transformation in the rôle of South Africa in the continent. They began with the massacre of Sharpeville and the brutalities which followed in various parts of the country. The worldwide outcry which resulted from these events undermined the self-confidence of Afrikanerdom and deterred many international investors from risking their capital in such an unstable state. The following year (1961) a Commonwealth Conference forced Dr Verwoerd to withdraw his country from the Commonwealth. It seemed that South Africa was at the nadir of its international reputation, that her slow but steady diplomatic gains during the 1950s had been destroyed. Many anticipated revolt within the country, aided by intensified international ostracism and a flight of the capital on which her government depended to keep the white community content and to provide the resources for its apartheid policy.

Yet by the end of the decade the situation had radically altered. South Africa was supremely self-confident, not only sustaining the rebellious Ian Smith in Rhodesia and supporting the Portuguese in their three colonial wars, but taking the initial steps in a policy of imperial expansion into black Africa. Her government had cowed both the Africans and its own white opponents and had so far recovered its reputation amongst its own supporters as to be able to sponsor a state visit from a black president – Hastings Banda of Malawi – without serious opposition.

The 1960s thus saw Afrikanerdom breaking out of its traditional laager. Nothing had seemed less likely at the start of the decade. At that moment of disruption the international community probably had its best chance of either coercing South Africa's Nationalist régime into modifying its policies or of assisting the forces of revolt. But it soon became apparent that Western capitalism had no intention of sacrificing its known rewards in South Africa for a gamble with the unknown. Racial policies were irrelevant in this calculation. By the middle of the decade capital was flowing into the country once more. Before it ended, the progress which South Africa's manufacturing and engineering industries had been making ever since the war reached a stage at which they were seeking markets to absorb excess production. As inflation and balance of payments difficulties combined with an ideological refusal to extend the domestic market to the mass of non-Europeans, pressures for export trade steadily mounted.

Meanwhile, at this point in the mid-sixties, political needs began to coincide with those of the economy. The breach between Britain and Rhodesia in 1965 was unwelcome to South Africans. Their government had to succour Ian Smith in order to satisfy its white electorate; yet this involved a cooling of relations with Britain at a time when diplomatic and economic friendship was being sought. In addition, the support given to Smith dangerously extended South Africa's lines of defence. It was bad enough to have to support the Rhodesians economically, but when it became necessary to give them military assistance, many South Africans realized that one of their buffers was disintegrating. The para-military units sent to guard the Zambezi were certainly serving the white man's laager; but they also bore witness to the fact that the laager's frontiers had become much longer, whilst the Rhodesian situation had brought black guerrillas to South Africa's doorstep.

In these circumstances it was therefore essential for the South African government to divide its black opponents as deeply as possible. Thus the diplomatic offensive dovetailed with economic expansion. The new South African policy was to offer African states economic aid in return for diplomatic friendship which would diminish the hostility focused on apartheid. At the same time, this would promote South Africa's new policy of internationalizing the Bantustan concept.

These temptations were first offered to the ex-High Commission Territories, Lesotho, Swaziland and Botswana. As each of them had been left by Britain heavily dependent on South Africa, the temptation was so much greater. Lesotho was entirely surrounded by South African territory whilst Swaziland had only one other frontier, and that with Mozambique. So neither had much chance of escape. As it happened, the ruling group in each showed little inclination to avoid South Africa's embrace.

Botswana was a different case. She was equally dependent on the Republic economically, yet the discovery of mineral wealth gave her some prospect of future independent action. Moreover, she had a tiny boundary with Zambia which enabled her to retain some slight thread of contact with black Africa. And out of the traumatic experience of the Khama case, in which the young chief-designate had been exiled by British governments for marrying a white British girl, there emerged in Seretse Khama a leader courageously combining a realistic concern for the interests of his people with a principled repudiation of apartheid. Botswana was not in a position to act as a bastion against apartheid; but she repudiated the rôle of its servant.

The next country to be wooed by the South Africans was Malawi. Again her poverty and geographic situation made her an easy target. Moreover, her leader, Hastings Banda, although having fought courageously for his own people's right to govern themselves against the white-ruled Central African Federation, seemed much less convinced that Rhodesian, South African or Portuguese Africans were equally entitled to the same rights. At all events, he gladly accepted South Africa's proffered hand of friendship, denounced the policy of the freedom fighters, and exchanged state visits with South Africa's president. As he received financial aid to build his favourite project, a new capital city at Lilongwe, as well as military assistance, he no doubt considered that the contempt shown to him by his fellow African leaders was worth the price.

Similar attractions were offered to the Malagasy and the Mauritians.

They were accepted in both cases, though in somewhat different circumstances, but Malagasy public opinion eventually forced a change. Of greater import was the success of the South African diplomatic offensive farther north. A number of African leaders began to propound the theory that apartheid should be met by discussion between themselves and South African ministers. The main proponent of this policy was Félix Houphouet-Boigny of the Ivory Coast. As he could command a considerable degree of support from the Entente countries, his value to the South Africans was multiplied. He was joined by Philibert Tsiranana of Malagasy and, as we have seen, Hastings Banda of Malawi adhered to the concept in practice as well as in theory. Kofi Busia of Ghana also toyed with the idea, though it was never clear how far he was prepared to put it into practice.

For a time the new policy of "dialogue" with the South Africans succeeded in achieving one South African objective: it caused dissension amongst black Africans and played some part in undermining their prospects of unity. Yet, by the beginning of the 1970s, it had made little headway. It had been directly challenged and rejected at African conferences, particularly by Julius Nyerere. His insistence that discussion with South African leaders would be welcomed, as outlined in the 1968 Lusaka Manifesto, but only provided that apartheid was on the agenda and South Africa's own non-Europeans fully represented, could hardly be refuted. The "dialogue" concept found few serious adherents, even amongst Houphouet-Boigny's clients in the Entente. Both Malagasy and the military régime which deposed Busia in Ghana repudiated it. Nevertheless, it remained a potential weapon for the South Africans, both in undermining African unity and in fomenting dissension within African states from those who would have liked to enjoy South African patronage.

Offering the hand of friendship to black Africa was only one part of South African imperial policy; the other hand presented a mailed fist. Expenditure on internal security and military strength increased tremendously during the 1960s. Sabre-rattling echoed behind seductive words. South Africa's Prime Minister, Johannes Vorster, frequently warned Zambia that the activities of freedom fighters could lead to South African forces invading her territory. Violations of Zambian frontiers often took place, not only by South African forces, but also by the Portuguese and Rhodesians. Ian Smith hoped to bully the Zambians by closing his border in 1973, but his tactic rebounded. For Zambia was first prize to the South Africans. They believed that if they could draw this copper-rich country into their web, the freedom fighters would lose their bases and black Africa its spearhead. This was the prime objective to pursue, whether by fomenting internal dissension, by economic seduction, or by military intervention. Once they had captured Zambia, the way would be open to the Congo; pressure on the Portuguese would be relieved; it was expected that Tanzanian opposition would then crumble, leaving a clear road to the rest of black Africa.

South Africa directed this policy; but Rhodesia and Portugal were also members of the alliance. The Rhodesian quarrel with Britain may have embarrassed the South Africans, but at least it demonstrated where the line was drawn against independent African rule. When challenged, British governments were not prepared to use their military power to impose democratic decolonization south of the Zambezi. Despite all the verbiage and double-talk, behind the headlines on sanctions, negotiations and "agreements", this was the only significant factor which emerged from the Anglo-Rhodesian imbroglio. Rhodesia was to be treated by Britain as South Africa had been; power over her future was to be left with the white community. Africans noted the contrast between this policy and that of de Gaulle in Algeria; between appeasement towards the white Rhodesians and the military intervention in Stanleyville to save white hostages.

The Portuguese, meanwhile, were fighting increasingly bitter wars in Guinea-Bissau, Angola and Mozambique. Although little reported, these countries were the scene of the only serious military confrontation between black and white after the end of the Algerian war. The fact that they involved southern Africa was significant. For this indicated a battle-line between white and black. The central issue of international politics in Africa would henceforth be the confrontation across the Zambezi and within the Portuguese territories. It would involve the rest of the world.

There were other theatres where scenes from this drama were being played. As the Indian Ocean and South-East Asia became a power vacuum from British withdrawal and American embarrassment, the east African coast again assumed an Asian as well as an African rôle. The Russians began to probe the ocean with their naval vessels. The Chinese supplied both equipment for the Tan-Zam railway and arms for freedom fighters through Dar es Salaam. Zanzibar offered opportunities for the activities of several Communist states. British Conservatives used the presence of Russians to justify their intention of providing arms to the South Africans. The Portuguese took advantage of their membership of NATO to arm their forces to fight the guerrillas. South Africa, Rhodesia and Portugal desperately proclaimed their adherence to the West. The West constantly sought to safeguard its vast investment in the south.

Thus all the elements of international conflict appeared in east, central and southern Africa. The ambivalence shown by the West to the racial struggle could be punctured at any moment by one incident on the frontier or on the east coast. It only needed intervention by the southern whites either in Zambia or in the Indian Ocean to force each member of the international community to have to declare its allegiance. If the South Africans were consistent, for instance, they would try and intercept Chinese supplies to the freedom fighters bound for Dar es Salaam. Southern Africa had become a court in which attitudes to the basic racial issues of the world were on trial.

Despite the comparative absence of racial or colour antagonism amongst Africans, racialism was a dominant factor in the affairs of the continent. The sense of conflict between black Africa and the white supremacists of the south was always present, even if overt violence only flared occasionally. For the foreseeable future the overwhelming strength of the South Africans in military and economic power made it impossible for African governments to mount an open offensive. They had to content themselves with mobilizing what support they could for the guerrillas who fought in the Portuguese territories, Rhodesia and, occasionally, in South Africa and Namibia. Yet, as the African states developed, there seemed little doubt but that confrontation with the south would become certain. Much would hinge on the success of states like Nigeria, Zaire and Zambia, with large wealth potentials, to solve their internal problems and build modern economies. For once they approached this objective, they would attain the strength to challenge the might of South Africa. And as military logistics progressively reduced the handicap of distance, South Africa would become increasingly vulnerable from anywhere in the continent.

The fact was that apartheid, racialism and colour discrimination affronted the dignity of the Africans throughout the continent. They felt profoundly bitter over the oppression of their brothers in the Republic, Namibia, Rhodesia and the Portuguese territories. They resented the evidence that many Europeans and Americans considered southern African white racialists to be their "kith and kin", certainly closer relatives than any blacks. The airlift to Stanleyville, the refusal to use force against rebellious white Rhodesians, the attempts to recognize Ian Smith's independence without any prospect of majority rule, the supplies of arms to South Africa and Portugal by Britain, France and NATO, the constantly mounting investments in southern Africa, all convinced Africans that the Western world secretly sympathized with the white supremacists whilst mouthing hypocritical opposition to apartheid. The minor exceptions, such as the support given to the freedom fighters by Scandinavian, German and British socialists and by church groups, prevented a blanket condemnation of the West as racialist; but there were other Western politicians and publicists who openly supported racialism.

If, therefore, as seemed probable, racial or colour confrontation became a crucial issue in international society during the later years of the twentieth century, Africa would certainly provide its main stage. The resolution of the basic racial issue in that continent, the conflict between Africans and the white supremacists of the south, would affect race relations throughout the world, whether it be between coloured and white Britons or blacks and whites in the United States. It would also vitally influence the development of every state within Africa itself, as well as their relations with every country outside the continent.

African Soldiers

Nothing in post-independent African society has changed so radically as attitudes toward the army. During the years of anti-colonial agitation most African nationalists, at least in the British territories, adopted the conventional European liberal posture of anti-militarism. The approach of French Africans was rather ambiguous, reflecting the more militaristic traditions of the French Left. Some years before independence I asked Julius Nyerere what special contribution he would like independent Africa to make to social engineering. His answer was that he hoped Africans could show the world that it is possible for societies to live together harmoniously without military forces. He carried his ideal into practice when, in one of his first actions after Tanganyika's independence, he abolished his country's contribution to the small east African navy.

Long before the end of the first independence decade, however, Africans, leaders and people, had learnt that their armies had become ambitious members of the ruling group. Along with the civil service and the politicians they participated in a triumvirate of rulers whose relations with each other vitally affected the fate of every new African state. As military coup followed military coup, it dawned on Africans that military control of governments were not isolated aberrations but common factors in the power struggle universal to the nation-state. This had to be accepted as a political reality, leaving former anti-militarist sentiments to the nostalgia of the pre-independence idealistic era.

It was hardly surprising that the army should play a political rôle within the power-structure of the new states. In both traditional and colonial periods armies had been accepted as integral parts of the ruling groups. Whilst their main function in traditional Africa had been to defend society from external aggression or to use their own power for conquest, they also had some responsibility for internal order. Under colonial rule, once colonial frontiers had been determined between the European powers, their rôle was almost entirely confined to that of domestic policeman.

In both instances, however, although the army was a unit of the ruling group, it was almost always subordinate to a superior authority. There are very few instances in African history of military government. In colonial times there were occasions on which the army took greater responsibilities than the civil authorities, but they were exceptional and even then ultimate power rested in the metropolitan capital. It was almost universal practice in both traditional and colonial societies, therefore, for the army to take its orders from the political rulers and use its monopoly of physical force to execute them.

Since independence, the rôle of the army in many African states has perceptibly changed. From being one of a group of ruling units, with a usually subordinate status, many armies found themselves on an equal footing with the other elements of authority. The new states had been created, as we have seen, from conglomerate communities. They had been left with the skeleton structures of government which were often inappropriate to local circumstances and with insufficient experience to have created general acceptability. There were therefore few states where rules for changes in government were so established that the rôle of force could be excluded. So long as co-operation prevailed between politicians, civil servants and soldiers, civil order in the state could be maintained. Yet even within such co-operation rivalry between the three elements of authority was latent. When resentments arose, especially prevalent over decisions which civil servants suspected were taken in the self-interest of politicians, the tripod of authority often collapsed. This disintegration was frequently hastened by the failure of politicians to solve the most insistent national problems bequeathed by colonial rulers, particularly when those politicians appeared to be mostly concerned with their personal or ethnic interests.

When such situations arose the soldiers found themselves in possession of unique sanctions. They had guns, whereas civil servants could only wield administrative authority and politicians had to rely on the support of the people. As we have seen, few politicians had achieved mass mobilization behind either themselves as individuals or the policies they represented. Where they had attained a substantial degree of mobilization, as in east Africa in 1964, in Zambia during the inter-communal quarrels, or, to some extent, in the Ivory Coast and Senegal, politicians were able to withstand military pressure even in a crisis. Even then, they usually only succeeded with the aid of external forces. But these civilian successes were exceptional. In most cases the guns of the soldiers prevailed. Army intervention in the political processes was welcomed or tacitly accepted by most inhabitants. The soldiers then formed an alliance with the civil servants to administer the state, excluding politicians from the decision-making process.

We have been considering the army so far as though it was monolithic and divorced from the political stresses of the new state. This is a false picture. Just as communal considerations greatly influenced political parties, governments and civil services, so they caused tensions within armies. It had been a frequent practice of colonial rulers to recruit soldiers from particular ethnic groups. Sometimes this was politically motivated. For instance, in Kenya it was thought dangerous to seek recruits from the two most politically minded communities, the Kikuyu and Luo. The Kamba traditionally provided the most reliable soldiers for colonial armies. So, at independence, the Kenyan government, which was largely based on Kikuyu and Luo leadership, found itself with an army in which its two major communities were gravely under-represented.

Sometimes the predominance of one community arose from more fortuitous circumstances. Where educational achievement could lead to commercial, civil-service or academic employment, service in the army was often regarded as socially degrading. Thus in Nigeria it was the more backward Tiv who proportionately provided the highest number of recruits to the ranks. Yet this same factor also worked in a contrary direction. Educational attainment increasingly opened the doors to army commissions as decolonization evolved measures of Africanization. So, although the Tiv provided large supplies of other ranks, it was the educated Ibo who dominated the officer class. They had the advantage of Christian missions to provide modern education, in contrast to the Hausa, who were commonly offered only traditional Muslim training. The commercial opportunities enjoyed by the Yoruba were not available to most Ibo. Although many entered the civil service or the academic world, whilst some became small-scale traders, army commissions provided chances of social preferment unavailable or unattractive to the other major communities. At the time of independence, about three out of four officers in the Nigerian army came from the Eastern Region. The action of the federal government in recruiting specially heavy quotas from the other communities to redress the balance inevitably caused additional resentment; and when the new recruits found their way to promotion blocked by young officers appointed previously, another cause of friction was added.

Armies were thus influenced by many of the same factors which applied to politicians and bureaucrats. Some soldiers faced an additional handicap. In almost every new state political power passed at independence from colonial rulers to those who had led the anti-colonial campaigns. But these rarely included members of the armed forces. There were exceptions, such as the Magreb states, Egypt, and Cameroun; but in most cases the soldiers had obeyed the orders of colonial rulers to combat anti-colonial movements. Occasionally this experience taught political lessons. In his autobiography, Waruhiu Itote, more widely known as the Mau Mau

"General China", recalls the time when he was a member of the King's African Rifles and was sent to Uganda to suppress a revolt against colonial authority. He met an old man from the Baganda community who asked him, "Why have you come here to plague us and punish us for trying to get our freedom? Why aren't you helping your own people to get theirs ... You should be making your own armies and your own roads and building schools for your own kind of education. If you don't fight for Kenyatta to become your Kabaka you will be a useless lot of people." "General China" learnt the lesson taught by the old Maganda; but few soldiers did so, for they were trained to serve unquestioningly the colonial government. Those who were already in the army before independence brought a legacy of antagonism towards the nationalist leaders who had inherited political power; they themselves were often suspected of anti-nationalist sympathies.

This factor was especially significant in the ex-French colonies. The British generally used their colonial recruits only in their own regions, except in time of world war. But the French recruited Africans for their national army. They were sent to any area where France was at war. Many Africans thus served in the campaigns in Indo-China and Algeria. They became French rather than African soldiers, absorbing many of the sensitivities of the French army. This hardly fitted them to become stalwart defenders of post-independence African establishments.

Moreover, at independence France made defence agreements with most of her ex-colonies. These left about 300,000 French troops in Africa in bases which they retained after independence. It was clear that these troops would come to the aid of those independent régimes favoured by French governments. They did so in Senegal in 1962 when the Prime Minister, Mamadou Dia, attempted a coup against President Senghor. They restored President M'ba when he had been deposed and imprisoned in Gabon in 1964. In the previous year France's favourite African son, President Houphouet-Boigny, had been helped to suppress an attempted coup against his régime.

Yet during the 1960s there were signs that this French rôle was perceptibly changing. Troops were withdrawn until only about 7,000 were left, although certain bases were retained so that military action could still be taken. However, it seemed likely that the immediate help which had been forthcoming in Senegal, the Ivory Coast and Gabon would no longer be available. The French army still assisted the government of Chad to suppress the efforts of her northern secessionists to defy its authority; but the succession of coups in French-speaking west and central Africa no longer brought French troops to the rescue of deposed régimes.

Another factor which distinguished French from British practice was the post-war institution of the gendarmerie d'outre-mer. This was a special force organized for the purpose of maintaining internal security. It therefore relieved the regular troops from the task of confronting rebels except in the most extreme cases. At the same time, however, this arrangement obstructed that personal contact between soldiers and local populace which, in British territories, had its beneficial as well as a destructive effect on relationships.

The gendarmerie was usually retained after independence and its French officers remained with it. This was significant in the Gabon crisis of 1964. It was the Gabon army which deposed M'ba; the gendarmerie remained loyal to him. Here was an illustration of how the French system, by dividing the armed forces, could split the power of the military section of the ruling group. In anglophone countries similar tensions resulted in divisions within the army itself, as witnessed in Nigeria.

One example of division within the military force was seen in Sierra Leone, another illustration that the army, no more than other ruling units, should be considered as monolithic. Here three separate actions were taken by different sections of the army, each activated by political motives. First, the army commander personally prevented the Governor-General from swearing in Siaka Stevens, who had just won an election, as Prime Minister. The commander acted as a supporter of the defeated previous Prime Minister, Sir Albert Margai. Secondly, a group of officers arrested the commander and set up their own National Reformation Council in place of civilian government. Thirdly, a year later, a group of warrant-officers arrested members of the Council, together with all army and police officers, and called Stevens back to restore representative government.

The fact that the conflicts which affected the political scene also divided groups within armies could hardly have been more starkly demonstrated. It was illustrated again in Sierra Leone in 1971 when another commander and his followers in the army tried to assassinate Stevens, only to be arrested by other officers.

This incident also provided evidence of a further feature of the struggle within the ruling group. Alarmed by the superior power which armies displayed in their rivalry with political rulers, many leaders sought means to defend the political against the military section of the ruling community. The Congo set a precedent when Kasavubu and Lumumba asked for United Nations help. Their force publique had mutinied, the Belgians were deploying troops on their own initiative and the province of Katanga was attempting to secede. In these circumstances the United Nations organized a military force which was sent to the Congo. There it helped to pacify the force publique and bring some form of discipline to its ranks. Inevitably it became involved in local politics between

Kasavubu, Lumumba, Mobutu, Gizenga and Tshombe. As the United Nations Force included many Africans and as the whole of Africa was watching the Congolese situation, lessons were learnt which were later to be applied elsewhere.

Both politicians and military leaders saw in the Congo the power which support from outside Africa could offer them. The Belgians backed Tshombe and made his secession possible. The Russians supported Lumumba and his successors. The United States assisted Kasavubu, Mobutu and Adoula. Foreign mercenaries were used by all sides. No general external intervention was to be seen again on such a scale; but the Nigerian civil war found the Russians, British and Americans supporting the Federal cause, the Portuguese, French, Rhodesians and South Africans the Biafrans, who also employed mercenaries from wherever they could be recruited.

In Sierra Leone the example of the Congo was hardly relevant. Yet Siaka Stevens, first as Prime Minister and then, from April 1971, as President, felt compelled to adopt the same policy of calling in foreign troops to defend his régime. As he saw army officers first conspiring with opposition politicians and then trying to assassinate him he realized that he could no longer rely on his own armed forces to obey government orders. He therefore made arrangements with Sékou Touré of Guinea for a detachment of Guinean troops to come to his aid. They acted as a personal bodyguard and remained as a form of fire-brigade lest further treason arise amongst the Sierra Leonean army.

Kwame Nkrumah was another who looked to foreigners for protection. At the time of the 1966 coup which deposed him, his President's Own Guard Regiment consisted of 50 officers and over 1,000 men; they were partially dependent on Soviet arms and had Soviet security advisers attached to them. The fact that this guard had been detached from army authority and was directly responsible to Nkrumah himself formed one of the military causes of complaint which led sections of the army to join with police in the coup.

Houphouet-Boigny also created a presidential guard after the coup attempt of 1963, but in his case it was recruited from men drawn from his own area. The secretary-general of the party seems to have considered this an idea which should have wider application. He insisted that he be allowed to form his own party militia. The project of a militia drawn from the ruling party or from its youth league was widely adopted. Again it represented attempts by the political wing to break the monopoly of force possessed by the army. Again, also, the attempts to establish a rival power organization antagonized the army, at times provoking it to take pre-emptive action before such bodies could build their counter-weight to the regular military.

Except for the east African mutinies, where foreign forces intervened, African armies were always successful in direct trials of strength with the politicians. Although they shared in post-independence tensions, they usually possessed a coherence far in excess of most political parties. Their officers often had common experience, in French wars, at Sandhurst, or in Fréjus. It is true that many of the younger ones had also shared their education in Africa and Europe with politicians or civil servants of the same age-group. To some extent they were members of the same post-independence élite. Yet often some of their training in austere living and discipline survived to set them apart from the civilians in a coherence which no other section of the ruling group could match.

So when the army asserted itself in the political arena it was almost always decisively. As we saw earlier, in most post-independence African states a very few soldiers strategically deployed could seize control of the state nerve-centres. Surround the presidential palace, seize the broadcasting station, the post office communications, the airport, and a new régime was in power.

Yet, despite the fact that coup techniques were similar, it should not be assumed that the coups themselves took place in identical circumstances. There were coups provoked by army discontent, others where the military forces emerged from a disturbance as the only remaining coherent unit, some supported politicans no longer able to command authority and there were interventions by soldiers claiming puritanical rectitude to sweep away corrupt politicians.

It is significant that no successful military intervention was met by mass resistance from the populace. Politicians had not endeared themselves either by charisma or by their policies sufficiently for any substantial number of citizens to risk their safety in order to keep them in office. Nor had the political parties so mobilized their followers as to present any serious resistance to the armies. Usually, the military coup seemed to bring an initial sense of public relief. Africans demonstrated that they were more concerned with jobs, incomes and public probity than with their own participation in the kind of politics they had been offered – though many found that their aspirations were no better achieved by military rule than they had been under civilian government.

It was General Neguib and Colonel Nasser who initiated military intervention in the state affairs of Africa. Their 1953 coup against Farouk set an important precedent. It proved that an army could overthrow a civilian government if the local circumstances were propitious. At the time this may not have had much effect on black African soldiers, for it was in a period when personal contact between Arab and African was rare. But Farouk had been so despised by African progressives that Nasser soon took on the guise of a new Atatürk. His military régime had removed the monarchy with the claim that it would root out corruption, end the gross ostentation which had been flaunted before the people, and introduce radical agrarian reform. It never succeeded in its revolutionary aims, but by its destruction of the worst forms of privilege, the austere life of Nasser himself, and some attempts at social reform, it retained a radical reputation. As Nasser was accepted first into the non-aligned community of Bandung and later into the inter-African fraternity, his stature remained high. The fact that his had been a military revolution, that his army remained a focal point of his régime, became more significant when Africans south of the Sahara began to run into political frustrations during the 1960s.

In 1958, with the Sudanese government in crisis, its Prime Minister asked General Abboud to suspend parliament in order to save him from opposition. The Prime Minister had also been in the army and was an old colleague of Abboud's. This may have facilitated the General's consent, but it did not prevent him from replacing the Prime Minister's government with his own military régime. Again the army had stepped into the political arena and abrogated the constitution. Later the army itself was to suffer from conflicts within its corps of officers, culminating in 1969 when a group of them allied with popular opposition to remove Abboud's régime and establish a popular front government.

There were therefore already two precedents for military action in the political sphere before the Congo erupted in 1960. Each of the features seen in other African military coups was present in the Congo. The army mutinied over rates of pay and the presence of expatriate officers. Once discipline had broken down, armed bands were available to any politician who could pay them to support his cause. Outside intervention appeared regularly and from a variety of sources – the United Nations, the Belgians, Americans, Russians, Chinese, mercenaries from a dozen countries. The soldiers of a number of African countries, enlisted under the United Nations banner, witnessed all these events. They could not help but be impressed by the ease with which Congolese forces arbitrated the fate of their countrymen. Eventually, in 1965, it was the Congolese army, under General Mobutu, which turned the politicians out and took political control of the state.

Perhaps every succeeding African coup would have taken place even if the events in the Congo had never occurred. That is idle speculation. But it is impossible to suppose that the soldiers from other African countries who saw or heard about the failure of the Congolese politicians, the ease with which they were overthrown by armed forces, the intervention of foreign powers, the military skills of mercenaries and the final victory of the army, were unaffected by these events. For the next dozen years military revolutions became a commonplace of African political experience.

As early as December 1960 the continent was shocked by an attempted coup in Ethiopia, generally considered as a revered elder state in African nationalist circles. A conglomerate consisting of the Imperial Guard, leading members of the security services and police, and university students attempted to take advantage of the Emperor's absence abroad to depose him. Very broadly the educated élite tried to replace the Emperor's feudal régime with a government of modern reform. The loose alliance failed to attract mass support or sufficient approval within the armed forces. It was defeated by the army and air force, assisted by American advisers. In this case the power of the regular forces was used to defend the existing civilian régime.

If Emperor Haile Selassie, the venerable supreme "Paramount Chief" of Africa, could be challenged, no one could feel safe. In 1962 President Senghor was threatened as a result of a political quarrel with his Prime Minister. Here the army was divided in allegiance; only the superior physical force of the paratroopers saved the president. The following year Sylvanus Olympio of Togo was less fortunate. He was the victim of his army's discontent, caused by the consequences of French decolonization policy. There had been a few hundred Togolese in the French army. When they were demobilized by France they expected to be enrolled in the Togo army. Olympio refused, understandably, as they would have multiplied his tiny army fourfold. Whereupon a number of them went to his house and shot him. There had been a certain degree of political unrest, with French, American and West German influences in the background. The army set up a civilian government after the President's assassination in 1963 and selected Olympio's rival, Nicholas Grunitsky, to lead it. He was supported by the French and by northern Togolese. Three years later an attempt was made to overthrow the Grunitsky régime. It came mainly from civil servants, largely southerners. The army quelled it. The following year, 1967, the soldiers took over from Grunitsky.

The year 1963 was a year of coups in Africa. At the beginning of the year Olympio was assassinated by the soldiers. In August, Fulbert Youlou was deposed in Congo-Brazzaville. In October President Maga was removed from office in Dahomey. Although the circumstances were different, in one respect a common factor linked the action of the three armed forces. They were all still at the stage of interfering in the political process in order to change control over government. They supported parties or personalities, rather than yet aspiring to assume political responsibility themselves. Thus Grunitsky was selected to replace Olympio; Massemba-Débat succeeded Youlou; and S. M. Apithy and M. J. Ahomadegbé followed Maga.

In each case physical force was used or threatened as a sanction in political, communal or economic conflicts. In Congo-Brazzaville, in fact, it was the police, not the army, which deposed Youlou. Here there was rivalry between the two armed sectors. The party and its youth section, along with the trade unions, secured support from Cuba, China and Russia. They created a civilian militia to counter the strength of the army. The military forces, on the other hand, retained their traditional links with the French. At the same time, the army was largely drawn from northern communities, whilst the Bakongo of the south were dominant in the party. Eventually, by 1968, the army emerged victorious from its struggle with the party, Marien Ngouabi, a northern major, becoming head of state. By this time African armies were playing their own separate political rôle, discarding alliances with political parties.

Dahomey in many ways presents the most complicated and intriguing pattern of military activity. The ethnic divisions between north and south, and in the south, between east and west were reflected in rivalry between the three leading politicians, Maga, Apithy and Ahomadegbé. The army also was divided, young, middle-rank officers frequently showing themselves unwilling to accept the rule of successive commanders. The fact that the economic situation remained parlous constantly added urban and civil service discontent to the political confusion. Unemployment mounted at an alarming rate, swollen by Dahomeyans expelled from other countries where they had been accustomed to live and work, and by soldiers declared redundant by the French army.

The immediate cause of the first military intervention was an arrest of trade-union leaders. The army commander, General Christophe Soglo, stepped in to try and get the three main leaders to work together. But the trade unions, though not prepared to allow the government to control them, were unable to provide a common base for civilian government. The civil service particularly proved itself unwilling to meet the demands of the national situation and rebelled whenever measures were taken to deal with economic problems. The 1963 crisis was provoked by a general strike against a ten per cent reduction in the salaries of government employees; the following year 25 per cent cuts were proposed and another general strike resulted. When General Soglo intervened in December 1965, he insisted on enforcing the austerity measures; he, in turn, was deposed in 1967 when the unions again organized strikes against austerity. Still the army sought a civilian to head the state, eventually turning to Dr Emile Zinsou, who had been comparatively remote from the earlier struggles. His fate again revealed the schisms in the army, for when the commander arrested and imprisoned him the younger officers joined with the Cabinet in demanding his release and the summoning of a general assembly. This assembly then arranged elections in which all former political aspirants were entitled to stand.

This may seem a labyrinth of politico-military intrigue, and, of course, in one dimension this is an apt description. At the same time, the experience of Dahomey revealed both the intractable problems which have been faced by all African states and the desperate endeavours made by many Africans to overcome them. The state bequeathed by the French made no kind of sense, geographically, economically or ethnically. Its budget was always in deficit, and in the franc zone, unlike the sterling area, deficit budgeting was heavily frowned upon. So austerity was demanded, but the French had also left a legacy of inflated administrative expense which rapidly increased as Dahomeyans had to return home after the African states where they resided became independent. A birth-rate of 5.5 per cent constantly aggravated the problem. Economic growth was minimal, only about 0.2 per cent annually; imports usually cost twice as much as export receipts; state debts mounted astronomically; and wide differences existed between the various ethnic communities.

In these circumstances it was hardly surprising that no politician or government was able to satisfy the constant demand for improved living standards. The military were as helpless when they tried to govern. Yet, although the first decade of independence saw nine heads of state and four republics, the efforts made were not entirely in vain, nor did the political situation degenerate into complete shambles. Indeed, Dahomey eventually demonstrated that, despite quarrels between politicians, soldiers and civil servants, given the will some degree of co-operation could survive. (Nigeria provided further evidence for the same lesson.) Eventually a constitution was devised which provided for the main political contenders to take turns as head of state. Maga was the first, and, in 1972, office passed peacefully from him to Apithy. Meanwhile, the constitution was guaranteed by the army. Dahomeyans had learnt, at least for a time, that the services of all with national interests at heart were needed in a common effort. Unity between the military and the politicians still remained fragile, however. Late in 1972 the army intervened again, once more taking control of government.

In the second half of the sixties, African armies began to consider themselves more as distinct political units than as mere arbiters between political groupings. In January 1966, the army in Upper Volta took over power during another conflict between a civilian government and trade unions agitating against cuts in salaries. Initially intending to hold power only until a new civilian administration was formed, before the end of the year Colonel Sangoulé Lamizana declared that military rule would continue for the next four years.

In the same month Colonel Jean-Bodel Bokassa overthrew the civilian government of the Central African Republic and a group of young officers destroyed the federal government of Nigeria. In both cases military government was established, called on the assistance of some politicians and civil servants, and retained political authority into the 1970s.

The following month, February 1966, saw the deposition of Kwame Nkrumah's régime in Ghana. Here an alliance between the army and police provided the physical force which tore up the constitution and substituted a joint régime. Its only sanction was that of physical power, though it met with little popular opposition. Nevertheless, the tradition of representative government seemed to have sunk deeper roots in Ghana than elsewhere. General Joseph Ankrah and his successor, Brigadier A. A. Afrifa, made it clear that they wished the country to return to civilian government. Although they banned Nkrumah's party and dismantled his government structure, as early as September 1968 they prepared for a new representative constitution by providing for registration of voters. A year later, after parliamentary elections, they voluntarily handed over power to an elected civilian government headed by Kofi Busia. This remained in office until the beginning of 1972. But it had failed to solve the same endemic problems which had led to Nkrumah's downfall. High unemployment, the servicing of huge foreign debts, heavy dependence on cocoa with its fluctuating price, inability to diversify agriculture, a high birth-rate and the constant menace of ethnic politics brought Busia widespread unpopularity within two years. At the beginning of 1972 other army officers stepped in, deposing Busia, suspending the constitution and re-introducing military government. The tradition of representative government was not strong enough to survive failure to solve national problems.

So the story continues. In 1966 Captain Michel Micombero deposed the young king of Burundi whom he had helped to replace his father a few months earlier. As we have seen, in 1967 the army took power in Sierra Leone in the midst of political conflict, only to return power to the civilians in the following year. In 1968 young officers in the Mali army removed Modibo Keita who had been trying with little success to break away from the economic domination of France. The following year the Libyan monarchy was overthrown by army officers; young officers seized power in both the Sudan and Somalia. Dissension within the Moroccan army provoked two attempts on the life of King Hassan in 1971 and 1972, an attempted new coup was frustrated in the Sudan and (the then) Colonel Amin used his influence over some sections of the Ugandan army to depose President Obote during his absence at the Singapore Commonwealth Conference.

It is from the exceptions to this general pattern that we can complete the picture. If there were so many clamant reasons for military intervention in the political process, why were coups not universal? The armies we have been discussing were almost all tiny bodies; the largest was that of Algeria with about 65,000, until the massive expansion of Nigerian forces during the civil war. With the exception of five other states, Ethiopia, Zaire, the Sudan, Ghana and Somalia, they were numbered in four figures during the 1960s, those of Gabon and Togo only in three figures. Yet even the smallest had proved that the possession of guns could be decisive in political combat.

Algeria was one exception from the general pattern, but here experience was such that it illustrated little for the rest of Africa. Her peasant armies had won independence in battle. Yet the two forces were separated from each other during and after liberation. It was politicians who negotiated independence with the French, but behind Ben Bella's first government of independent Algeria lay the power of a highly organized professional army which had been built up in neighbouring countries. The peasant forces had no part in the settlement, had no cohesion amongst themselves and were quickly taken over or dissolved by the regulars. As soon as Ben Bella began to build himself a people's militia which might have acted as a counter to the army itself, Colonel Boumedienne stepped in with his regular soldiers to depose the President and establish a military government. Thus, although the military and political history of Algeria was quite different from that of the rest of Africa, a form of military coup took place here also. It was provoked by the jealousy of the army for its own power and assisted by the economic failures of the government.

Zanzibar was another exception which illustrates little. Here the supremacy of a minority party considered to represent Arab landlords against African workers was overthrown by a band of armed Africans. There was no army on the island; it was the police force which was defeated by the bizarre Okello's small group.

It was in east and central Africa that the exceptions to the general pattern were most significant. In Kenya, Uganda, Tanganyika, Zambia and Malawi the same tensions existed after independence as in the rest of the continent. In the case of Kenya the pressures were more severe than most, for the Mau Mau rebellion had not only shaken colonial rule but set African against African. Recriminations and revenge against collaborators could be expected once those who had fought in the forest or been imprisoned gained power.

Zambia was also subjected to above average tensions. Her copper wealth beckoned aspirants to offices which could offer lucrative rewards.

The illegal declaration of independence in Rhodesia and subsequent economic sanctions against that country dislocated the Zambian economy, creating resentments against the government which could be accused of sacrificing national interest to futile international action. Her geographic position on the front line of guerrilla warfare against the southern white supremacists made her a hostage to their actions, whilst quarrelling exiled nationalist movements could disturb her domestic politics. There were many Rhodesians and South Africans in the country who were potential fifth columnists, many refugees amongst whom spies could be infiltrated. In the midst of this exposed situation Zambia had her own ethnic conflicts, any of which could become associated with the ambitions of external aggressors. The situation seemed constantly ripe for intervention from the armed forces.

In Malawi the passion of opposition to the Federation, which led to over 50 deaths in 1959, might also have been expected to cause disturbance after independence. Within a few weeks of independence in 1964 the dismissal of three ministers and the consequent resignation of three others, all with a long record of anti-colonial activity, provided a situation which in many other African states had resulted in military intervention. Moreover, Dr Hastings Banda is one of Africa's most egocentric leaders; he antagonized many Africans by his friendship with the South African government and his contemptuous references to the freedom fighters, and offended many of his own people by flouting local susceptibilities in his attitude towards young women and personal financial dealings.

In Uganda, as we have seen, the army eventually destroyed civilian government nearly ten years after independence. For much of this decade the internal situation was precarious. President Obote inherited a country in which the Kingdom of Buganda had been accorded special privileges by the British. Uganda has also always been important in European affairs because of her command of the Nile waters. The fact that she bordered the southern Sudan, where a secessionist movement was fighting against the Khartoum government, brought Middle Eastern affairs into her national life. The Israelis, in particular, were anxious to keep the war going, for it weakened the Arab world. The British Conservative government also bridled at Obote's trenchant criticisms of Mr Heath's stubborn decision to sell arms to the South Africans. As, meanwhile, the country had to act as host to a large number of refugees from the Sudan, Zaire, Rwanda and Burundi, it was little wonder that Obote's government eventually fell. But when it did so it was the result of internal intrigues within the army on which Obote had placed so much responsibility, rather than of civil discontent. Moreover, there was considerable evidence of foreign intervention in the 1971 coup. It was still remarkable that the army had not intervened earlier.

Stability within a state may be described by the term "civil order". Concise definition is difficult, but, among other factors, it implies that a large majority of inhabitants are prepared to recognize the validity of laws passed by a legitimate government, to accept a strict limitation on the practice of violence in political issues, and to have a sufficient sense of common interest to place public order above particularist tactics. The colonial powers ensured such order by limiting political activities and holding in reserve sufficient physical force to suppress and punish any breach. But independent African governments had no such powers. They were expected to open political opportunities to the whole population, to provide employment and better living-standards for all, and at the same time, were pressed to supply privileged positions for their kinsmen. The armed forces became increasingly unwilling to accept civilian authority as they realized their strength as one of the rivals for political power. As the removal of colonial authority had also eradicated the sanctions it used, whilst respect for political order had hardly become customary, it was not surprising that the post-independence pressures brought a collapse of peaceful politics.

What was it, therefore, which marked off the above exceptions from the usual pattern? In the first place order was not preserved in these states by identical measures. Dr Banda, for example, insisted on retaining European military officers and government servants. He was believed to have an arrangement with the South Africans for military assistance. This policy no doubt saved his régime when an attempt was made in 1967 by his exiled ex-colleagues to overthrow it. Whether his people, and particularly the younger generation less susceptible to his charisma, would accept his autocratic rule remained to be seen.

In a different manner, the presence of President Kenyatta in Kenya did much to cushion the effect of post-independence tensions in his country. Although, as we have seen in the case of Ethiopia, the presence of a venerated leader did not necessarily insure against revolt, during the post-independence decade the severe ethnic and ideological strains in Kenya were contained by Kenyatta's massive influence. He was also able to use it to prevent the frequent tensions within the East African Community from precipitating collapse.

This charismatic quality, though projected in very different ways, also acted as a catalyst in both Tanganyika and Zambia. Nyerere's quiet, persuasive personality and his constant proximity to his people, was matched by Kaunda's ability to remain above the ethno-political conflicts which assailed his embattled state. It might be added that both Houphouet-Boigny in the Ivory Coast and Senghor in Senegal shared this identification with their people, though again in vastly different ways.

Nevertheless, there were other African charismatic leaders who fell to no more severe stresses than those experienced by these exceptional men. Why did the army of Nkrumah depose him whilst those of Tanganyika, Kenya and Uganda returned to their barracks in 1964? Why were subsequent emergencies in these countries never utilized by their armies to execute coups, until the collapse of the Obote régime in Uganda, whereas lesser strains in a dozen other states produced military régimes?

The answer to these questions seems to lie within the somewhat shadowy borders of public hope, confidence and awareness. The armies of the east African states mutinied in 1964 over pay and conditions which could be remedied. Yet, in Tanganyika certainly, they were attacking a cardinal principle of state policy. They demanded Africanization in place of localization; preference for African citizens over those of other races. This had been a bone of contention expressed both by the trade unions and by a small opposition party.

Africanization could have been a sufficiently populist cause to have unseated any government in east or central Africa. That it did not do so suggests that a sufficient majority of the public put greater store by the policies their government were pursuing than in their personal prejudices. Nyerere, Kenyatta and Kaunda were able to persuade most of their people that the price of the progress they were making was suppression of racial discrimination. An atmosphere had been created in which a large enough number of people recognized national problems and identified themselves with the efforts at solution to create a sense of common purpose. In each case this feeling appears to have been shared by some of the soldiers, whilst most of them must have been made aware by their experiences in the mutinies that it was general amongst the public.

Of course, the action of British forces in supporting the governments against their mutineers was a major immediate factor. But it does not explain why the armies subsequently did not take advantage of crises. Each of the east African governments and Kaunda's in Zambia quickly learnt the main lesson of the mutinies. They recognized that so long as their armies remained divorced from political ideology as they had been taught by colonial rulers, they would neither share responsibility for national policies nor feel committed to the national effort. The deliberate politicizing of the soldiers, the introduction of political education and the integration of the armed forces into party activity, thus bridged the gap between politician, civil servant and soldier. But this policy could not have succeeded without there being a general consensus of opinion that the government represented the interests of the people. There was an absence of this confidence in government in virtually every state where a military coup took place.

Finally, there is the normal responsibility of the soldier to defend his country to be considered. There has been little inter-African conflict at a military level so far. Yet the duty of defence against external attack is by no means negligible in the continent. Certain small wars have been fought, like that between Algeria and Morocco, or the skirmishes between Somalia, on the one hand, and Kenya and Ethiopia on the other. The tensions between Uganda under Amin and Tanzania broke out into military raiding in 1972 and the following year threatened an international war. Certainly with a paranoiac character like Amin as a head of state, and a fanatic such as Gadafy of Libya prepared to interfere at random, Nyerere's hopes of a continent free from the burden of military forces must have vanished.

Yet the most serious dangers to African security remained in the south. The attack by the Portuguese on Guinea in 1970 brought this menace sharply home to all African governments. A conference of military representatives was quickly called in Lagos, resulting in renewed demands for greater regional co-operation in defence. As the guerrilla wars against the Portuguese continued in Guinea-Bissau, Mozambique and Angola, with sporadic raids across the Rhodesian border, Guinea, Zambia and Tanzania remained under continuous threat of reprisal invasions. South Africa, Rhodesia and Portugal had established what amounted to a military alliance; African politicians constantly called for support to the freedom fighters; it remained to be seen whether Africa's soldiers could sink their national amour propre and form a genuine joint command.

9

Zambia — A Case Study

The experience of the Republic of Zambia since her independence in October 1964 illustrates each of the major issues we have discussed and which had to be faced by newly independent African states during the 1960s. At the moment of attaining independence, out of a population of about 4,000,000, only 100 Zambians possessed any kind of university degree and 1,200 had school certificates. She was left with virtually a single commodity economy, copper providing 40 per cent of gross domestic product, 95 per cent of export value and more than 65 per cent of government revenue. Her leaders had scarcely any experience of governmental responsibility, President Kaunda and his ministerial colleagues having been entrusted with office only since 1962. Until the late 1950s only a handful of Africans had been given the right to vote. And Zambia, like all other African states, was a European creation. Its frontiers had been drawn in Europe according to European considerations; they delineated no distinguishable entity, dividing members of ethnic communities from their fellows in surrounding states, enclosing communities with different cultures, languages and origins, often with a history of mutual antagonism. The relevance of these general problems will be discussed later in this chapter.

Copper provided Zambia with greater resources for development than were available to any other black-governed state at the moment of independence. The average per capita annual income of her inhabitants in 1964 was estimated at 126 Kwacha, or approximately £63.* This can be compared with a figure of £18 in neighbouring Tanzania and even less in Malawi. But this high average concealed the fact that the majority of Zambians were peasants living like their fellows in the rest of Africa. The additional wealth available to Zambia only served to highlight the problems she shared with the rest of post-colonial Africa. The companies which controlled mining were assured of strong political influence as they were indispensable to economic life; revenues and foreign exchange were at the mercy of fluctuations in world prices; and demand

* The Zambian Kwacha is tied to the US dollar. The 1973 average rate of exchange was 1.7 Kwachas to £1.

for the product could diminish at any time according to external factors such as the conclusion of wars or the development of synthetics.

Of still greater significance were the implications of the dominant mining industry on the social structure of the nation. The 40,000 African copper-miners earned much less than white miners, but a great deal more than other citizens. It is roughly estimated that at the time of independence the African miner was paid ten times less than his white colleague, but ten times more than the average income of his fellow African. The mining families, together with those who settled in the Copper Belt to provide goods and services, thus comprised an economic and social élite. They tended to set standards which wage employees in other industries attempted to match.

Moreover, the wealth produced by the mines proved a mixed blessing to Zambia's development efforts. Whilst it provided more capital and revenue than was available to most African states, it increased the money supply in a manner which gave many people the impression that they could rely on government subsidies instead of their own efforts, increased the consumption demands of the élite and offered prizes to those in public life which diminished the concept of service. At the same time, because of this unusual wealth, industry was attracted to Zambia irrespective of planned development. The extent of industrialization and construction which followed independence often distorted the government's efforts to plan the economy according to its philosophy of social justice.

President Kaunda and his colleagues were well aware that the system they had inherited was socially unjust and publicly promised to reform it. The President, for instance, wrote in his introduction to the First National Development Plan:

A constant preoccupation of my Government is the disparity in the standard of living between the rural masses and the comparatively limited urban and industrial sector.

He added:

The structure which we have inherited from the colonial era resulted in many situations which have to be put right ... So it is, by opening a frontal attack on these inherited structures ... this first National Development Plan lays the foundation not only of economic independence but also of growing prosperity.

Yet the pressure for increased incomes from that small proportion of Zambians who earned wages – only 269,000 in the year of independence – was bound to negate the government's efforts to build a society based on social justice. The gap in living-standards between urban and rural inhabitants, a crucial threat to peaceful development throughout Africa, would widen instead of closing. But the pressures proved impossible to resist.

In the first place, as in the rest of Africa, the wage employees could organize because of their social proximity. The Zambian Mineworkers Union, with 35,000 members, was probably the best organized African trade union in the continent. Soon after independence it merged with other African unions into the Mineworkers Union of Zambia. Moreover, it had conducted a campaign over more than a decade to break the dual wage policy adopted by the mining companies. This policy had been initiated at a time when it was necessary to attract expatriate miners for skilled work. The white miners themselves, supported by federal politicians, had entrenched their privileged position, even when the companies sought to break down the colour bar in employment to secure higher productivity. The colour bar itself was abolished by independence, but the duality remained de facto because of the lack of skilled Africans. To the African miners, however, this seemed a continuation of colonial racialism.

So the union continued to call strikes after independence. It could not be easily condemned by the government, for it had played an important part in the anti-federal and anti-colonial movement. Its agitation against the Central African Federation enlisted international aid through the International Mineworkers Federation and significantly stimulated the drive to independence.

Following a strike which closed the industry, the government appointed a commission under Roland Brown, the Tanzanian Attorney-General, to investigate the whole issue. In 1966 the Brown Commission criticized the companies for continuing to discriminate against Africans and the union for calling strikes during a time of national crisis; but it also awarded the African miners a 22 per cent wage increase. This certainly lowered tensions on the Copper Belt, reducing criticism of the government; but it also inevitably retarded the government's efforts to secure national social justice and added fuel to the flames of inflation.

Before independence, little planned development had been attempted in Zambia. Not only was the country regarded by the British as Europeans usually viewed their African colonies – i.e. as suppliers of raw materials as cheaply as possible – but Zambia was specially handicapped as a member of the Central African Federation. Emphasis had been placed on the growth of Southern Rhodesia, with Zambian needs taking a distant second place. Indeed, although during the period 1956–64 Zambia's gross domestic product had risen by 66 per cent, the annual rate of 5.8

per cent, when population increase was taken into account, fell to about two per cent per capita. From 1961 to 1963, during the dissolution of the Federation, it was stagnant. The first task of the independent government, therefore, was to increase production in order that, when plans for more equal distribution took effect, the shares would be substantially larger than the meagre K126 (£63) of 1964.

President Kaunda's attitude to this economic problem has been revealed in several long speeches explaining his philosophy, to which he has given the name "Humanism". This is essentially based on a profound concern for people, as distinct from statistics or the mere production of goods. He put this in two succinct queries: "How do we now organize our society on the basis of the individual, and how can we ensure that what the individual does is for the good of society as a whole?" and "How do we preserve what is good in our traditions, and at the same time allow ourselves to benefit from the science and technology of our friends from both the West and the East?" He appended one answer: "We refuse to be dogmatic about anything ... We choose to be constantly looking for and devising new ways by which to encourage the hastening of material advance while ensuring that the principles of traditional man-centred society are preserved." In short, increased material wealth was to be encouraged by expanded production, but not for the purpose of some abstract concept of "national growth"; rather in order to ensure that the individual lives of Zambian citizens were improved.

Even before independence the basic needs had been visible. The campaign against Federation and colonial rule had largely concentrated on the racial discrimination which both systems practised. Yet the majority of Zambians were mainly concerned with improvements in their standards of living. They were persuaded that school places, higher wages, hospitals and clinics, more houses, water supplies, roads and buses were being denied through the dominance of European interests in the Federation or by British imperialism; they expected them to be provided by the substitution of African for white government.

Kaunda and his colleagues had been warned of what was expected of them when, in 1963, a commission appointed to investigate growing violence on the Copper Belt published its report. Unemployment and lack of educational opportunity were emphasized as the main causes of the violent outbursts. But the commission reported in addition "the opinion was also expressed that there was disappointment that the coming into power of a nationalist government had not resulted in immediate and widespread benefits to the mass of the people." As Kaunda's party was represented on this commission, the relevance of its report for his government was unquestionable.

In 1964 an Economic Survey Mission representing the United Nations, the Economic Commission for Africa and the Food and Agricultural Organization, prepared an analysis of the Zambian economy. Its report began with the sentence, "The great majority of the people in Zambia are poor, under-educated (if not illiterate) and unhealthy." It proceeded to pinpoint specific economic weaknesses which could cause social or political unrest: the contrasts in living-standards between black and white, town and country, the areas in proximity to the railway line and those remote from communications. The objectives of economic policy following independence must therefore be: to increase employment, promote greater equality in standards of life, build on existing social forms where possible to avoid disruption, and to integrate Zambian development into the development of the African continent. The Mission significantly asserted that Zambia "can have big increases in wages or big increases in employment, *not both*".

President Kaunda himself did not need such evidence to convince himself that the responsibility of those who had gained political independence was to use it for the benefit of the common man. He had a deep conviction that it was his duty to build a new society based on his understanding of African values:

> African society has always been man-centred ... We in Zambia intend to do everything in our power to keep our society man-centred ... I have always defined the common man as that man who, without help from the people's party and Government, is likely to become a victim of exploitation in this merciless world, and goodness knows he is by far, far in the majority ... I do not want, even in economic terms, the government of Zambia to think of our people as if they were mere pawns in a game. I want them to participate fully in everything that we are planning and doing. How can it be done? To be effective we must think in terms of the smallest unit in our social and political organization – the village.

Yet:

> I must admit that I hesitate to interfere to any great extent with village life as it is today for the very reason that culturally we may be committing suicide – we might, without being aware of it, destroy some of the very best things in our national culture. At the same time, to leave our villages as they are today means stagnation, and the last may well be worse than the first.

When President Kaunda led his nation into independence he thus had a set of imperatives which, from expert reports, conversations with his intimates and listening to his people, he recognized would determine the success or failure, probably the survival, of his régime. He had to increase national wealth in order to provide the means for expanding the economic and social infrastructure; he had to outlaw racial discrimination, bridging the gap between white and black incomes, yet without creating a black élite imitative of white life-styles; he must halt and then narrow the rapidly widening differentials between urban and rural living-standards, between employed and unemployed in the towns; he must provide massive educational facilities to supply the nation with sufficient trained Zambian personnel to replace expatriate experts, whilst recruiting still more foreigners during the period necessary to accomplish this task; he had to grow more food, limit imports, encourage exports, develop industry, diversify from dependence on copper, build new communications to escape from the stranglehold of Rhodesia, Portugal and South Africa. He had to forge new diplomatic contacts with the various sections of the communist and non-aligned worlds in order to avoid being trapped into dependence on the Western society in which his country had been anchored by Britain and the Federation. All this had to be accomplished whilst building the nation's defences against threats of aggression from the heavily armed South.

From listening to President Kaunda and his leading ministers during the early years of independence I was never left in doubt that all these crucial issues were fully appreciated. Various experts – perhaps too many – were set to work on discovering the means to solve the problems. A stream of reports were written, though often they contradicted each other and were rarely complementary. A considerable number of people appeared in Lusaka, anxious to jump on the Zambian bandwagon on the strength of previous acquaintance with the President. Yet, although the enormous challenges were recognized, certain influences were undermining the single-minded efforts to meet them. One of the major problems was the isolation of the President himself. He had a clear vision of the kind of society that he wished to build in Zambia, and had every reason to believe that his vision would satisfy the ambitions of the vast majority of his people. He was prepared to be empirical, experimenting to discover solutions. But he was never able to collect around him an inner group of either politicians or public servants on whom he could always depend both to share his objectives and to devote themselves to their attainment. Consequently he remained a solitary unifying, directing catalyst, often a lonely figure, forced to recognize that few of his lieutenants could be relied on to take burdens from his shoulders, or confident that agreed policies would be pursued.

Much of this failure to mobilize a team devoted to a common goal was due to politicizing taking precedence over the execution of policy. Ethnic considerations frequently influenced political appointments and interfered with collective action. Immediately following independence, there was also some necessity to reward loyal colleagues from the anti-colonial struggle – a necessity common to all ex-colonial régimes. Yet the qualities which distinguish a warrior in the battle against colonial rule are different from those needed by the successful administrator of programmes in a new state. Moreover, certain differences of view concerning central policy issues soon appeared amongst Kaunda's colleagues. The most important of these arose over the part which Zambia should play in the imposition of economic sanctions against rebel Rhodesia. It was obvious that Zambia would suffer severely from any immediate diversion of trade from her southern neighbour. Nor did anyone in Zambia believe that economic sanctions could defeat Ian Smith's rebellion. There were ministers and civil servants, therefore, who would have ignored the British request for the boycott of Rhodesia, on the grounds that the interests of the Zambian people must take precedence over an international policy which was bound, in any case, to fail.

At independence, therefore, Zambia faced all the conventional economic problems of young developing countries. She was left with a mono-crop, copper, corresponding to the cocoa of Ghana, the cotton of Egypt or the groundnuts of Senegal. Her manufacturing potential had been ignored in the interests of colonial rulers, in this case not so much the British as the white Rhodesians. Communications had been directed southward towards the coast to facilitate exports and imports, thus again ensuring dependence on the white south to the neglect of internal development. Most of her people had been left to exist on subsistence, cash agriculture being largely confined to European and Afrikaner immigrants. Those Africans employed in modern economic activities were used as unskilled or semi-skilled labour, virtually no attempt being made to train them in skills.

In dealing with this legacy and trying to turn it into the kind of society demanded by his people, Kaunda and his colleagues were handicapped by two other factors common throughout the continent. Zambia's governmental structure, like that in the rest of Africa, had been devised by the imperial power. Was this suitable to meet the tasks of independence? Secondly, again in common with other African states, Zambian boundaries had been drawn by the European colonialists. They confined within a single state different communities with little common history, some with previous experience of conflict. Could they work together in the interests of the new nation, subordinating communal separatism to national interest?

The administrative machine bequeathed by Britain had the great virtue of comparative honesty. The value of this characteristic became increasingly apparent throughout post-independence Africa. Bribery and corruption, or, in blunter language, personal stealing of public money, became the most corrosive element in public life. But the British had built a civil service which was largely immune from corruption. It was also reasonably efficient in conducting the administration of the country.

Yet there were two aspects of the British-type civil service which cast doubts on its suitability to face the tasks of independence. In the first places, its probity had been preserved by paying its higher grades such large salaries that they were removed from temptation. This method accorded with the British assumption that a select élite should set the standards and values of society, with a solid middle class imitating them and thus defending the social rules. But could a new nation afford such high salaries or an élitist concept when trying to build a socially just society?

In any case, with increased government activity the civil service expanded rapidly after independence. Appointments proliferated, not only to meet increased needs, but as rewards to friends and relatives. Many of the newcomers had little training or experience. Standards of efficiency therefore rapidly declined, but salaries continued to increase. Over the first four years of independence government expenditure rose by 20 per cent a year, and four-fifths of this was spent on civil-service salaries. Supplementary budgets – the financial bane of many African governments – plus unauthorized spending became commonplace. When Kapwepwe, then Vice-President, attempted to defend the civil service he was sharply contradicted by President Kaunda, who roundly declared, "I must indicate how disgusted I have been in the past by the apathy, sheer lack of initiative and indiscipline which has been prevalent in the civil service." But where were the personnel who could be given authority to clean the Augean stable? It was the early 1970s before Aaron Milner, head of the service, could undertake the task.

Still more significant was the political outlook of a British-type civil service. In accordance with British practice, the colonial civil servant was supposed to be apolitical, to serve every political master with indiscriminate devotion. In fact, this attitude, as in Britain, tended to encourage the characteristic conservatism of the civil servant. He was content with his privileged lot, any change threatened his contentment and incidentally made for extra work. In any case, the colonial service had participated in the pre-independence efforts to suppress the nationalists who now took office. Moreover, administrative conventions might be undermined by innovation, and the new régime was led by ex-rebels who were dedicated to changing the structure of society. Could such a remote bureaucracy promote the objects of economic development and social revolution?

Similar doubts arose over the political sector of the governmental struc-

ture. The idea that a double or multi-party system was essential to democratic representation was firmly fixed in British minds. In Zambia's case
there had been three parties during the short period of domestic self-
government preceding independence. Kaunda's UNIP was opposed by
Harry Nkumbula's African National Congress, the original nationalist
party from which UNIP (actually its prohibited predecessor) had split.
The third party represented most of the white community, a survival from
the Federation. It soon dissolved after independence.

Already, before independence, the dangers of this system had been
exposed. The threat of racial politics, if not of social racialism, quickly
disappeared with the dissolution of Federation; but factionalism and
communalism survived.

For a time Nkumbula flirted with the idea of forming a coalition with
the white party. This would have left UNIP, the majority party, in
opposition. The frustration felt by its supporters, who had borne the brunt
of the anti-Federation and anti-colonial struggle, would almost certainly
have led to violence. A system which allowed the will of the majority of
electors to be subordinated to its technicalities would soon have
foundered. It was saved by Nkumbula's eventual decision to combine
with Kaunda.

Yet this decision did not remove the more dangerous aspect of the
multi-party system. For Nkumbula's party drew its support almost
entirely from the south, where the Tonga community was dominant. In
the British and European context political parties had usually sprung
from socio-economic classes and broadly represented their contending
interests. In Africa such class formation had scarcely begun. Parties were
therefore likely to represent communal loyalties, and communal politics
presented a direct menace to nation-building.

It therefore seemed probable that some changes would have to be made
to the forms of government, politics and administration after independence. This was in fact recognized before independence when Kaunda
and his colleagues decided that the new state should come into being as a
republic with an executive president.

The menace of communalism was not confined to inter-party rivalry.
Its threat was as obvious within the ruling UNIP as between that body
and the ANC. Although UNIP was certainly a national party, it had
never gained a strong foothold in the south. Moreover, in the west,
Barotseland had been granted a privileged position under colonial rule, a
separate treaty between its Litunga and the British monarch providing it
with a claim to special treatment. For some time there was open talk of
Barotse secession. In the east were the Ngoni-speaking peoples, some of
them descendants of the Ngoni who had broken away from Shaka's Zulus
in the nineteenth century and successfully invaded the east of the

continent through Rhodesia, Malawi, Zambia, Mozambique and Tanzania. These communities were to remain solidly loyal to Kaunda and UNIP. The northerners were in some respects the most crucial to communal peace. They are often described as Bemba, but a distinction should be made between the Bemba community proper and the Bemba-speakers. Most workers on the Copper Belt are Bemba-speakers, but they are drawn from many communities. The Bemba themselves are probably the most cohesively organized of these communities, but even they should not be regarded as monolithic. One division within their ranks is that between the educated and the semi-literate or illiterate, who are often also unemployed. These latter have always displayed envy towards the former and regarded Simon Kapwepwe, the tall, bearded, toga-clad boyhood friend and lieutenant of Kaunda, as their usual champion.

Although UNIP was a national party, its policies representing national interests, it was composed of an uneasy coalition. In party elections, crucial to government as well as party offices, manoeuvring and bloc voting on communal lines became frequent. The Bemba group tried to gain control of the party hierarchy and had been opposed by a loose combination of the Ngoni-speakers and the Lozi from Barotseland.

Between 1967 and 1969, however, new alignments were negotiated which almost destroyed UNIP by the communal conflicts they provoked. Nalumino Mundia, a Lozi from the party leadership and Minister of Labour, was forced by the President to resign for acquiring shares in companies receiving government loans. He formed the United Party, which attracted various malcontents and a number of discontented Lozi.

In August 1967 an alliance between the Bemba and the Tonga deposed Reuben Kamanga, an easterner, as vice-president of party and country and replaced him by Simon Kapwepwe – the Bemba. At the same party elections, Mainza Chona, a Tonga, replaced Sipalo, the Lozi, as secretary-general and Elijah Mudenda, another Tonga, ousted another Lozi, Arthur Wina, as party treasurer and Finance Minister. The Bemba, claiming with some justice that they had borne the brunt of the anti-federal and anti-colonial struggles, had mobilized votes with the help of the Tonga alliance, to defeat the pretensions of both easterners and Lozi.

By early 1968 communalism had become so rife within UNIP that Kaunda actually resigned as president of party and country. For a moment the party was shocked rigid. Kaunda was persuaded to change his decision on condition that communalism was exorcized from party activities; but the party and the nation had been forced to face the awful prospect of a battle for the succession. It was recognized that Kaunda alone could hold party and country together.

So strong were communal tensions, however, that even this salutary lesson did not serve to end them. Munu Sipalo, another Lozi minister, was openly accused by the Bemba of supporting the United Party. He was insulted in the Northern Province and refused an apology by party officials.

Much now depended on the general election to be held at the end of 1968. The allocation of seats, the results and subsequent Cabinet appointments would determine the communal balance of power for the future.

In the event UNIP suffered severely for its internal conflicts. Arthur Wina, Munu Sipalo, both experienced ministers, were defeated, along with three other Lozi ministers, in Barotse seats. Ironically it was Congress which defeated them, taking advantage of the attacks which had been vented on them by their own UNIP colleagues. Congress, indeed, capitalized on the communal conflicts of UNIP, not only consolidating its hold on the south, but getting Mundia elected, even though he was still in restriction, and gaining eight Lozi seats. The power balance between Bemba and Lozi in UNIP and government had been shattered by internal, communal strife and the party itself dangerously weakened as a national force. The even deeper fear was that the elections had exposed the communal emotions of the party's lower ranks and of the electors. If its national image were to be restored, the party itself would have to be reformed.

Kaunda himself was the one man amongst the party-government hierarchy who stood above communal allegiance. He was helped by the fact that, although born in Bemba country, his parents came from Malawi. This gave him the strength of being seen to be genuinely noncommunal, as the unique symbol of national unity; at the same time, it denied him a power-base within any one community. So long as the momentum towards building a national entity could be maintained, the whole country recognized that Kaunda was the only man capable of leading it; but if communal emotions ever began to supersede the national drive, the President would find himself without a political army. This fact was realized abroad as well as at home; in the white south renewed efforts were planned to discredit and then remove Kaunda, to replace him with a Hastings Banda-like leader who would co-operate with the South Africans, Rhodesians and Portuguese.

The communal tensions within UNIP gravely affected the conduct of government. In neighbouring Tanzania, the closest parallel to the Zambian political arena, Nyerere had been able to gather a team of colleagues which, with occasional exceptions, had lent him constant support through the difficulties of guiding his nation towards social justice despite the threat of external attack. Kaunda, in contrast, had to be constantly changing his ministers and chief civil servants from one office to another in order to maintain communal balance and avoid the creation of any dangerous ethnic power bloc which an enemy could use against his nation's security. This hardly made for single-minded or efficient government, tending to divert effort from the paramount economic and social problems to a concentration on political manoeuvring.

It is possible that these communal distractions could have been reduced by the creation of a single-party state. Yet, as was demonstrated in Tanzania, Ghana and many other African states, whilst a single-party structure might obviate the danger of the political arena becoming a battleground for communal parties, it could only succeed to the extent that a basic political philosophy was commonly accepted and party discipline well established. Otherwise factions would be enabled to use the party itself for particularist purposes.

In Zambia the two-pronged struggle against Federation and colonial rule had never allowed the kind of wide-reaching campaign of political education on which Nyerere had been able to base his national policies. A general concept of national unity did exist, characterized by the national slogan, "One Zambia, One nation". Nor were factionalism or greed so powerfully disruptive as, for example, in Uganda and Ghana. Yet Bemba ambitions, closely attached to the wealth opportunities on the Copper Belt and in rapidly developing Lusaka, constantly undermined a general acceptance of national idealism. The activities of the élite in all the urban areas increased the cynicism with which Kaunda's philosophy of "Humanism" was regarded in influential circles. Nor could the party be safely used to attack these dissentient elements. Party discipline was far too loose and local sections of the party were frequently able to take the law into their own hands, often antagonizing the populace by irresponsible actions.

In any case, Kaunda was anxious to attain a base from which he could create a single-party state by consent rather than through legislation or coercion. He hoped that his old friend Nkumbula would join him in establishing a single party devoted to pursuing the interests of the nation as a whole, discarding sectional or personal ambitions. Yet Nkumbula, although often flirting with such unpopular causes as a "dialogue" with South Africa and the British supply of arms to the South Africans, despite frequent quarrels and defections in his party, still survived as a separate political influence. In spite of his personal aberrations, he was regarded affectionately by many Zambians, including the President, although his political whims could be infuriating.

When, in 1972, Kaunda, conscious of growing dangers from external subversion, internal factionalism, and economic crises, decided that a commission should be set up to hear public opinion and report on the best way of introducing a single-party system, the ANC refused an invitation to be represented on it. The menace of communalism still loomed heavily over Zambia's political horizon.

One other problem plagued Kaunda and his colleagues in their early years of independence. Alice Lenshina was born in Kaunda's own district and attended his father's mission church. In 1954 she claimed to have risen from the dead and founded her own sect. This became one of the messianic groups to which men and women throughout the world have turned for comfort and security when they feel there is little to live for. The sect refused to co-operate with authority and became an object of derision and hatred for many members of UNIP who felt that its members were traitors to the nationalist cause.

Despite attempts by Kaunda to prevent bloodshed, in the months preceding independence clashes between party members and the Lumpa sect became more serious. Eventually the police stormed Lenshina's church. The Lumpas became desperate and resorted to witchcraft. In the ensuing battles between the sect and the police over 700 people lost their lives. Alice Lenshina was first imprisoned and then restricted to a remote district. Many of her followers fled to the Congo, refusing all appeals for reconciliation and representing a constant threat of violence or subversion from across the frontier.

These events profoundly grieved Kaunda. He was a deeply religious man, gradually developing from Christianity to a more universalist spirituality which he termed "Humanism". He was especially influenced by the life and teachings of Gandhi, which gave him a sincere belief in non-violence and the sacred nature of man. Like Gandhi, he has forsworn alcohol, tea, coffee, tobacco and meat. He tried to apply this spiritual outlook to his political tasks, telling his people that "We in Zambia intend to do everything in our power to keep our society man-centred. For it is in this that what might be described as African civilization is embodied and indeed if modern Africa has anything to contribute to this troubled world, it is in this direction that it should."

Yet he found that he was often faced by the choice between protecting his nation from disintegration by means of force or of maintaining his principles inviolate and risking disaster. He once said to me after a mission abroad to seek missile protection against the threat of bombing from the white south, "Doesn't it seem ironic that I, a convinced pacifist, should be buying the most modern weapons of destruction?"He also recognized the irony of his own son choosing an army career, becoming a Sandhurst cadet. (Although he was very proud when the young man declined an invitation to dinner at Buckingham Palace as he was too devoted to his studies.) Kaunda also had to recognize that the freedom fighters in Rhodesia, the Portuguese territories, Namibia and South Africa had no option but to meet violence with violence, all constitutional avenues for attaining their rights being closed. The Lumpa episode came into the same category: the preservation of the nation had to take priority over his personal beliefs. But it hurt him profoundly; he comforted himself with the perspective that man is imperfect but still trying to climb to a better life; that it is his responsibility to assist the ascent and that this demands priorities, the first immediate one being the creation of a just national society.

These were some of the chains which fettered Kaunda and his colleagues as they attempted to transform Zambia from a retarded colonial client of white Rhodesia into a state offering equal opportunities to all its citizens, supplying its inhabitants with increasing quantities of nutritious food, more varied amenities, improving health, a balanced rural and urban life, a full education, and training Zambians to run national life, to defend their new state from aggression. The handicaps have been described with hindsight, for an understanding of them is essential to comprehend the attempts made by Kaunda's government to achieve these objectives. Her problems represent a fair cross-section of the difficulties encountered across the continent in the post-independence era. For, although Zambia possessed the massive advantage of her copper wealth, this only raised greater expectations amongst large sections of her people, highlighting the gap between anticipation and actuality. Each of the handicaps Kaunda encountered in his efforts to build a nation based on social justice were duplicated elsewhere; the greater resources at his disposal only brought his difficulties into sharper relief.

In addition to these common African problems, Zambia had to face dilemmas unique to herself, which still illustrated the kind of difficulties faced by most African leaders. Against the wishes of most articulate Zambians, she had been thrust into the Central African Federation in 1953. One of the purposes of the Federation was to marry the copper revenues of Zambia (then Northern Rhodesia) to the more diversified economy of Southern Rhodesia, thus creating a strong, white-dominated federated state capable of attracting external capital. This purpose was achieved to the extent that, according to the Central African Statistical Office, Zambia suffered a revenue loss of £98 million during the decade of the Federation's life.

Secondly, at the time of the Federation's dissolution it was agreed that most of its armed forces should revert to Southern Rhodesia. Of special significance was the transfer of the federal air service. This had been trained and equipped as part of the British Royal Air Force. Thus the Southern Rhodesians gained a modern, well-armed force which enabled them to defy any threatened coercion from British governments whilst constantly menacing the security of Zambia.

Thirdly, and most crucially, Zambia was left at the time of

independence with her economy inextricably tied to Southern Rhodesia (usually called Rhodesia after the dissolution of the Federation). As a land-locked state she depended on the railway through Rhodesia to export her copper and obtain most of her imports. The coal on which her copper mines relied came from Wankie in Rhodesia. The oil which fuelled most of her transport was brought from the Mozambique coast through Rhodesia. Most of her electricity was drawn from the Karibo hydro-electric plant, the power-house of which was on the Rhodesian shore of the dam. Airways, railways and the electricity grid were operated as common services. In the first full year of independence, 1965, Zambia bought £35,538,000 worth of goods from her southern neighbour, or 34 per cent of her total imports. In normal circumstances Zambia would have been in a precarious situation following independence. Her economic lifelines passed through Rhodesia, Mozambique, and Angola, the latter two countries governed by Portugal. Friction over racial policies could have been expected from all three sources, with the Zambian economy at the mercy of her opponents. But the circumstances were not normal. Less than 13 months after Zambia's independence, on 11 November 1965, Rhodesia was declared by Ian Smith to be independent. This declaration flouted international law and represented overt defiance of the British government's authority. It was met by the imposition of economic sanctions by Britain and the United Nations. All members of the United Nations were first requested and then commanded to sever their trade with Rhodesia.

This decision to try and defeat the rebel régime of Ian Smith by economic boycott rather than by armed compulsion was bound to damage the interests of Zambia more severely than those of any other country. To others Rhodesian trade was marginal, to Zambia it was crucial. Some argument took place amongst the Zambian leadership as to whether sanctions should be applied. There were those who argued that the quarrel was between Rhodesia and Britain, that Rhodesia was still a British colony, therefore that it was Britain's responsibility to defeat the rebellion; that the sanctions' policy could not destroy Mr Smith's power and therefore that Zambia should not jeopardize her own interests for the sake of a British face-saving device. The majority, however, though equally convinced that sanctions could never defeat the Smith régime as no action was to be taken against open violation by South Africa, decided that Zambia should co-operate with Britain and the United Nations. President Kaunda himself was an enthusiastic supporter of the United Nations and took the view that loyal members should apply its policies, even when they appeared inimical to their own immediate interests.

Despite the heavy dependence on Rhodesia which Zambia had been bequeathed by her former British rulers, she now made strenuous efforts to comply with the sanctions policy. In 1966 her imports from Rhodesia fell from the 34 per cent of the previous year to 19 per cent, and in 1967 to 11 per cent. Exports during the same period fell from nearly £5½ million to about £1 million. This was a tremendous effort for an infant nation at the beginning of its attempt to create a modern way of life for its people. It was accepted by Britain and the United Nations that it was impossible for Zambia to sever trade completely. The British government headed by Harold Wilson offered some compensation for the losses incurred, but never attempted to cover more than a fraction of the cost. Even more important to Zambians than the financial burden of seeking new communications and alternative sources of supplies was the diversion of economic direction. Instead of being able to plan a phased expansion of production and devise new, socially just methods of distribution, all resources had suddenly to be mobilized for the single purpose of meeting the insistent demands arising out of sanctions. Even though this situation attracted some foreign investment in manufacturing which might not otherwise have been directed to Zambia at this moment, it also was unplanned, often adding distortion to the social economy.

The first action taken by Kaunda's government, within a few weeks of independence, was to introduce a transitional development plan. It was to bridge an interim period of 18 months whilst a full plan could be prepared. This transitional plan envisaged an expenditure of £35 million. This, in itself, bore testimony to the strength of the Zambian economy. Few, if any, African countries could have found such a sum from their own resources at the time of their independence. But during 1964 Zambia had achieved a visible trade balance of over £89 million. Moreover, foreign investors had already begun to recognize the potential of the Zambian market now that it had been separated from Rhodesia. During the same year manufacturing industry had grown by 13½ per cent.

The government first concentrated on two sectors which it believed should have priority. It felt that higher education should be immediately expanded in order to provide a base from which to meet the extensive need for trained Zambians. It therefore made strenuous efforts to build and staff new secondary schools, whilst making provision for the new University of Zambia to be opened early in 1966. The success of these plans can be measured from the fact that whereas at the time of independence there were about 10,000 African children in secondary schools, this number had been more than doubled when the transitional plan concluded.

Yet this policy raised its own problems. There simply were not nearly enough Zambian teachers to staff the existing secondary schools, still less a greater number. The expansion could only be achieved by recruiting a large number of foreign teachers. That they were non-Africans might be of little account, for Zambia was aiming to become a non-racial society; but the fact that they brought with them alien cultural patterns could be a handicap, for Zambia needed young people trained for her specific needs. Above all, the young men and women students had to build bridges between the traditional culture of their country and the modern technical life essential for economic progress. The educational methods of foreigners could divert them from this task, leading them into élitist assumptions which would separate them from their own people. Yet the need for trained personnel was so urgent that the risk had to be taken.

A similar problem arose very early in the life of the university. For several years before independence I had participated in long discussions with Kaunda and John Little (Permanent Secretary in the Ministry of Education and then secretary to the university council) about the purpose, structure and character at which the university should aim. They agreed that the Oxbridge–Sorbonne style adopted by most African universities should be eschewed. Zambia's priority needs were for administrators, mining engineers, agriculturalists; it was the primary task of the new university to supply such people as quickly as possible.

The university began its life dedicated to this general principle of supplying the country's needs. Entry qualifications were to be low, so as to enrol the maximum number of students, which would allow a substantial number of students to graduate each year. Yet, within a short time, different voices were heard. The conventional academic claims were made – that Zambia must have a university of international standard, comparable to universities elsewhere in the world, original research must be encouraged, traditional standards of entry and graduation imposed. And the significant feature of this criticism was that it emanated from Africans, not Europeans, on the council, and was supported by sections of the students. So the university soon followed the path taken by other African universities, within the general pattern of institutions in the metropolitan countries. Students, however militant in theory, became a privileged élite; the engineering department trained civil or electrical engineers who could make large salaries on graduation, rather than preparing Zambians for responsible posts in the mines; political science attracted large numbers with ambitions in politics or the foreign service; perhaps the only survival of the functional principle was the appearance of its buildings, which amply justified the claim of its Yugoslavian architects to have applied their "ugly style".

The second priority was accorded to a government building programme, to cost £27.5 million. The objects of this scheme were twofold. First, there was an obvious and immediate need for new buildings, for extra houses, schools, clinics, hospitals, offices and factories essential to an expanding economy. The second need, equally urgent, was to provide employment for the urban population, already growing at a rapidly increasing rate. Although the attractions of town life might lure a swelling stream of migrants from the countryside – especially of the young – employment opportunities were never increasing fast enough to provide all of them with jobs. Thus the problem of growing urban unemployment threatened to disrupt social peace and hinder economic development. The government hoped that its building programme would provide 40,000 new jobs, halving the numbers of urban unemployed it had inherited.

Before the transitional plan had run its course, the crisis of Rhodesian UDI with its accompanying sanctions' problems had broken. Nevertheless, despite the menace of the new situation, President Kaunda and his government continued to pursue a policy of trying to plan their economy. The First National Development Plan was ready to come into operation in 1966; it was to cover the period 1966 to 1970. What did Zambians expect from their President and government; and what were the aims of the country's leaders? It is on the results of this first substantive plan that the ambitions and difficulties, the successes and failures of Kaunda's régime can be seen most clearly.

The government undoubtedly lost its first battles on the urban–rural front. According to one estimate, between 1964 and 1968 the earnings of peasant farmers increased by a mere three per cent, compared with 35 per cent for African miners. Wage earners outside the mines secured even greater increases, averaging 52 per cent. At the end of 1968, whilst peasant farmers were earning an average of K145 a year, miners were paid K1,300 and other wage earners K640. According to the calculations made in the Second National Development Plan, in the total rural areas the average per capita real income had increased between 1964 and 1970 only from K23 to K34, whereas wages and salaries in the urban areas had more than doubled.

Moreover, all the signs pointed to a continuation of this trend. Whereas manufacturing industry was increasing at a rate of about 16 per cent a year during this period, the growth rate of the agricultural sector was a mere 2.5 per cent, despite the first development plan's target of nine per cent. In short, although the government tried to devise a policy which would stimulate agricultural production and raise the standards of rural life, economic actualities had mocked their attempts. In relative terms rural inhabitants were becoming poorer and urban peoples richer.

Of course, all these figures are approximations. It is impossible, for instance, to measure accurately the monetary value of subsistence agriculture. Yet the reality of the trend cannot be gainsaid, and it produced further consequences unpalatable to the government.

Although wages had increased substantially, productivity had not kept pace. During the first four years after independence, for instance, whilst average wages increased by 54 per cent, productivity was only raised by 12 per cent, causing an increase in labour costs per unit of 38 per cent. The inevitable result was a bad dose of inflation and rapidly rising prices, with consequent need to introduce deflationary budgets, retarding the attack on unemployment.

Even in the midst of its struggles to apply sanctions to Rhodesia and create new lifelines to supply the economy with essential fuels whilst finding the means to get its copper to external markets, the government did not blind itself to these economic dangers. Nor did it take the easier road of relying on external help and thus burdening itself with future debt payments. Indeed, in April 1968, President Kaunda proclaimed an "economic revolution". He announced that his government was taking a majority interest in over a score of the large, foreign-owned companies. A state Industrial Development Corporation would henceforth ensure that the operations of major industry and commerce would serve the nation, instead of making excessive profits and sending them abroad. At the same time Zambian citizens were to be encouraged to engage in the business world, instead of leaving it under the domination of foreigners. At this stage the President felt that the copper industry was too big to handle, though he strongly criticized the low level of investment of the companies.

This action was calculated to strengthen the sense of nationalism, but inevitably it reduced the attraction of foreign investment on which a substantial part of the national plan depended. Nor did it reduce the level of government expenditure, of high wages, of mounting imports, all of which were contributing to the inflationary spiral which damaged most of the poor – i.e., the rural inhabitants.

Early in 1969, therefore, the government decided to introduce a deflationary budget. It was entrusted to Simon Kapwepwe, who imposed higher taxes and heavier duties on non-essential imports. This did not endear him to the miners, despite the fact that a substantial section of them were Bemba and considered him as their spokesman. This left him in a difficult position. He did not improve the chances of the mining community co-operating with the government in solving the national problem by accusing the press of inciting its readers against his budget. He managed to stave off a miners' strike, but at the price of storing up further dissension against government policies for the future.

Then again, the contrast in urban and rural living-standards naturally induced constant migration from countryside to town. From the 1969 census figures it appears that over the previous six years the urban population had increased by 65 per cent, an average of 8.7 per cent annually. By

1969 the 18 main towns of Zambia had a total population of 1.1 million, or 27 per cent of the country's inhabitants.

Social services could not keep up with this rate of mobility. It was estimated that 100,000 urban families were badly housed. Massive shanty communities spread round the towns. Nor could this growing army of migrants be absorbed into employment. By 1970 wage employment had grown from the 269,000 at independence to 390,000, but over a third of the working-age population were seeking work. It was estimated by the development planners that during the 1970s between 30,000 and 40,000 new jobs would have to be created every year; during the first plan only about 10,000 a year had been provided outside the agricultural sector.

The record of the first development plan should be considered within the perspective of all the difficulties we have discussed. There can be no doubt that the economic effort yielded substantial gains. Whereas during the decade preceeding independence the domestic product rose by 66 per cent (at constant 1955 figures), with an average annual rate of 5.8 per cent, during the period of the first plan, 1966–70, it increased by 84 per cent, or 10.6 per cent a year. Moreover, if population expansion is taken into account, the increase works out at only two per cent per capita in the former, colonial period, compared with 8.2 per cent after independence. As a result, the average per capita domestic product (at 1969 prices) rose from K126 ($176) to K303 ($424).

At the same time, we need to be realistic about these figures. A large proportion of the increase is attributable to unusually high copper prices. If the price of copper had remained as estimated in the plan, the actual rate of growth would have been reduced from 10.6 to six per cent. The crucial effects of copper price fluctuations can be seen in 1970–71. At the start of 1970, cash copper wire bars were selling at £700 a ton. In 1971 the price fell for a time below £400. As a consequence, whilst average per capita domestic production reached a figure of K303 in 1970, in the following year it had fallen to K246. Moreover, the low price threatened to render some Zambian mines uneconomic for production.

The high price of copper during most of the plan period, and the favourable trade balance it provided, enabled the government to achieve striking successes in certain social provisions. Budget expenditure rose dramatically, enabling it to embark on a large public investment programme. The transitional plan had raised employment from 269,000 in the year of independence to 313,000 by mid-1966. The first national plan aimed to increase this figure to 407,000 by the end of 1970. In fact, it only reached 390,000, yet this represented nearly a 24 per cent increase.

It was in health and education that the most spectacular successes were achieved. In addition to doubling the number of hospital beds and substantially increasing the supply of doctors and nurses, one of the greatest achievements was the attack on fatal disease. In 1964, 189 people died from smallpox; in 1969 only three; by the end of the period the disease had been virtually wiped out.

In education the figures speak for themselves. In 1964 there were 368,000 children in primary school; in 1970 the estimated figure was 904,600. In 1964 there were 14,000 children in secondary schools; in 1970, 52,000. At the start of the period there was no university and only about 100 graduates from foreign institutions; by 1970 over 1,200 under-graduates were studying at the new University of Zambia.

Yet each of these successes brought its own residual problems. All of them were achieved under the shadow of rapid population increase; between 1963 and 1969 the Zambian population rose by 17.3 per cent, an average annual rate of 2.7 per cent. Inevitably, this raised the propor-tion of young people in the community; by the end of the plan period about 46 per cent of inhabitants were under 15 years old. When older, non-working persons are added, and this section increased as medical care extended life, it will be seen that more than half the nation had become dependent, though many children still participated in some form of pro-duction. The burden of social services had thus become progressively heavier – just at the time when resources were most needed for productive investment.

So the increase in educational opportunity, taken in conjunction with a rapidly rising population, produced an employment crisis. This was aggravated by a migration to the towns, induced by the rise in wages as well as the ambitions of the educated and the social attractions of urban life. There was an 8.7 per cent increase in the urban population. As a result, the need arose for the creation of at least 30,000 new jobs a year, a figure that would inevitably rise. Despite the efforts made by the govern-ment, only about 10,000 new non-agricultural jobs became available each year under the plan. By the end of the period, at least half of wage workers were seeking work.

The most crucial issue raised by this economic expansion was the distribu-tion of wealth. The total wealth of the country was substantially increased and a greater proportion of it made available to Zambians. But to which Zambians? Wages in the money economy consistently rose, some very rapidly. Between 1964 and 1970 money earnings of Zambian employees increased by 130 per cent – given a rise in prices of eight per cent per annum. As productivity in every sector rose at a lower rate than wages, the rise in prices was hardly surprising. Statistics in the subsistence sector for both production and consumption have not yet been officially pro-duced; yet no one believes that they have kept pace with those in the cash economy. The majority of Zambians still live in this sector; they are also those most seriously affected by increased prices as the cost of consumption goods rise much faster than the prices paid for primary products. (A domestic reflection of the situation between developed and developing nations.) One estimate suggests that by the end of 1968 the earnings of peasant farmers had increased by only three per cent over 1964.

Nor is this situation surprising. In the first plan, lip-service was paid to the objective of narrowing the gap between rural and urban areas. Yet in the plan estimates for government capital investment 69 per cent was allocated to the three provinces which border the railway line; but they are inhabited by only 50 per cent of the population. In practice, these three provinces absorbed 82 per cent of capital expenditure, the other five having to share the remaining 18 per cent. If the expenditure is divided strictly between urban and rural areas, it is found that, whilst the plan envisaged spending K188 per capita in the urban provinces, K286 was actually spent, whereas the anticipated K104 to be spent per person in the rural areas sank to K82 in actuality. Thus the first plan, even if implemented as intended, could only widen the gap between country people and townsfolk; as carried out it stretched the gap into a chasm.

These consequences were certainly not intentional. Kaunda and his colleagues were entirely sincere in a desire to achieve their objectives. Rather do the results bear witness to the difficulties facing developing nations in achieving their conceptions of a just state from the starting point of the colonial legacy, the diversionary influence of obsessive politics, often intermixed with ethnic considerations, and the power of an urban-based élite.

The two former elements have already been portrayed; the latter deserves attention. Lack of trained personnel in all walks of national life left Zambia, like other newly independent nations, largely dependent on a small coterie of those with qualifications and experience. These technocrats, intellectuals, the educated and sophisticated, carried on much of the country's administration, both in government service and in private business, controlled educational institutions, and negotiated with international firms. After the economic reforms of 1968–70 which gave the government power over large sections of national industry, commerce, mining and finance, they also took control of these new powerful bodies. Gradually a number of Zambians joined the expatriates who first dominated their ranks, so that the small community cut across colour lines. But in their outlook they remained homogeneous. They were impatient of politics, tribalism, inefficiency, often cynical towards idealistic objectives. Their ambition was limited to "success", measured in terms of material gains and efficiently organized institutions. With the large copper revenues they not only ensured that their own salaries matched the standards of Europe, but encouraged the government to spend at a rate which would mortgage the future if copper prices were to fall – as they did.

These men, with a cosmopolitan perspective and a life-style drawn from the developed world, grew into an élite in the years after independence. Their monopoly of skills made them virtually indispensable. They took their opportunity to consolidate high incomes, to ensure that their children secured the best educational opportunities, that their international contacts would always guarantee their future.

The danger of the formation of such an élite class in a developing nation such as Zambia was not simply that it tended to set social standards inimical to the proclaimed national objectives, nor only that their display of wealth provoked envy and cynicism. More serious was their influence on national policies. Because they were either brought up in towns or adopted their life, they tended to concentrate on those policies which showed success in the urban environment. The same attitude was evident in the parastatal organizations. Instead of integrating the activities of these institutions into national policies, at times restraining their potential growth according to determined priorities, their success as entities was the main aim.

Above all, this élite was fundamentally conservative. It would prefer to maintain the status quo in which it flourished than risk innovation. Some of its members might talk or write theoretically about the need for "rural renaissance" or an "agrarian revolution", but as they had no genuine communication with the countryside, their plans remained intellectual exercises, remote from the practicalities of rural life.

President Kaunda tried to circumvent the influence of this élite in various ways, but never fully succeeded. He had neither the time to supervise its activities nor the personnel to diminish its power. One such instance was apparent in the preparation of the second development plan. The President had tried for over two years to involve the villages in the new planning by trying to set up a pyramid of committees down to the ward and village level. The planners were supposed to consider the proposals made from all parts of the nation by these committees. To my personal knowledge, at least one planning group simply ignored the pile of proposals set before it, preferring to rely on its own theoretical ideas. There is reason to suppose that was the general attitude. So the élite, usually remaining outside actual party activity, became an often decisive force in obstructing the radical action essential for dealing with the country's major problems.

The failure of the first plan to achieve its central objective did not apparently serve as sufficient warning. The second plan, which was hurriedly prepared during 1971, repeated many of the errors which had been exposed in its predecessor.

We can see the continuing inability of Zambian planners to overcome the massive difficulties facing them by taking a few examples of the contrast between declared objectives and measures proposed in this second plan.

In his Foreword the President wrote:

> Our deliberate emphasis, in our Second National Development Plan, is on rural development. The objectives in this programme will be mainly to correct the anomaly of lop-sided development that we inherited from the pre-Independence era ... For us, developing the rural areas is a matter of life and death ...

The planners themselves declared that the first of their main points of strategy was, "The expansion of agricultural production as a top priority ..." Yet in their provisions for expenditure over the five years, the rural sector was allocated K151.5 million, whereas mining was given K402 million, industry K253 million, transport and communications K373.2 million. The agricultural growth rate was planned as between five and six per cent, that of manufacturing for 14.7 per cent. Agricultural wages were to rise by 5.9 per cent, those of manufacturing and construction by 12.9 and ten per cent respectively. The plan actually provided for agriculture to fall from 15.2 per cent of gross domestic product to 13.9 per cent. Once again, on the one hand there is a declaration of intent, on the other provision for a clearly contrary result.

The same dichotomy was evident in provision for employment, probably Zambia's most serious problem during the 1970s. After calculating that about 67,000 persons would enter the labour-force each year during 1971–6, the planners deducted an arbitrary number of self-employed and unpaid family workers, reaching the conclusion that 46,000 new jobs would have to be found every year. Yet the plan provided for only 20,000 jobs a year. Despite a certain amount of sophistry, any rational reading of the document would have to conclude that unemployment would be considerably higher after the plan had been implemented than the very large figure which already existed at its start.

These criticisms of Zambian planning should not give the impression that nothing had been achieved. Considering the extreme difficulties, the nation had performed miracles during its first few years of independence. National wealth had been greatly increased, educational opportunities offered to unprecedented numbers of children, communications considerably improved and diversified from the vulnerable south, new power and water supplies provided, new hospitals, clinics, doctors and nurses made available. Moreover, the attempts to grow more food and diversify from copper had achieved certain successes. Sugar, cotton and poultry all showed remarkable advance, with the President's favourite target of an egg a day for every citizen being achieved. Industry had also taken advantage of sanctions against Rhodesia to build factories and workshops in Zambia, including textile production using the country's own cotton. Construction boomed with the essential building programme, whilst during the first six years of independence about K100 million was spent by the government on housing programmes.

Moreover, the President announced a series of economic reforms between 1968 and 1970 designed to provide the government with stronger machinery to control economic direction. The government took majority holdings in a collection of foreign firms and in the mining companies, set up industrial, mining and financial corporations, and laid down frontiers for private, state and mixed economic activities. The objects were to provide Zambians with opportunities they had never possessed in local business and to give the government the means of guiding the economy towards its declared objectives. The weakness of this kind of economic machinery, as mentioned above, was that these massive corporations might attain a momentum of their own, influencing government policies irrespective of national needs.

The President and his colleagues had certainly learnt some hard lessons during the course of their experiences. They had tried, for instance, to inject some new energies into agriculture by heavily subsidizing co-operatives and state farms. They quickly found that too much easy money could actually retard farming and induce a lax attitude to debt repayment which created anti-social attitudes. An Israeli team was encouraged to experiment in the Luanshya area of the Copper Belt, settling unemployed from the towns on the land. It found that the kibbutz model conflicted with local customs and turned to the moshav, or smallholders' co-operative. This experiment might point to an important future method of combining peasant independence with the community spirit essential to the humanistic philosophy. Yet even here muddle and lack of co-operation hindered progress. When I visited the projects at Kafubu and Kafulafuta at the end of 1970, I was told by one village committee that 6,000 dozen of their eggs had gone bad through marketing difficulties, that only 12 of their 18 tractors were in working order, that the stores were selling their tomatoes for five times the price paid to their co-operative, whilst the state trading organizations were not buying their produce to the extent they felt they had a right to expect.

These are the kind of teething troubles a new country with little basic organization and a shortage of experienced technicians has to suffer.

Zambia has been awakening to the brash energy of youth since independence. In many ways it is the most virile society in Africa and may well set many examples for its companions in the search for maturity. Yet the central issue has still remained unsolved. It was graphically demonstrated in the critical years, 1971 and 1972. These saw not only the exposure of the failure of the first plan to move the society towards social justice and the publication of the second plan which appeared to be equally avoiding that issue; they also witnessed a series of events which demonstrated the fragility of the efforts being made to achieve this aim, the quicksands which at any time could engulf those in charge of national policies.

A chronology of the setbacks suffered by Kaunda and his colleagues during these two years clearly reveals how suddenly and unexpectedly the policies of a developing nation can be undermined. First the copper price collapsed, drastically reducing government revenue and draining foreign reserves. Then, through a mixture of inefficient distribution and Portuguese refusal to deliver Zambian goods from their ports, a maize famine grew to such proportions that the humiliation of buying from Rhodesia had to be accepted. The South Africans next demonstrated their avidity to take advantage of any weakness in Kaunda's position by accusing him of secretly negotiating with Mr Vorster whilst professing to be an unrelenting enemy of apartheid. Kaunda's publication of his correspondence with Vorster neatly turned the tables on the South Africans, but the incident diverted energies from more urgent issues. At Mulungushi, in 1971, the party assembly ratified a new constitution which replaced the party president and vice-president by a secretary general, while removing the power of the Bemba to dominate through their numerical superiority. But Kapwepwe had opposed the changes and few expected him or his Bemba followers to accept the defeat. Three months later the fears were confirmed when he resigned from government and UNIP, setting up his own opposition party. Even before Kapwepwe's move, signs of trouble had appeared when university students organized anti-government demonstrations which provoked the usual angry counter-demonstrations from party youths. Following Kapwepwe's resignation, violence spread as UNIP and members of the new party clashed in a series of brawls. There was evidence that Kapwepwe had received aid and encouragement from foreign sources: the East German trade mission was asked to leave the country, the Russians replaced a number of their diplomats in Lusaka and a purge of exiles from southern Africa took place. Many of the leaders of the new party, though not Kapwepwe himself, were detained in 1971. Yet some of the younger UNIP activists were not satisfied. They mounted a campaign of confronting citizens in the streets, in their houses, at market or in buses and demanding to see their party cards. If they were not produced harassment and interference with daily life ensued.

Before the end of 1971, economic analysis established that the urban–rural gap was still rapidly widening, unemployment growing, foreign reserves vanishing and resources for the next period of development diminishing. The political situation was deteriorating under the effects of violence and continued ethnic rivalries, whilst the party itself had shown dangerous signs of indiscipline.

By now Kaunda himself was convinced that he must mobilize from the bottom, seeking to activate the rural peoples in the villages to a sense of national purpose based on increased agricultural production and self-help in improving rural amenities. Yet to pursue this policy demanded a cadre of persuasive leaders content to devote themselves to village life, eschewing the richer rewards of urban political life.

Everything pointed to the necessity of creating a single-party state to halt a degeneration into mob politics and concentrate the energies of the party members on leadership in national development. Yet Kaunda himself had always hoped that the one-party system would emerge from the electorate, through a withering away of support for opposition, rather than necessitating coercive legislation. The 1968 elections had disappointed him in this regard. At the end of 1971 another test was to be held, as 12 by-elections were due. If UNIP could score spectacular victories over Nkumbula's ANC and Kapwepwe's United Progressive Party, the ground would be cleared to institute a single-party system on the foundations of massive popular support. The fact that neither opposition party offered any coherent alternative to the government ought to have given UNIP a substantial advantage. In the event UNIP won seven of the seats, one unopposed, ANC retained four and Kapwepwe narrowly won Mufilira on the Copper Belt. This certainly did not represent the resounding victory for which Kaunda was hoping.

Nevertheless, with a paramount necessity for discipline if the new development plan were to achieve anything but an increasing polarization between élite and masses, with the growing need to take unpopular measures, to impose austerity on the few for the benefit of the many, with escalating violence in the political arena, Kaunda decided that he should proceed towards the one-party state. He appointed a commission to take evidence of public views and to propose the best means of instituting the system.

The year 1972, brought little comfort to Kaunda and those who wished the nation-building attempt to succeed. Nkumbula refused to allow his ANC to be represented on the commission, a decision which probably excluded most southerners from approving a single-party constitution. Violence continued in politics, leading to the detention of Kapwepwe and most of his colleagues early in the year. Although the copper price increased slightly to over £400 a ton, neither this increase nor a small devaluation of the Kwacha was sufficient to bridge the gap between a rising import bill and falling values in exports. In May it was found necessary to halt all imports except those absolutely essential, in order to stem the drain on overseas reserves, which had fallen by two-thirds in just over a year.

These economic reverses intensified the dilemma which had constantly faced Kaunda and his colleagues since 1965. Zambia had been left by Britain heavily dependent on Rhodesia for her economic essentials. The application of sanctions after UDI in 1965 forced her to seek other sources of supply. The only viable alternative for many goods was South Africa. If she could no longer buy Wankie coal for her copper mines, for instance, she could only obtain it from South Africa, though making valiant efforts to develop her own more expensive and lower quality resources.

The President saw the issue with absolute clarity. The Rhodesian and South African régimes were each enemies of Zambia. Freedom fighters would be supported against both. But it was unrealistic and could be suicidal to try and defeat them simultaneously. The international community had outlawed the Smith régime, so it was common sense for Zambia to treat it as her priority enemy. This might involve increasing Zambian trade with South Africa to obtain essential supplies. In 1969 South Africa exported $10,649,000 worth of goods to Zambia, three times the size of trade between any other two African countries.

The new economic crisis of 1972 intensified the necessity for Zambia to trade with South Africa. Many of the goods she needed could be bought more cheaply in South Africa than anywhere else, and she needed to economize. The Minister of Finance urged importers to seek the cheapest markets. Kaunda had no desire to encourage trade with Africa's chief enemy; he knew that his critics could use it against him; he also realized that this might be used by the South African government to try and blackmail him; but economic necessity left him no choice.

The turn of the year 1972–73 again highlighted Zambia's problems and equally her crucial rôle in the future of the continent. The institution of a single-party state in December was accomplished without serious opposition. It paved the way for a more coherent, planned direction of policy based on the accepted national objectives of increased wealth production and greater social justice. At the same time it would reduce the opportunities for the country's enemies to use political factions in order to subvert the state.

Of even greater significance was President Kaunda's courageous decision to introduce a Leadership Code at the same moment. His insistence on public figures making a choice between business ambitions and public life challenged the whole concept of élitism. Because so many leaders had entered into obligations, an interim period of five years was allowed for them to disengage from the enterprises in which they had participated. The success of the policy would clearly depend on the vigour with which the principle laid down by the President was pursued in practice over this period.

Yet the gauntlet had been thrown down. If Zambia, with her unusual supply of money, could insist that her leaders in all sectors of public life resist the temptations of forming an élite class, her example would reverberate throughout the continent, inspiring the new generation of Africans.

Early in 1973 the country's exposed position facing the hostility of white southern Africa again came into the spotlight. Ian Smith, apparently in desperation over his internal hazards, unable to secure recognition from Britain and frightened by the increasing activities of guerrillas within Rhodesia, closed his border with Zambia. It was known that he had been urged by some of his followers to conduct an Israeli-type air strike against the Zambians.

President Kaunda displayed immense coolness in this crisis. Not only did he contemptuously reject Smith's offer to except copper from the blockade; he seized the opportunity to divert his trade entirely from Rhodesian routes and to declare that the diversion would be permanent. It would certainly be costly to achieve this objective at such short notice. Yet the spirit of Zambia's national solidarity which arose under this threat revealed that Smith's aggression had back-fired, that he was left under even greater economic pressures, whilst Zambians, by tightening their belts, could gain long-term economic and political advantages.

It was at this time that copper prices again took an upward turn. The dangers of too much money floating around the country have already been described. They were revived in 1973. They could undermine Kaunda's objectives of seeking a rural renaissance and preventing the consolidation of an élite. The essentials for achievement of these objectives were now more clearly seen. Rather than a slavish dependence on traditional copper revenues, the country needed to recognize the poverty of most of its citizens, the necessity to concentrate on producing for their needs, on gearing its economy to its own potential market.

In short, Zambia illustrated the general African picture of high expectations at independence being overtaken by austere realities. The fact that expectations were higher than general in Zambia because of her greater wealth only brought the lesson into clearer focus and intensified the disappointment. During the 1970s the country faces the politically dangerous but crucial task of persuading some of its people to postpone increases in their standard of life in order that resources can be concentrated on helping the less fortunate to gain some prospect of equality. And this task has to be achieved by such means that it does not provoke revolt, as has happened in so many other African states. Throughout the continent ethnic rivalries, personal ambition, foreign economic control all exacerbate the resentments which measures to achieve social justice inevitably produce. In Zambia, the situation is aggravated still further by the activities of foreign agents determined to secure the downfall of President Kaunda. Fortunately, the President has observed the experiences of other régimes; his trust in his armed forces is witnessed by his introduction of political education amongst them, confident that political understanding will strengthen their support for the policies he is pursuing.

The year 1973 witnessed President Kaunda and his colleagues making further moves in the battle to gain control of economic life for the people. The institution of a single-party state was designed not just to disperse ethnic rivalries, but to concentrate positive leadership on economic development. The adherence of Harry Nkumbula to the government party removed one core of dissension, leaving Simon Kapwepwe as the last isolated dissident. But the success of this measure would still depend on the quality of leadership which the party could provide, the relationship its members could forge with the mass of the people, especially in villages.

Recognition that nationalization of copper had still left major decision-making with the multi-national companies was reflected in steps taken to secure greater governmental powers. Since nationalization, government revenues from mining had fallen catastrophically. Yawning gaps were left in the nationalizing agreement through which the companies continued to make large profits for their shareholders, much of which were sent out of the country. The President revealed his awareness of this weakness by redeeming the bonds forming part of the previous agreement and thus opening the door to re-negotiation. The Zambian president demonstrated that he was determined to prevent the multi-national companies from fleecing his people or sabotaging his development plans. The outcome of this battle would crucially affect Zambia's and Africa's power to deal with the multi-nationals.

Zambia can expect a rough, often turbulent, always exciting decade. So can the African continent. Zambians are likely to influence the course of their continent's history more than most of their fellow-Africans. The successes they achieve and the failures they suffer in the use of their above-average resources will be closely observed as lessons for others. Their ability to withstand the threats and bribes from the white south may well determine the course of the African racial battle with its crucial impact on race relations throughout the world. Their success in rejecting the values of a consumer society and building on the spirit of service associated with co-operation is crucial to the future character of African society.

International Relations

Much of the passion which inspired anti-colonial movements in Africa arose from an intense conviction in the fundamental unity of African peoples. Indeed, some of the feeling extended beyond the continent. The Caribbean and America supplied notable recruits to the leadership of African nationalism. Edward Blyden was one of the early pioneers to cross the Atlantic and become a prophet in Africa. He was followed by men like Du Bois, Padmore, Milliard, whilst the ideas of Marcus Garvey travelled in the same direction.

These political thinkers provided one source of inspiration. The other came from Africa itself, from men such as Kenyatta, Nkrumah, Azikiwe, Abrahams, Wallace Johnson. It is noteworthy that they held two characteristics in common: they were all devoted to African liberation from colonial rule; and they all believed that the central purpose of this objective was to create a united Africa. This belief was partly engendered by the common struggle against European colonialism in the continent. But it also arose from a form of idealism. Observing the conflicts between nation-states in other continents and the world wars which they had produced, Africans determined that they would avoid following this fatal example. They aimed to prevent the existence of the state frontiers imposed by European colonialists from inducing the kind of nationalist emotions that had produced international warfare in the rest of the world. Africa would gain her independence from the efforts of anti-colonial movements throughout the continent, where possible in co-operation with each other; then Africans would unite across the artificial boundaries in one United States of Africa.

There was thus always a strong strain of internationalist sentiment in the anti-colonial movements. Pan-Africanism, from its inception at the beginning of the twentieth century, reinforced the determination to rid the continent of colonial rule and was itself strengthened by the common purpose of the movements against colonialism.

In the event, the cause of African unity languished in the years following nationalist independence, though it never died. At first Nkrumah was the leading exponent of continental unity. This was partly because he was intellectually and politically convinced of the principle, and partly because he gained a special kudos from being the leader of the first black nation to gain independence. For some years this gave him the ear of the continent. In the year following Ghana's independence he was able to hold two conferences in Accra, the first for African states already independent, the second for the nationalist parties of countries still under colonial rule. He thereby assumed the leadership of the anti-colonial and Pan-Africanist spirit of the continent.

This leadership did not remain unchallenged. It was never accepted by the majority of French-speaking leaders, nor by the Nigerians. Nor did Nkrumah offer any serious practical proposals by which the desire for unity between African states could be translated into administrative reality. He talked somewhat vaguely about a common parliament, but how it should be elected, what its powers should be or how responsibility could be divided between it and sovereign states remained unconsidered.

Meanwhile, the period in which most African states were attaining their independence was marked by two features, both of which appeared hostile to Nkrumah's concept. In a manner similar to that of other continents, African governments began to form alliances between themselves. The francophone states, led by the Ivory Coast, but with Guinea and Mali as exceptions, created a loose political and economic association known by the name of the city where it was initiated, Brazzaville. The object was French-speaking, rather than African unity. Ghana and Guinea then led the way in forming an alliance between what were supposed to be like-minded governments. As this "Casablanca" group included the Moroccan and Libyan monarchies, the military régime of Egypt, together with the three west African states proclaiming devotion to democracy and socialism, it seemed doubtful whether its formation was based on much more than expediency.

Originally conceived as an effort to prevent the Brazzaville and Casablanca blocs from seriously dividing the continent, another, "Monrovia", alliance was quickly formed. This consisted of the Brazzaville group, together with most other independent states. Its attempt to attract the Casablanca members failed. For two years, therefore, between May 1961 and May 1963, independent Africa was divided into two alliances with a considerable degree of tension between them.

But there were other African leaders, just as devoted as Nkrumah to the principle of African unity, who approached the issue differently. In particular, Julius Nyerere in the east believed that the unity of the continent could be more realistically pursued through associating, in the first instance, within regions than by trying to leap directly to a continental parliament. Nyerere had the advantage that a regional association already existed in east Africa. The Common Services Organization provided a certain degree of economic foundation for closer association between the countries of east Africa. But both Nyerere and Tom Mboya realized that genuine unity required a political commitment leading to political institutions.

In 1958, therefore, the initiative was taken to set up an organization known as the Pan-African Freedom Movement of East and Central Africa. Its original members were Tanganyika, Kenya, Uganda, Zanzibar, Northern and Southern Rhodesia and Nyasaland. Its initial objective was to ally the anti-colonial movements of the constituent countries in the battle for independence. But later, when independence rose into sight and then when it had been achieved, the horizons of the movement broadened. It began to represent an alternative road towards the goal of African unity. The opportunity presented by PAFMECA for the leaders of east and central African states to meet regularly and exchange ideas on common problems encouraged them to consider the prospect of an association between their countries on a regional basis. They therefore were led to propound the theory that continental unity should be pursued initially through regional associations. Later the chances of association between the regions could be further explored.

Even before independence Nyerere had revealed that he recognized the dangers which would result from national sovereignty. Because of the national unity he had organized in Tanganyika, allied to the fact that the white community of his country had never developed such political ambitions as could seriously obstruct African advance, Tanganyika approached the threshold of independence as early as 1961. Yet neither Kenya nor Uganda seemed likely to reach this position for several years.

Nyerere therefore knew that he faced the prospect of gaining national sovereignty at a time when his neighbours still remained under colonial rule; and that this situation was the logical consequence of his nationalist efforts, that his people had been led by him to seek sovereignty as their major objective. Yet if he continued along this path Nyerere knew that he would have to accept the structure of a nation-state. By the time that Kenya and Uganda achieved independence many of his own colleagues would have established a vested interest in the preservation of the state apparatus. Their opposite numbers in the two neighbouring states would be anticipating similar opportunities. The chances of dismantling a large enough sector of that apparatus to enable an east African federation to supersede the individual sovereignty of each state would have become minimal.

So Nyerere offered to postpone the independence of Tanganyika. This was an act which probably no other African leader would have had the courage to take or the personal authority to sustain. He had mobilized his whole population to the purpose of removing colonial rule and gaining national sovereignty; yet when the prize was actually within grasp, he suggested that they retract their hands from it.

This audacious proposal revealed not only Nyerere's authority but the priority of his commitment to African unity. For the purpose of his offer and the condition for it was simultaneous independence for the three east African states as partners in a federation. His offer was rejected and the consequences he foresaw ensued. Although some measure of economic and political co-ordination was maintained, each state set up its separate national structure and any prospect of a genuine federation was indefinitely postponed.

If the federal concept failed to materialize, there was certainly a greater degree of co-operation and consultation in the east and central regions than anywhere else. The PAFMECA association enabled the governments of its associate states to continue to meet after independence and it was also extended to include the nationalist movements of the south. The "Mulungushi Club" also brought together a number of heads of state on the initiative of President Kaunda. The presidents of Kenya, Uganda and Tanzania met frequently to order the affairs of the East African Community until the Amin coup caused a rift, whilst the personal friendship and similar ideals of Presidents Nyerere and Kaunda enabled them to work closely together. Before his deposition this regional approach to African unity seemed to anger Kwame Nkrumah who always maintained that his centralized, continental-wide concept provided the only formula for success. This led to a coldness between him and Nyerere which seriously handicapped the search for unity.

Despite the degree of accord reached in the east and centre and the various temporary alliances formed elsewhere, African leaders seemed to accept that national sovereignty was inviolable. It was briefly challenged in the Ghana-Guinea union of 1958, extended to Mali in 1960, and in the abortive federation of Soudan and Senegal. Neither of these exceptions succeeded and their failures tended to entrench the notion of national sovereignty.

On the other hand, thousands of ordinary Africans took scant notice of this Europeanized concept of nationality. All over the continent they continued to cross boundaries at will, as they had done for centuries. They took their sheep, goats or cattle to favourable watering and grazing districts, sought seasonal employment, fished rich waters or simply migrated to where work was available. In doing so they ignored the frontiers which European colonial powers had drawn on their maps, now inherited by African national rulers. And where violence erupted, many more thousands of Africans crossed these borders to seek asylum amongst their friends, neighbours or kinsmen. In this sense, although by the end of the decade hundreds of thousands of Africans were living in lands of which they were not nationals, the status of refugee was unknown in the continent. It was only when national governments sought extra employment for their own citizens that the migrants were compelled to recognize the nationality thrust upon them through the cruel practice of forcible deportation.

Nevertheless, it was the leaders, not the people, who made international agreements. So when Africa made its greatest step towards unity it was still based on recognition of the individuality of nation-states and national sovereignty. The formation of the Organization of African Unity in Addis Ababa in 1963 created a form of continental association unknown to other continents. Europe had sought in vain for a central forum of inter-state decision-making over a thousand years. The Americans had merely succeeded in establishing a continental association dominated by the United States. Asia had never seriously tried. Yet, within a few years of the start of European withdrawal and even before many countries had attained full self-government, Africans succeeded in creating an organization to which every African government became affiliated. It still recognized the sovereignty of each member state and expressly disclaimed any right to interfere in their domestic affairs. It therefore adopted an entirely international posture. Yet its stated purpose, considering matters of common concern, at least proved that African governments were anxious to act collectively in their external policies rather than claim absolute sovereignty over their foreign policies.

The OAU had a chequered history during its first ten-years' existence. It helped to mediate in certain international conflicts within the continent. It was successful in this rôle in the border disputes between Algeria and Morocco, between Somalia, Kenya and Ethiopia. Within its agency some of Africa's elder statesmen, like Haile Selassie and Jomo Kenyatta, were able to reconcile states in conflict with each other. This was successful, for instance, in disputes between Ghana and Guinea, the four states which recognized Biafra and the Nigerians, Uganda and Tanzania.

Yet, despite its self-denying ordinance against interference within the domestic prerogatives of its members, it was internal conflicts which most seriously worried African leaders. Chaos in the Congo, civil wars in Nigeria, the Sudan, Chad, Ethiopia, Burundi, Uganda, all shattered the peace of the continent. These tragic events undermined progress towards African unity. They detracted from the claim of Africans to be humane people bound to each other by fundamentally common bonds of brotherhood. The OAU therefore felt a sense of responsibility to mediate not only between states in conflict but also between rival communities within member states. Here the organization was much less effective. It assisted in eventually building a bridge between northern and southern Sudanese; but in the other cases it was totally ineffective. This was particularly the case during the Nigerian civil war. The OAU, like other agencies which attempted mediation, such as the Vatican, the Commonwealth Secretariat, the Americans, and the Emperor of Ethiopia, never succeeded in persuading the two sides to talk seriously of peace.

Unfortunately, the attempts at mediation in these internal conflicts usually damaged the OAU itself. Schism arose within its ranks over the Nigerian war, recognition of Boumedienne as Ben Bella's successor, the military régime which deposed Nkrumah, Amin's replacement of Obote, and Mobutu's claim to represent Zaire.

External events also caused dissension within the organization. The conflict between the Arabs and Israel proved a constant source of tension amongst Africans. The Arabs of the north claimed to be Africans and were accepted as full members of the OAU. Yet Israel had established close relations with many African states and provided valuable help, especially in technical aid, to many of them. Strenuous efforts were therefore made to avoid meetings of the OAU being used by Arab members to solicit diplomatic support for their cause. Usually the Arabs recognized this desire, particularly so long as Nasser was alive. They generally contented themselves with securing resolutions supporting their demand that Israel vacate conquered territory. The Israelis, too, showed themselves sensitive to the dilemma in which their African friends were placed. In 1971 the OAU actually took the initiative, sending a mission to both Tel Aviv and Cairo. It had a greater success in suggesting compromises than anyone expected.

After the death of Nasser, however, the Arab-Israeli issue began to become more menacing towards African unity. Nasser had acquired a reputation as one of the early African radicals who both inspired and attracted African nationalists. As an associate of Nkrumah, Tito and Nehru in the initial non-aligned conference at Bandung he lent international stature to leadership within the African continent. He made friends with several African leaders and understood the sensibilities of African governments towards the Middle East conflict. His death removed this modifying influence. The appearance of President Gadafy of Libya as a leading Arab spokesman in African affairs appeared to accentuate the change. For Gadafy was an Arab fanatic, intent at all cost on pursuing a Muslim jihad, unconcerned with the delicate balance of Arab-African relations. His open antagonism towards King Hassan of Morocco, at a time when the king was chairman of the OAU, aroused African resentment. When he materially intervened in the Uganda-Tanzanian conflict by sending Libyan troops and planes to assist General Amin the clouds on the horizon of Arab-African understanding became perceptibly darker. The concept of continental unity, which inevitably embraced Arab as well as African, receded still farther.

A more surprising divisive issue was that of policy towards the white-dominated south. If one factor had provided a sure foundation for African unity it was universal determination to rid South Africa, Rhodesia, Namibia and the Portuguese territories of white minority domination. Whenever the OAU appeared to come under centrifugal pressures, this issue could always be relied on to establish a focus of unity. Most member states might not be prepared to sacrifice any of their own interests to assist the freedom fighters, but they appeared to be unanimous in moral support to the guerrillas and the various nationalist movements.

The unanimity began to show fractures at the end of the 1960s. Dr Hastings Banda, President of Malawi, had displayed a curious ambivalence towards the southern whites from the time of Malawi's independence in 1964. He had been one of Africa's most vociferous anti-colonial spokesmen during the 1950s. Despite more than 20 years' absence from his own country, he remained revered in Nyasaland, leading the fight against federation from abroad. On his return home he was immediately accepted as leader of his country, his lieutenants, Chiume and Chipembere having ensured that his reputation was maintained amongst his people during his absence. During the disturbances of 1959 he was imprisoned in a federal gaol, sealing his acceptability through martyrdom.

Banda was entirely singleminded in his determination to take Nyasaland out of federation. He associated little with other anti-colonial or anti-federal leaders, although during a period of residence in Ghana he came to know Nkrumah. There was no doubt, however, that to the vast majority of Nyasas his charisma was unlimited. There were a few murmurings about his personal behaviour when he first returned, but his personification of the nation's aspirations was unchallenged.

One personal experience illustrates the hold which Banda exercised over his people even at a time when he had not been seen by them for many years. In 1951 I visited Nyasaland at the same time as Jim Griffiths, then British Colonial Secretary, was in the country testing African reactions to the proposed federation. I spent some days in Lilongwe where the African Congress was meeting to prepare its submission to Griffiths. I attended the meeting, held in a small, wooden school. At first I was angrily attacked as a British spy. On producing a letter of introduction written by Banda in London, however, I was immediately accepted as a friend and fêted as an ally of Africans for the rest of my visit.

The other side of Banda's personality was revealed by another personal incident ten years later. On the way to Tanganyika's independence celebrations I called in Zomba to see Dr Banda. Immediately before meeting him some of his closest associates waylaid me and earnestly sought my aid in persuading him to agree to attend the events in Dar es Salaam. Apparently he was reluctant to go, in their opinion because he was jealous of Nyerere's success. Two days before the functions began he still could not be persuaded to attend. In fact, his colleagues' persuasions eventually succeeded, but he only arrived at the very last moment.

Considering his obviously divided personality, other African leaders were prepared for Dr Banda to act erratically after Malawi's independence; what they did not anticipate was his entire reversal of the principles he had preached concerning the white régimes of the south. In July 1963, as Prime Minister of Nyasaland, he had declared, "As an African nationalist I hate the present régime in South Africa and will have nothing to do with it when this country is independent. There will be no diplomatic or commercial dealings between us." In September 1967, as President of the now independent Malawi, in discussing the possible invasion of South Africa and Rhodesia, his policy had turned 180 degrees. He now announced, "In self-defence – all is fair in love and war – we must join with South Africa, Rhodesia and Mozambique to form a solid laager around southern Africa." In the same year he opened full diplomatic and commercial relations with South Africa and allowed the Republic to station a military attaché in his country. He was later to visit South Africa himself and to receive a return visit from the South African President. He signed an agreement with Portugal and made joint commercial arrangements with her. This policy was accompanied by constant sneering references to the freedom fighters engaged in conflict with Rhodesia, Portugal and South Africa. It became abundantly clear that not only was he not prepared to support those who were fighting for the same rights he had demanded for his own people, but that he had joined the camp of their white adversaries.

Many Africans attributed this reversal of attitude to the fact that the South Africans and Portuguese were prepared to provide Dr Banda with substantial economic and military assistance. This may well have influenced him, but those who had known him longer recognized a personal in addition to an economic factor. Banda always wanted to be the centre of attention, to be acknowledged as supreme in any association in which he participated. His minor rôle in the OAU irked him. The arguments of his own colleagues in his government caused him to expel them. He was also a natural authoritarian, profoundly impressed by the monarchy and establishment when living in Britain. He could feed these emotions by becoming hailed as a great man in South Africa; in the OAU and other African organizations he was relegated to the shadows.

Dr Banda's Malawi was therefore regarded as an irresponsible maverick by most members of the OAU. Its eccentricities, along with the

o

more understandable reluctance of Lesotho and Swaziland to offend their giant South African neighbours, were insufficiently important to reduce appreciably the combined assault of the rest on white supremacy. But when Houphouet-Boigny of the Ivory Coast began to diverge from received policy towards southern Africa, its cause could be more seriously damaged. Houphouet-Boigny began to talk about the need for a "dialogue" with South Africa's government. If this meant anything practical it had to be interpreted as a willingness to enter discussions with South African ministers whilst the vast majority of South Africans remained unrepresented. This would obviously be considered by the non-European majority in South Africa as a betrayal by African leaders who had risen to power through demanding identical rights for their own people. It was seen as such by most African leaders themselves.

Houphouet-Boigny's deviation was considered much more menacing to African unity than the aberrations of Banda. For the Ivory Coast influenced other francophone states. Tsiranana of Malagasy favoured the new doctrine and gave the South Africans concessions in his island. Some allies of the Ivory Coast appeared equivocal over following Houphouet-Boigny's initiative, but Busia in Ghana accepted it for a time.

Even more menacing was the guiding influence behind this heresy. As we have already seen, the French retained far more direct control over their former colonies than was ever attempted by the British. And although British governments reneged over their responsibilities in Rhodesia, whilst British investors supplied South Africa with three-fifths of her foreign capital, the British Labour government did ban arms sales to the Republic. French governments openly sold arms to the South Africans and enabled them to manufacture weapons themselves. The French also actively participated in breaking sanctions against Rhodesia.

Few francophone governments or leaders ever criticized French foreign policies. Yet, through historical convenience a general convention was accepted that African states should concentrate on criticizing their particular former masters whose weaknesses they knew best. So a situation was created in which anglophone Africans vociferously condemned British policies in the continent, whilst the more serious menace of French policy was left largely unscathed, except by such international missions as that undertaken by President Kaunda in 1970.

It was the French desire to maintain and increase her trade with South Africa which lay behind Houphouet-Boigny's "dialogue" initiative. No aspect of foreign policy emerged from Abidjan without previous reference to the Quai d'Orsay. It was no coincidence that Houphouet-Boigny began to talk about the necessity of "dialogue" with Mr Vorster just at the moment that France was intent on expanding Franco-South African trade.

The "dialogue" issue itself died a fairly quick death. By 1972 it had disappeared from the OAU agenda. Yet the deeper menace survived. French-speaking Africa had been held within the franc zone. This deliberately handicapped efforts to expand inter-African trade between francophone and anglophone states on which growing political unity could have been based. Francophone Africa was forced of necessity to accept associate status with the EEC. This again militated against African unity, provoking rivalry between states whose prosperity and independence demanded a complementary relationship. Under General de Gaulle, a charismatic figure to French-speaking Africans, and his adviser on African affairs, Jacques Foccart, these economic manacles forced francophone Africans into a political strait-jacket. Throughout the 1960s, virtually every aspect of French foreign policy was automatically supported by almost all governments of French-speaking Africa.

This feature of post-independence Africa obviously affected international relations in the continent, profoundly undermining efforts to secure a uniform approach to policies concerned with issues common to the continent. But it also produced a more serious effect. In their efforts to escape from the endemic economic dependence in which they had been left, the more progressive African governments sought to work out strategies with Third World countries in Asia, Latin America and the Caribbean. Through associations like the Non-Aligned Conference, UNCTAD and the United Nations, attempts were made to forge some form of unified action amongst the developing nations of the world. The closed French community within which francophone African states had to operate constantly frustrated African efforts to present a united front within the Third World context. Membership of the franc zone, association with the EEC and the political inhibitions arising from these economic imperatives raised insuperable barriers to united African action. The prospect arising from British membership of the EEC appeared to extend such barriers across the entire continent.

Yet, despite all these debilitating influences, the OAU survived. Its heads of state continued to meet every year, their meetings varying in harmony and value, but their regularity always providing an opportunity to face the issues common to the continent. In spite of dissension over the "dialogue" issue, the OAU never wavered in its support of the freedom movements attacking the régimes in South Africa, Namibia, Rhodesia, Mozambique, Angola and Guinea-Bissau. Frequently schisms appeared in these organizations; the Liberation Committee of the OAU, sited in Dar es Salaam, tried to heal them. The continued existence of the OAU served notice on the white régimes of southern Africa that, however weak and divided Africa might appear, they would have to face the implacable hostility of black Africa and any allies it could attach to its cause.

The divisions and frictions which appeared within the OAU during its first ten years often diminished Africa's impact on other international bodies. At the United Nations, Africans could legitimately claim that their appearance increased awareness of the problems of their continent and especially produced greater concern with racial issues. South Africa had first been put in the UN dock by the Indians. The prosecution was strengthened by the presence of African delegates, particularly over the question of South African intransigence towards the administration of Namibia. Too few African states were represented at the time of the Congo crisis to make much impression on that policy, but over Rhodesia their impact was more substantial. Britain was the offender here for her refusal to discipline Ian Smith's rebel régime. Africans took a prominent rôle on the sanctions committee which was supposed to detect and report any breaches of the economic boycott which the UN imposed.

Yet, as the Africans became more experienced in the affairs of the UN, they tended to lose the idealistic conception of the organization which they had held at the time of their election. They found, as others had discovered before them, that resolutions did not often result in action, that speeches appeared in the records and then became little more than historical documents. Moreover, when they tried to expedite action, as, for example, on sanctions, they found that their own continental divisions frustrated them. The English-speaking states were never able to secure genuine support from francophone Africans when French interests were at stake.

In the Commonwealth, African influence was much stronger and had greater practical effect. Even before Tanganyika became independent, and therefore eligible for membership, Nyerere's public warning that his country would not join a Commonwealth which included South Africa strengthened the hand of those who were trying to exclude Dr Verwoerd's new republic. The second half of the sixties were largely devoted to Rhodesia, and here the presence of an increasing number of African members prevented the issue from being avoided or sidetracked. Yet, at the same time, concentration on Rhodesia and then on Mr Heath's determination to sell arms to South Africa, and the amount of time taken at successive conferences over these issues, tended to obscure other areas of policy where the Commonwealth could have been effective. In 1971, for instance, when President Kaunda submitted his Declaration of Commonwealth Principles, the debate was diverted into channels relating to conflict over Britain's right to determine her own policy towards South Africa. Yet the principles themselves affected much wider issues. They could have been discussed in a manner more calculated to strengthen the Commonwealth association and less concerned with national sovereignty.

Another issue appeared at the 1971 Singapore conference, though it was only visible on the horizon to those less preoccupied with the immediate. The British government had cited the danger of Russian penetration in the Indian Ocean in defence of their support for South Africa – although some of its own members exposed this as a canard. Yet to the Indians, Ceylonese, Malaysians, Singaporeans and Pakistanis the Indian Ocean was seen to be of vital importance. Indeed, its links to the Pacific embraced the interests of Australasia, Canada and the United States as well.

It was at Singapore that it gradually became apparent that the Indian Ocean also had east African shores. A new centre of strategic concern emerged in the background of the more publicized issues. Yet it was not totally divorced from them. For as a realization of common concern began to affect Asians and Africans, so a greater common danger became recognized. The Chinese and other communist states were supplying the freedom fighters against white southern Africa through Dar es Salaam. The Chinese were also sending materials and technicians to Tanzania to build the Tan-Zam railway from Dar es Salaam to Zambia. If the South Africans ever interfered with Chinese shipping, as their foreign and defence policies implied, an incident of international significance could occur. The effect of this realization taught the more thoughtful Africans that east Africa had resumed her medieval rôle as an integral part of Indian Ocean commercial-military strategy; that Africans must expand their associations with Asian states and that the Commonwealth provided them with the best forum for doing so.

Africans were new to international affairs. Since international organs first became seriously developed during the nineteenth century, Africa had been a mere pawn in the Euro-American power-game, her interests supposedly represented by her masters. It was inevitable, therefore, that the inexperienced African representatives should require time to discover the best methods of furthering their countries' interests, particularly as all African states were so short of skilled personnel.

Yet the future of Africans within international society seemed to depend on something other than the performance of their diplomats or politicians in the various gatherings of international organizations. The independence decade was also marked by a relaxation in the Cold War. Thus, whilst in earlier years it was possible for some African states to play off the Russians and the West against each other in securing aid or diplomatic support, this avenue of policy was almost closed by the end of the sixties.

The situation had radically changed. Now the option lay between some form of client association with the developed world as a whole – including the communist states – and establishing a front amongst the developing nations strong enough to challenge the domination of the industrialized states. The Third World concept had been born from a belief that developing states should not have to choose between dependence on communist or capitalist worlds. As these two drew closer together towards the end of the sixties the term "Third World" ceased to represent its original significance. Yet the basic problem of the developing world became even tougher. No longer able to play off one section of the rich world against the other, it was left as the victim of the new amalgam unless it could discover strength within itself.

Very few Africans recognized this reality. Conferences held under such auspices as UNCTAD remained platforms for political demagogy, leaving the central issue untouched. The Economic Commission for Africa produced reports and plans, but was never considered by African governments as a potential supranational body to be used to enable them to escape from the shackles of national economics. The oil-producing countries, the producers of copper, cocoa and coffee, all made tentative efforts to co-ordinate their policies with fellow producers, but these efforts were never given high priority in national policies.

For the crucial factor was that Africans had been brought up under colonial rule to accept the nation-state and its apparatus as an immutable fact of international life. Yet in a continent divided between some 40 states, varying from a few hundred thousand inhabitants to 60 million, all composed of disparate communities, the nation-state concept itself barred the way to providing the needs of the people or achieving their ambitions. Africans were challenged to seek new forms of society, new associations between themselves and with peoples in similar circumstances outside Africa. Until such radical and unconventional channels of thought were opened, Africans were bound to remain on the periphery of international society, passive spectators of actions vitally affecting them, rather than active participants in international action.

Africa in the 1970s

The future of the African peoples cannot be divorced from that of the rest of the human race. Speculation as to the fate of particular nations or societies, as to where the next coup will occur, whether specific experiments will succeed or fail, the location of further inter-communal or international warfare, is a useless gamble. Yet it is reasonable to suggest that if certain trends continue, if particular alternatives are chosen, the consequences are predictable. Every policy followed in Africa, however, each choice made, all the efforts mobilized, and each of their end-products, will inevitably be conditioned by their relation to events in the rest of the world.

It is Africa's fate to have to mould her destiny in a unique period of human experience. For 7,000 years Euro-Asian men have been engaged in a massive experiment to transform society from the hunting-gathering primitive into "civilization". The indications today are that this experiment is finally collapsing. Scientific technology has escaped from the control of all but a tiny group of men and they are hypnotized by its momentum. So the human race lives on a precipice of nuclear annihilation, hundreds of millions are daily being poisoned by the pollution of their environment, vital ecological balances are upset, psychological disorders proliferate as people are herded together amongst offensive city buildings, essential natural resources are spent at prodigal rates, population expansion far exceeds the growth in food production.

Above all, most human communities have abandoned any sense of idealism. The "consumer society" of the second half of the twentieth century finds itself on a treadmill; it is impelled to run progressively faster, attaining diminishing quantities and qualities of satisfaction. Yet it has no hope of dismounting. The Utopias which in the past led human beings to strive towards visions of happier societies have disappeared. Many people recognize the signs of disintegration in human society; many of the young reject its degraded values; but no one any longer tries to construct an alternative image, for the established powers are seen to be in unrestrained control.

Even the abstract concepts which used to provide a general guide to moral effort have lost their meaning. Throughout human history it has been assumed that "peace" is preferable to "war". "Peace" today represents little more than the absence of organized national violence. It does not even retard the major elements of social disintegration. To large sections of society, therefore, "peace" no longer represents the antithesis of "war". To some, warfare even offers release from the tense frustrations of "peaceful" society; as do many other forms of violent behaviour.

Few Africans have been involved in this unsuccessful experiment. In one way or another peoples in each of the other continents have played some rôle in it, but in Africa only insignificant groups within the towns of north, west and south Africa have actively participated. The vast majority of Africans were long isolated from the activities of other societies and, until very recently, scarcely affected by them. Consequently, most African communities have retained a continuity of life-style unparalleled in other continents.

Nevertheless, Africans can no longer immunize themselves from all effects of events elsewhere. Their deserts, mountains and oceans, which for centuries insulated them from other societies, are no protection against nuclear fall-out. The operations of foreigners who have increasingly penetrated their fastness over the past four centuries have begun to add pollution, ecological imbalance, urban tragedies and exponential population growth to the natural hazards of tropical existence. Some African countries have come to depend on the export of materials whose production and sale depends crucially on foreigners; others retain the relationship of clients to their former colonial masters. All remain subject to those whims of nineteenth-century European politicians which fragmented the continent with their boundary lines. The idols of the consumer society are being imported by returning students, diplomats, politicians, businessmen, through the aegis of radio, television, advertising, foreign educators and advisers.

Above all, whether Africans desire it or not, the external world will not refrain from interfering in their affairs. A succession of societies in Asia, Europe and America, at various stages in their development, have coveted the products of the African continent. Gold and iron left the east coast ports 1,000 years ago. More recently, human cargoes, palm-oil, gold, diamonds, copper, rubber, iron ore, uranium, groundnuts, cocoa, coffee, cloves, sisal and a score of other materials have poured out of the continent into the maws of industrializing society. Now the world's thirst for oil has added a new dimension to the flow from the north and the west.

In contrast to demands made by the industrial world on Asia and America, however, the impact on Africa has been slight. Nowhere in Africa has treasure been looted on the scale experienced in India or Latin

America. Nor has African society been undermined or destroyed to the degree that was experienced in the Americas or the Caribbean. In contrast to the societies of these continents, most communities in Africa have hardly been disturbed by the most recent technological phase of social engineering.

The weight of this external impact is now rapidly increasing. International companies have been involved for nearly a century in gold, diamonds, copper, rubber, iron and fats. As South Africa has industrialized, such companies have increased their influence. Now they are exploiting the opportunities in newly independent black-governed states by supplying a whole set of goods and services which, although only peripheral to their own massive operations, become indispensable to the governments concerned. In the search for and extraction of oil, of course, they are dominant.

Yet the character of international capitalism is changing qualitatively as well as quantitatively. The extent of operations by the multi-national corporations which increasingly dominate the economic life of humanity is staggering. General Motors, for instance, has a larger annual sales revenue than the combined gross national products of all African-governed states. The annual turnover of Unilever, a company with multiple interests in Africa, is greater than the GNP of Nigeria, with her 60 million population.

It may not be the size of the economic control exercised by these corporations which presents the greatest menace to Africans, however. The power which it supplies certainly threatens democratic decision-making throughout the industrialized world. But so far their activities in Africa are puny in comparison with those they undertake in developed states. Yet as they search for ever-greater profitability, including tax-dodging, labour-saving, cutting costs, moving capital, so they increasingly look towards the developing countries. Here they may be able to secure government co-operation, find cheap labour, move capital and profits without hindrance, escape taxation. It may be, and often is, only a fragment of the total process which is manufactured in a developing country, one component out of scores. To the corporation it represents an infinitesimal fraction of its investment; to the country concerned it forms a crucial element of its economy; it creams off the surplus created in the Third World, preventing serious capital formation; and to the labour-forces of both industrialized and developing states it presents a mutual threat.

Africa is a continent where idealism has not yet been smothered by the cynicism of blinded visions. Together with a few groups in Latin America and Asia – and with more valid expectations – some Africans believe that

they can build better societies by combining the best of their traditions
with a careful selection of technological innovations. They may even find
the means of using scientific knowledge to meet their particular needs,
instead of merely accepting the instruments it has created in industrialized
society. The extent of their success depends on many factors; but unless
they recognize the threat presented by the inevitable logic of multi-
national capitalism, their utopias will be still-born.

It is easier to state the obvious fact that if Africans are to govern their
own destiny they will have to control the operations of these giant
corporations in their territories than to suggest how they may do so. After
all, none of the long-established institutions of the developed states has
yet found the means, and most show little sign of even trying.

The formula adopted by Tanzania, described previously, is only
marginally relevant to this task. Tanzania possesses few minerals, so far as
is known, has little commerce or industry, whilst the low incomes of her
inhabitants offer scant opportunities for investment in consumer goods.
She is setting high moral standards, charting a path towards a genuine
form of African independence. Her emphasis on self-reliance is inspiring
other Africans to adopt the principle in vastly different circumstances. She
may also offer a model to those African societies, which, like her, are
largely confined to rural activities. Yet this only provides a broad skeleton
of principles to guide those countries which have to face the immediate
threat of domination by the multi-national corporations.

Zambia and Zaire, in their different ways, have made a start in bringing their giant copper companies under government control. But they face
enormous difficulties. Compensation to the companies, Anglo-American,
Selection Trust and Union Minière, is considerable; management is still
controlled by them, with expatriates in the key positions; and the sale of
copper still rests with the world market dominated by international financial giants.

Nor should it be assumed that when an industry is nationalized (when,
for instance, the Zambian government took 51 per cent control over its
copper), the companies inevitably become servants of the people. These
huge multi-national corporations are able to command the most skilled
lawyers and economists in the world. The negotiations which take place
between them and governments are crucial. All too often it is discovered
later that the companies have skilfully evaded any threats to their profits.

Take the case of Zambia as an example. Between 1969 and 1972 her
government's revenues from copper fell from K234 million to K54
million, despite nationalization. It is true that the world price of copper
fell drastically during this period; but that did not account for more than
half the decrease in revenues. The companies were able to use the agreement they had negotiated to deny the government revenue it had pre-

viously received. Cost increases were recorded out of all proportion to reality. New capital invested each year was given a tax-free concession; it is not difficult to borrow capital abroad, repay it from profits and so escape taxation; it can even be borrowed from an associate to the parent company so that the interest itself is never lost. In the case of Zambia, the profitability of the massive Anglo-American Corporation certainly did not suffer from nationalization; whereas it had only six per cent of its investment capital in copper, it drew 21 per cent of its investment income from this industry.

Moreover, when governments are desperately seeking resources to finance their national development, there is always a temptation to turn again to the source which has supplied them in the past. This may become even more insistent when revenues decline and when the government believes that it has harnessed a particular industry. So, although the Zambians and Zaireans have been trying to diversify their economies away from their heavy dependence on copper, both have encouraged exploration for further deposits. They may deceive themselves that by bringing in alternative companies or consortia to those which have traditionally controlled their mining they are escaping from increased dependence. Yet the essential point is that they are deepening the dependence of their economies on the industry itself, thus exposing themselves still more nakedly to the winds of world prices, export markets and international manipulation. In any case, the new companies may come from Japan or Italy; but essentially they are linked to the same system.

Yet there are more subtle influences undermining these countries' efforts to secure control over their economies. When the price of copper is high, foreign investment is strongly attracted. The local government is then tempted to expand its development schemes rapidly, leaving hostages to future fortune. The Zaire government, for example, invested heavily in its Inga hydro-electric scheme and in the development of its Atlantic port, Banana. This necessitated awarding large contracts to foreign firms – in the case of Inga to an Italian consortium. When the catastrophic fall in copper prices drastically reduced revenues, all government spending had to be severely pruned. And when, as often occurs, suppliers' credit has been used to raise the initial finance, heavy debt servicing greatly increases the burden, increasing the stranglehold of the supplying company.

Nor do the difficulties emanate only from the outside. When commodity prices are high government expenditure leads many people to become accustomed to easy cash and high incomes. Town élites, contractors, politicians, diplomats, large farmers, all improve their life-styles on the assumption that these conditions will continue indefinitely.

Ghana during the cocoa boom and Zambia when copper prices soared are two examples of this situation. When the prices fall there is not only disappointment as money becomes scarce, but often obligations have been undertaken which cannot be dishonoured. Mortgages, loans, school fees, responsibilities for relatives, machinery or hire purchase, have all been incurred. Expensive tastes have been acquired by families. Then suddenly incomes are reduced, money becomes scarce. It is little wonder that these circumstances often provoke discontent.

Yet it was in such a situation that President Kaunda of Zambia proclaimed his Leadership Code at the end of 1972. He insisted that national leaders in all fields of activity should dispose of their investment properties within five years and henceforth live on their government salaries or turn their businesses into co-operatives, live on the salary of a managing director and dispense with the income from government. In any case, leaders were not to be allowed two incomes. It was a brave effort to narrow the gap between the élite and the masses, to set an example to the rest of the nation, to divorce public life from profiteering. It recalled the similar policy announced by President Nyerere in the Arusha Declaration. But whereas there was little surplus wealth in Tanzania, there had been a great deal during the copper boom in Zambia and many people had become accustomed to living well on it. Whether Kaunda will succeed in extirpating commercial values from Zambian public life or whether his lead came too late will be an issue affecting a wider society than that of Zambia alone.

Then again, much government investment is in building an infrastructure, hydro-electricity, railways, harbours, and roads. These are facilities which can only become viable if used by industry. Whilst copper may be nationalized, many other industries remain in private hands. In Zaire Shell, British-American Tobacco, Tanganyika Concessions, Lonrho, and British Leyland, are all active. Even the new copper deposits at Tenke-Fungurume have been prospected and will be developed by the Charter Consolidated group, which is associated with the Anglo-American Corporation, and whose partners include a subsidiary of Standard Oil and Japan's Mitsui. The greater the government investment in a modern infrastructure, the higher the attractions for international capital to use it.

Another highly significant problem raised for the countries whose natural resources can be used for rapid economic growth is the emphasis which is inevitably placed on industrial and commercial expansion. A quick increase in GNP can only be achieved by encouraging investment, management and labour to concentrate on construction, mining, manufactures and services. This results in spectacular expansion – both Zaire and Zambia have achieved annual growth rates of over ten per cent. Yet the consequence is that the concentration of effort is largely confined to the towns. The vast majority of the population, living in rural areas, enjoys little if any benefit from the growth of the economy. Some of them migrate to the towns, aggravating the social burdens there and impoverishing the rural communities. The argument that an increase in the GNP, however obtained, will spread benefits to the whole nation has found no justification. In both Zaire and Zambia rural incomes have stagnated whilst urban wages have soared, expenditure on food imports has risen tremendously instead of the new demands of town-workers being supplied by home-grown products. It remains to be seen whether the governments of the two countries, both of which have declared their recognition of this danger, find the means to overcome it.

To understand how difficult it will be for African governments to escape from the tentacles of the multi-national company, however anxious they are to do so, we should look at west Africa. Take the case of Unilever, with its African subsidiary, the United Africa Company. At the end of the war UAC was responsible for a third of all Gold Coast (Ghana) and Nigerian imports and exports. After independence its opportunities actually increased. Colonial governments had refused to protect local production, being concerned to expand metropolitan exports. African governments, however, anxious to restrict imports and stimulate local production, were persuaded that protective tariffs would achieve these ends.

But UAC was so strong in west Africa that many of the import-substitute industries were under its control. Between the end of the war and independence, during the period when marketing and licensed buying agents were being instituted, it diversified its operations from buying local produce for export into the retail trade. Seeing independent governments moving towards Africanization of retailing, it then redeployed its capital into light manufacturing industries. In doing so it had the approval of the new governments. Timber mills, breweries, detergent factories, printing works, vehicle assembly plants, meat factories, ice-cream manufacture, cement production, and a score of other activities were undertaken by the company, often in association with other specialist foreign companies. It was particularly active in Ghana, Nigeria, and, through its French section, Niger France, in the Ivory Coast. But it also operated in 14 francophone states, in east and South Africa, in Rhodesia and in Zaire.

Unilever illustrates the general pattern taken by multi-national companies over the past two decades. Its main investments went to the developed world. Between 1951–5 and 1961–5 its capital expenditure in Britain rose from £32 million to £136.4 million; in the rest of Europe from £43.1 million to £144.6 million; but in Africa it only increased from £30 million to £39.9 million. Yet its influence in African economies had been strengthened. It had invested in 72 factories in tropical Africa, supplied commercial management in 55 and technical management to 34. Most of its profits were either re-invested, supplying new capital, or sent back to Europe. The surplus created was owned by it, under its control and deployed according to its interests.

Nkrumah's governments tried to harness the economic activities of Unilever as they did of other foreign companies. Restrictions on imports and campaigns against repatriation of profits, added to massive government expenditure, temporarily undermined its power. But the Ghanaians had little conception of how to plan their economy efficiently. The example given above of their blindness in the Volta Dam project provides one illustration. When it came to import control and supervision of government expenditure they almost bankrupted themselves without ever gaining control over the roots of their economic system.

In any case, Nkrumah's period of radicalism did not last very long. With his downfall foreign capital was again sought through multiple concessions. In Nigeria and the Ivory Coast no serious attempt was ever made to curb its activities. And as oil production in Nigeria multiplied several times during the 1960s, not only were the oil combines added to the multi-national community, but the incomes generated by them offered fresh opportunites for manufacturing production.

Even the most radically orientated governments will face enormous difficulties in trying to control the activities of companies with such a complex hold on every aspect of economic life. It was the received theory of anti-colonial nationalists that their economies must be diversified and expanded as soon as independence was attained. As little local capital was available, and as there was no local expertise in techniques, to achieve these objectives quickly necessitated using the services of foreign companies. Whether the pace of construction and industrialization need have been so fast; whether agreements with these companies need have produced such a degree of dependence; whether stronger local control could have been exercised – are arguable issues. The first independence decade has seen the entrenchment of these massive alien economic forces; if the Africans are to gain control of their own economic life they face a difficult, complicated task.

The major international attempt by Third World states to co-ordinate their strategy in facing this challenge is that mounted by the Organization of the Petroleum Exporting Countries (OPEC). This body first successfully demanded higher returns for the oil which was produced from their members' countries by the huge petroleum companies. Then it decided to press for participation in the process by the governments of those member states, eventually to reach majority ownership. Nigeria, Libya and Algeria are the main African states involved at the beginning of the 1970s, though there may well be others before the decade is over.

There is every sign that this strategy is succeeding. The crucial importance of oil to the industrial world, the fact that most of its known supplies are to be found in the Third World and the fear that supplies may become exhausted before a suitable substitute is discovered, have all given OPEC a negotiating strength previously unknown to the producers of raw materials. It seems probable that the power of OPEC will continue to grow, provided that its member states do not suffer from severe domestic conflicts (not unlikely when one looks at the variety of régimes existing amongst them) and that they continue to recognize their common interest. Even then, however, they will still be dependent on the expertise of foreign companies until they have trained their own personnel, which may well be their most important responsibility. As there is every likelihood of the seller's market continuing, provided no country breaks ranks to make a separate deal, the collective strength of the organization seems assured.

The experience of other bodies organized to protect the producers is not so happy. Zambia, Zaire, Chile and Peru established the Inter-Governmental Council of Copper Exporting Countries in the hope of finding the means to halt disastrous price fluctuations. Yet these member states have not yet overcome their mutual competition. Their expansion programmes remain unco-ordinated, whilst their differing production costs make cooperation difficult. As a consequence rivalry persists, with production or labour troubles in one country bringing advantages to the others. The difficulties experienced by Chile over Allende's nationalization of American companies, for instance, brought renewed hopes of higher copper prices. It will require a much stronger concept of transnational thought and a greater recognition of common interest before this organization attains the influence of OPEC. But these requisites are not impossible to achieve. It may well be that during the 1970s each of these four countries will recognize that in the battle between national economic independence and world capitalist forces, only unity can achieve success.

The cocoa and coffee exporters have had little greater success than the producers of copper. It took 16 years for the cocoa-growing countries to reach some sort of agreement with the chief cocoa consumers. Even that agreement, reached in the second half of 1972, appeared very fragile. It fixed maximum and minimum prices, but left it to the discretion of the governments concerned whether to sign. As two of the major consumers, the United States and West Germany, had strongly opposed the agreement, it remained doubtful whether the years of negotiation had produced any practical results.

In coffee, production gluts and shortages alternated with little success being achieved in agreement on production quotas or price. As with cocoa and copper, rivalry and competition were much more common amongst the producing countries than co-operation.

The success of African governments – and, indeed, of all Third World governments – in bridling the activities of foreign economic forces and gaining control over their own economies will depend heavily on their skill and foresight in using such international associations. Yet this issue is closely linked to the manner in which they harness their own economic forces. Governments in the African states are the only serious sources of capital. Unless they control its use it is inevitable that a variety of entrepreneurs will take advantage of the situation, usually by suborning some of those in positions of influence. That this has already occurred in many African states is well known. The process has led to some of the worst abuses of power, to mounting tensions between masses and élites, to gross mismanagement of economic resources and, often, to political upheaval. No doubt the situation can be duplicated in other states with longer and more stable histories; but the fact is that Africa cannot afford the luxury of such corrupt, debilitating practices; nor will Africans allow them to persist without revolt, as they have repeatedly demonstrated.

President Mobutu has taken a short step in the direction of government control over the major source of Zaire's wealth by the formation of Gécamines, the state-owned minerals company which runs the mines previously controlled by Belgium's Union Minière. President Kaunda, in neighbouring Zambia, has taken much longer steps. Not only are his copper mines controlled through the state corporation, MINDECO, but much of his country's major industries come under the umbrella of INDECO, the state's industrial corporation. As finance, insurance and banking are also under government control, all the strategic areas of the Zambian economy are, at least theoretically, controlled by the elected representatives of the people.

This may be the most important example in Africa of deliberate social control over the economic life of the nation. It has still to prove itself. It must show greater efficiency, more ruthless extirpation of corruption, deeper roots in the villages, greater political sagacity and stability than displayed by Nkrumah's experiment in state control. It may demand the courage to re-negotiate terms with the copper companies. Above all, it will be tested by the degree of genuine economic independence it can achieve; for if a state economic institution remains dependent on foreign capital, management, entrepreneurs, or markets, no matter what degree of Africanization it achieves, it rests in pawn to foreign interest. Kaunda has made a brave start, especially taking into account the uniquely dangerous circumstances in which he has had to operate. What the President has still to do is to resist the temptation to seek increased revenues from expanding copper production, which can only serve a short-term interest and deepen the dependence on copper. He must also halt the indiscriminate establishment of industries and services which have been attracted by copper wealth and consumer demands. For this has already created a dangerous imbalance in the economy and aggravated the division between town and country. It must be recognized by Zambians that they belong to a basically poor country, that if the nation as a whole to achieve prosperity, it must build its economic structure from the base, from the villages, not from a small copper-rich élite. This demands a concentration on the rural areas, on agriculture and on associating the growth of industry with agricultural needs. If Kaunda succeeds in this, Zambia will become the pacemaker in the race for economic independence.

The multi-national companies have already revealed a strategy designed to combat African interference in their activities: they move their African headquarters to South Africa. Although they remain governed from Europe, America or Japan, they can use the Republic as a base for operations throughout the African continent.

In South Africa such companies find a favourable economic climate, an absence of intervention from the government, and a foreign policy which perfectly suits their interests. They are able to rely on a stable though politically restricted domestic market, sustained by an advanced economy, and a plentiful supply of cheap, regimented labour. Capital is therefore constantly available, attracted from throughout the investing world. So long as such conditions persist, neither Britain nor America is likely to take measures which might undermine the political régime, whilst France positively embraces the opportunities of rich economic prizes. Japan and West Germany follow only a few steps behind.

The South African government and the economy on which it rests need black African markets for the agricultural and manufactured products, for they artificially restrict their domestic market through apartheid. During the 1970s they will also be seeking to sell capital goods to the African states. This precisely coincides with the perspective of the multi-national companies. If the European Economic Community succeeds in overcoming its difficulties and consolidates itself as a major capital-accumulating power, it is likely to reinforce the alliance between the South African government and the multi-national corporations. As these corporations are based in Europe or America – often in both – the possibility of competition developing between South African and

P

Euro-American salesmen can be discounted. South Africa will have been designated as an ally of the multi-national world.

This fait accompli will present black Africa with its greatest challenge. The South African government is anxious to keep black-governed states small, weak and divided, unable to offer much help to the freedom fighters. Its support of Tshombe in Zaire, of Ojukwu in Biafra, of Banda in Malawi and of Tsiranana in Malagasy amply illustrates this. The South Africans have spread a web of intelligence agents throughout the continent, concentrated particularly on fomenting dissension in Zambia and Tanzania, retain as much politico-economic control as possible over Lesotho, Botswana and Swaziland, and openly provide support for the Portuguese and Rhodesians. With the aid of the multi-national companies, themselves ensuring support from Europe and America, their strategy is to bribe those with public influence in black Africa, obstruct the efforts of the OAU, especially in its attempts to secure greater regional co-operation, and attempt to remove any African leaders who oppose their policies.

It may be that during the 1970s African leaders within South Africa will gain greater power to undermine the government's policies than hitherto. The only new factor in the struggle for African democratic rights, which has been unsuccessfully waged throughout this century, is the emergence of leaders of the new Bantustans. Chief Buthelezi, in Zulu-land, for example, is seeking to use his position in order to construct a strategy which will reduce the power of the white oligarchic government over the Bantustan which it imposed on his people. It may be that the very logic of apartheid itself can be turned against the practice of white supremacy. But with its massive economic and military power, constantly reinforced by external capital, it is unlikely that racial domination will be dented in this decade. The most that can be expected is that the hegemony of the white community may become less comfortably secure.

The tenure of the white rulers of Rhodesia is much more dubious. Not only is their community a great deal smaller in proportion to the African population, but they have been seriously weakened by economic sanctions and exclusion from the capital market. They have had to beg military and economic assistance from the South Africans, who have no desire to extend the black–white confrontation from the Limpopo to the Zambezi. Their help to the Smith régime has been based on nothing stronger than a faute de mieux.

Despite weak, schismatic and vacillating leadership, the Africans of Rhodesia demonstrated their determination to put long-term interests before expediency when they clearly rejected the Smith–Home terms in the test of opinion carried out by the Pearce Commission in 1972. The African National Council which emerged to represent African opinion during the visit of Lord Pearce and his colleagues seemed to offer more subtle tactics than had hitherto been employed by the older nationalist movements. The extension of guerrilla operations within Rhodesia in 1972–3 heralded increasing confrontation during the 1970s. Smith's reaction on closing the border with Zambia represented further escalation of the black–white conflict.

Nor should the fact be ignored that to the west of Rhodesia in both Botswana and Namibia stern opposition to the ethos of white supremacy had arisen. The Namibians had to face the strong battalions of South Africa, though they had the advantage of United Nations involvement. In Botswana, however, Seretse Khama had embarked on a policy of proving that the economic dependence of South Africa in which his country had been left did not necessitate acceptance of apartheid. With the discovery of new minerals and a socio-political policy of non-racialism, Botswana could well turn the flank of apartheid by quietly building an alternative and more attractive form of society. But she will have to be careful not to place herself under the influence of the multi-national companies which covet her mineral wealth.

Yet the most direct challenge to white supremacy undoubtedly comes from the African movements in the Portuguese territories. They alone present an immediate, serious, military threat to the white oligarchies. They have been waging war on their Portuguese masters since the early sixties and the fact that concerted military attempts by Portugal to crush them have failed, demonstrates the strength of their appeal to their countrymen. In Guinea-Bissau the remarkably modest, serious and dedicated leader, Amilcar Cabral, claimed to control more than half the country before he was tragically assassinated early in 1973. Schisms have weakened the efforts of the anti-colonial movements in Angola, but the main force, MPLA, also controls substantial areas of the country. A détente between the two rival groups at the end of 1972 may lead to more cohesive action. Perhaps it is FRELIMO, the movement in Mozambique inspired by Eduardo Mondlane, himself assassinated by a bomb in Dar es Salaam in 1969, which presents the most direct threat to the southern whites. For this organization has started to operate in the southern parts of the country, concentrating particularly in disrupting the construction of the Cabora Bassa dam. As Cabora Bassa is being built with the help of South African and international finance and is designed to supply electric power to the whole of southern Africa, the FRELIMO guerrillas are directly challenging the entire white supremacist syndrome. In doing so, they are also threatening communications between Rhodesia and the east coast, vital to her international trade. The road which leads from Salisbury through Malawi to Mozambique was mined, as were railways, forcing traffic to move in convoys under military protection.

In all three Portuguese territories the gauntlet of the freedom fighters has been thrown down not simply before the Portuguese military forces but at the government of Portugal itself. For once an area is occupied by the anti-colonial movements, an administration is established. Schools and clinics are set up, roads and markets built, agriculture organized, committees elected, laws agreed and courts created. The freedom movements are building alternative societies out of their revolutionary battles, founded on peasant values, democratic practices and popular involvement, even before Portuguese rule has been ended. They are already seen by many young Africans as a model for the future social organization of the continent.

Yet, despite the gradual growth of these African efforts to secure control over their social and economic future, the struggles against external economic forces are bound to be long and hard. South Africa will remain throughout the 1970s as the only self-sustaining modern economy, able to organize and maintain technologically advanced military forces. If, as seems almost certain, the Republic continues to attract vast amounts of international capital, its oligarchy is unlikely to be seriously challenged from within. It is too much to expect the OAU, or its member states, plagued with their own problems, to mount sufficient external challenge to do more than progressively embarrass it.

If the Africans are unable to overthrow the white supremacist régimes themselves, or, directly linked to the same issue, to control the activities of the multi-national corporations, what chance is there for them to secure external assistance? The Chinese will continue to help to strengthen indigenous economies and to supply the freedom fighters with training and equipment. As India solves some of her domestic problems, with the possibility of peace spreading, however uneasily, over the sub-continent, she may well be prepared to lend greater assistance to her African friends. This could lead to an involvement of the important Indian Ocean theatre in international activity over the southern Africa issue. Supplies to the freedom fighters come largely through Dar es Salaam, many from the Chinese. It is not difficult to imagine a Southern African naval or aerial attempt to interfere with this supply route. That would immediately become an issue of major international importance, involving not only the Africans and Chinese, but also all those states in the West associated with South Africa. In any case, east Africa and those countries of the hinterland using east African ports have resumed the rôle in the Indian Ocean they used to play in the Middle Ages. As two-thirds of mankind lives around its shores, the Africans are entering a zone likely to become as important before the end of the twentieth century as the Atlantic has been for the past four centuries.

The assistance of the Russians and East Europeans to Africans has always been marginal, whilst their barter agreements have often seemed to result in greater benefit to communist economies than to those of Africa. As the détente between the United States and the USSR progresses it is being increasingly accepted within the Third World that European communists have become part of the industrialized world. Not only has the possibility of playing off the communists against the capitalists to attract aid disappeared, but it seems as though Russia and her satellites are less willing to help developing countries to resist the incursions of capitalist economic forces. Assuming that the understanding between the two giants is maintained, the economic relations between them will increasingly exclude consideration of African and other Third World states.

Friendship between the United States and China is both younger and more fragile. It has not so far reduced Chinese interest in aiding Third World countries. Indeed, China regards herself as a member of the Third World and would like to assume leadership of it. Whilst she may be willing to accept economic relations with the Americans, as others in the Third World have done, she is unlikely to diminish her hostility to the American international posture during the 1970s. It is not only her parallel conflict with the Russians which leads her to condemn the Great Power concept of a world divided into twin spheres of influence. She certainly fears that this could be used against her, isolating her from taking an influential place in the international community, interfering with her independent actions and, in the last resort, endangering her security. But, more importantly, China is still in a state of revolution, envisaging a different kind of world from the two major powers; for many years yet she will continue to identify the interests of the Third World with her own, seeking their support for her policies and hoping that they will accept her leadership.

When China gains some experience at the United Nations and in other international bodies her global influence may well begin to be more seriously felt. This could lend additional weight to the demands of the Third World, if any substantial part of it should forge the means of common action. Yet it should not be assumed that the Third World will uncritically accept Chinese policies or leadership. Russo-Chinese rivalry has already undermined Afro-Asian conferences and persists in Somalia. Continued friction with India will not help China's cause and could cause fresh divisions within the already fragmented developing countries. Moreover, many Third World leaders have learnt sufficient about international politics to be sceptical over pretensions of altruism. The Tanzanian government, for example, although genuinely grateful for Chinese help in building the Tan-Zam railway and other technological projects, announced in 1972 that she would not accept any further aid from China for a period. Nyerere and his colleagues are aware of the dangers arising from too great a dependence on any foreign aid, no matter what its source.

If the Chinese continue to progress in transforming their own society, and if they are prepared to work in concert with progressive sections of the Third World, radical Africans can expect increasing support from them. They not only help the freedom fighters to maintain their pressure on the white south, but recognize the importance of supplying the kind of technological installations suitable for the present stage of African development and of training Africans to operate them. Their labour-intensive machinery is ideally suited to the present generation of African workers and offers the advantage of attacking the massive problem of African unemployment. Yet even Chinese assistance will not provide Africans with substantial means to undermine the white régimes or to halt the encroachments of the multi-national companies on their economies. If it is recognized that this twin menace is based in Europe, America and Japan, strategy becomes imperative.

The same multi-national corporations which increasingly control African economic life also menace all forms of social control over the economies of Europe and America. It would therefore seem sensible for Africans to attempt to associate with those sections of society in these continents which recognize the same danger to their own democratic freedoms. Admittedly, they are not very strong or coherent, whilst many of them remain blind to the realities of late twentieth-century economic society.

Nevertheless, within the labour movements of Europe, especially those of Scandinavia, amongst some sections of black political society in America, and, most significantly but as a more amorphous group, amongst the younger generation everywhere, are to be found potential friends. On the issue of white supremacy in southern Africa such associ-ates are often vague and muddleheaded. Nevertheless, their liberalism or anti-racialism can be used to pressurize their governments, even when they do not recognize the connection between apartheid and international capitalism.

In the long term, however, it is more important to convince the labour organizations that the multi-national menace, together with its South African component, threatens the interests of workers in the industrialized countries as much as it endangers African development. The multi-national structures have become so all-pervading that either they will be brought under social control or they will dominate the industrialized world, whatever political institutions exist in it. If, therefore, the peoples of the developed countries hope to establish any form of control over the economic basis of their lives, they will have to combine to do so in full recognition of where the danger lies. But, even if they mount this effort, they are bound to fail unless the radical forces of the Third World are included in their alliance. For already the multi-national companies have begun to use developing countries as refuges from restrictions encountered in industrialized states. It is therefore a common interest between the peoples of both developed and developing worlds to combine in a joint strategy.

Much of the success or failure of those African countries particularly exposed to the impact of the multi-nationals in bringing their economies under indigenous control will depend on the creation of such an alliance. Countries like Zambia, Zaire, Ghana, Nigeria, Gabon, Ivory Coast, Libya, and, to a lesser extent, a score of others, will find that the realities of economic independence will escape them unless they are able to weaken the Euro-American base of multi-national power. For their ability to harness their own economic resources, to provide their own people with the chance of a higher quality of life, substantially depends on this alliance.

At the same time, it would be foolish for African radicals or other members of the Third World to rely completely on the chances of awakening progressive movements in the developed world to this international imperative. It must be remembered that most of such movements have become deeply ingrained by the values of the commercialized, consumer society, whilst their followers are even more indoctrinated by the acquisitive society. The great trading blocs being erected during the 1970s, the USA, COMECON, the EEC, Japan, all protectionist-orientated, have so far experienced little internal opposition from radical critics. Each bloc is dominated by the multi-national corporations or the similar state institutions of the communists. They have beguiled many socialists into believing that they represent the kind of internationalism for which socialism has been seeking. Those who oppose them usually do so more on grounds of national sovereignty than through recognition of the dangers from international industrial finance. Nor do they at present perceive any socialist alternative. Their traditionally patronizing attitude to the Third World blinds them to the common threat aimed at industrialized and developing peoples alike, to the common interests which could offer the foundation of an alliance between working-class organizations in the developed world and those in the Third World seeking economic independence.

It would therefore be wise for African radicals to plan their socio-economic development contingent on continued absence of support from the industrialized world. If an alliance with its progressives materializes, it will then become a bonus. But the essential policy to be followed if economic independence is ever to become a reality is to integrate agri-cultural and industrial development, concentrate export revenues on purchases of essentials and co-ordinate trade policies between Third World countries.

It would be foolish to believe that this process can be easily accom-plished, or that it is likely to be achieved quickly. Yet time is not an African asset. For there are clear signs of a collapse of society in many parts of the continent; failure to attack their roots has already led to a spread of anti-social infection. It is becoming increasingly common in the continent for the individual African to find himself exposed to arbitrary assault, deprived of any institutional protection.

The brutalization of life which developed in Zaire, the CAR, Nigeria, Burundi and Uganda at various periods of the first decade and a half of independence were not isolated instances. They are mirrored else-where. They derived from frustration, fear, psychological stress, in the face of the immense difficulties bequeathed by colonial rule. But, what-ever their causes, they led to the torture and death of millions of Africans, inevitably extending the insecurities from which they originated.

Frantz Fanon once described this as a phase in which "the niggers beat each other up", bitterly using colonial words to emphasize the connection with the imperial legacy. Fanon, himself a psychiatrist, analysed the phenomenon as a form of avoidance behaviour, a reflex towards death in the face of danger. The fraternal bloodbath he saw as a substitute for getting to grips with those responsible for the Africans' intolerable frustrations.

Certainly in Burundi and Uganda it seems clear that large sections of the population were incited to attack scapegoats in order to turn their attention from the failure of governing régimes. This is a political tactic common to governments outside Africa, but it is particularly disastrous in African society where few institutions are firmly rooted and all states lack homogeneity. Inevitably the reaction of most Africans is to return to their ethnic consciousness, where they can expect communal protection. In those countries where society is multi-racial there is also a temptation to identify non-African racial groups as scapegoats, as in Uganda. In the light of racial attitudes in the rest of the world this is hardly surprising. Nevertheless, it makes for further chaos. With anger vented by commun-ity on community, whether of ethnic or racial origin, national societies have little chance of survival.

Yet the counter-measures taken may have even more disastrous conse-quences. One can sympathize with governments which, driven to despera-tion by armed robberies, assaults and murders, resort to public executions. They defend the use of capital punishment against those outside Africa who argue that the death penalty has never succeeded as a deterrent by asserting that conditions in Africa cannot be compared with those else-where. They claim that the executions must be in public so that there is no suspicion of secret favouritism, to impress people that the influential individuals behind much of the lawlessness are not escaping punishment. Yet the effects of these brutal sights on those who witness them must be dehumanizing and one trembles for the consequences on the thousands of children who are present.

Sometimes the counter-measures against anarchy represent a reversion to ancient custom. Colonel Gadafy of Libya, for instance, seemed to be reacting against his frustrations with the modern world when he restored the literal interpretation of the Koranic precept, "And the thief, male and female, cut off the hands of both, as recompense for what they have earned." It appeared that the Colonel's fanatical adherence to Mohammedanism was more responsible for this brutal degree than a desire for order. Yet such practices have been rejected by most Muslim authorities for many years as contrary to the true spirit of Islam.

Ancient traditions mingle with modern social problems in many parts of the continent. The bride price, for instance, formed a valuable social institution in traditional society. Yet it becomes degraded when practised in modern town life, where it often represents little more than the sale of women for money. Similarly, whilst polygyny played an important part in cementing rural communities and guaranteeing security to every member, in modern urban areas it usually becomes a form of concubinage with detrimental effects on families.

Nor can Africans view with complacency the effects of the transference of traditional attitudes towards women into modern society. The more progressive leaders, like Nyerere and Bourguiba, have always insisted that the second-class status traditionally accorded women must be changed in modern Africa. Yet in many parts of the continent the cruel practice of female circumcision persists. The degradation of women is then com-pounded by the addition of modern social disabilities. Prostitution is rife in the towns, whereas it was virtually unknown to traditional Africa. The spread of venereal disease is so severe that in certain regions of central Africa infertility is actually reducing the population.

Thus Africans have local social evils to combat in addition to those imported from abroad. As many in positions of influence were born to illiterate peasant parents, it is not surprising that psychological strain becomes unsupportable under the weight of the problems they have to face. Yet these social tensions, and the cruelties they promote, corrode the foundations of the societies all Africans are trying to build. Unless they can be overcome, the indications of social collapse which have appeared since independence can plunge the continent into chaos. They will certainly leave African society in no state to grapple with its external dangers.

The progress of events in Uganda seems likely to draw all these African threads together during the mid-1970s, if not for the entire decade. During 1971–2 Amin declared war on the concept of the non-racial African state, brought Islam's jihad together with the Arab-Israeli conflict into the heart of the continent, destroyed east African unity, menaced Tanzania's socialist experiment, utilized ethnic rivalries to build his own power and, by his massacres, gave ammunition to the southern white supremacists and those who support them. But to many ordinary Africans in his own country and elsewhere in the continent, he represented the common man against the élite, whether Asian, European or African. He could be heard denouncing the white supremacists of the south, calling for an international brigade to fight against them, he was seen to be attacking the Israelis for their wealth, their American dependence and their occupation of Arab lands. Above all, he appeared in the posture of a common, un-Europeanized African determined that the continent should be governed by and for black Africans. That is a populist appeal which could significantly affect every state in the continent.

If this mood spreads the future of Asians and Europeans in the rest of east Africa, whether they are citizens of their states of residence or not, will become extremely precarious. So will the position of the many Syrians, Lebanese and other non-Africans in west Africa. Kaunda's convinced non-racialism in Zambia and Banda's use of expatriates in Malawi will also come under attack, whilst eventually the position of over half a million Asians in South Africa could be placed in jeopardy.

Meanwhile, Islamic influence has already a strong foundation on which to build. If Amin, with less than ten per cent of Muslims in his country, can place them in controlling positions in his army and business, what are the prospects in Nigeria, where about half the 60 million population follows Islam? The Israelis made a fatal error in choosing to support Amin in his coup against Obote. Their intelligence must have been appalling. If they believed that Amin would be more likely than his predecessor to sustain the southern Sudanese in their war with Khartoum, thereby weakening the Arab world, they soon discovered their miscalculation. Not only was the Sudanese breach healed, but Amin surrounded himself with Sudanese soldiers as his personal agents within his army and expelled from Uganda the Israelis who had been actually training his forces. Supported by President Gadafy of Libya and King Feisal of Saudi Arabia, Amin then deliberately gave preference to the few Muslims in his country. His example in expelling the Israelis was soon followed by Chad,

Mali, Niger and Congo-Brazzaville. Rarely can a diplomatic decision have so catastrophically blown up in its originator's face.

Israel still retained a strong influence in some parts of the continent. The Ivory Coast, Liberia, Zaire, and Ethiopia, retained their trust in Israeli assistance, which has usually been of a more practical nature than that of the Arabs. Yet the danger had become apparent; if the Arab-Israeli conflict becomes a significant element throughout the continent it will inevitably dislocate African development and unity.

In Uganda itself the future seemed obscure. Most of the predictions made in Europe that the economy would collapse appeared unwarranted. The staple diet of Ugandans is made from bananas which are always plentiful. Rivers and lakes provide a constant supply of fish, whilst cattle-ranching and dairy-farming have expanded rapidly since independence. Coffee, cotton, tobacco and copper offer a varied supply of exports for which there are constant overseas demands. So the people have little difficulty in feeding themselves, whilst foreign reserves can be maintained through exports.

The expulsion of Asians and Europeans from commerce, business, the civil service, education, management and technical expertise will certainly dislocate the modernized sector of Uganda's life. Yet to the vast majority of Ugandans it will mean little but a welcome removal of foreigners. It seems possible that for a time Uganda will dispense with most of her modernizing ambitions. The élite and those who depended on them will be resentful. But for those whose affairs have hardly been changed by modernization, the vast majority, life will proceed as before, with the added enjoyment of knowing that an African common man is in charge. The test will be how many Ugandans will accept economic stagnation, minimal growth and diminished educational opportunities as a fair price for populist Africanization.

It would be idle to speculate how long this situation will last. Changes have occurred rapidly and without warning in many African states since independence. Yet nothing quite like the Amin phenomenon has appeared before. All previous coups have been followed by pledges of continued modernization by alliances between soldiers and civil servants, by the continuation of élite society. Amin antagonized virtually all the agents of modernization, outraged all sections of the élite and appealed directly to the ordinary people. He certainly shocked many sections of Uganda society by massacres of particular groups; the Langi and Acholi suffered cruelly, as did many Ankole and Baganda. Resentments are bound to fester amongst some of them. Yet as European and Asian assets are re-allocated, some will accept appeasement. How far the Christian churches will be prepared to bow before Muslim domination of the country, to what extent the lack of teachers will lead to a frustration in the widespread clamour for education, what reactions may come against the lawlessness of soldiers and gangsters, how long administration can survive on the basis of presidential decree, whether the economy can continue to bear the expense of a 14,000-strong army, are all matters of speculation.

What should be learnt from the example of Uganda, however, is the resentment simmering just below the surface of African society against the yawning gap between élites and people. Obote did not bridge it despite his nationalizing efforts. Indeed, recollections of his lavish wedding identified him with the ostentation of the élite. It may be that army officers and Libyan traders, filling the gap left by the deposed élite, will arouse similar resentment to that shown towards their predecessors. If so the populist attractions of the Amin régime will soon fade. In those circumstances the many nascent groups resentful of his irresponsible and often brutal methods might well overthrow the régime. Uganda could decline into a Congo-like chaos, with ethnic conflict aggravated by mob violence. It remains to be seen whether the popular resentment in Uganda against the élitist development of society is cured by the expulsion of Asians and Europeans or further provoked by the appearance of a new élite.

Yet, whatever happens in Uganda, it seems probable that the effects of Amin's impact will be felt in the rest of the continent for a long time. On the one hand, by arousing colour prejudices latent amongst the deprived of every nation, he has made the task of building genuine non-racial African societies infinitely more difficult; on the other, he has given an expression to popular feelings antagonistic against not only non-Africans but all élites. The repercussions may well variously affect the whole continent.

Africans face these enormous difficulties in a world which seems likely to suffer from profound traumas during the rest of the twentieth century. The crisis which has already developed is one in which over-development and under-development are inextricably linked. As the industrialized world continues to gyrate on its consumer-demand roundabout, so it requires motive power from ever greater proportions of the resources which could be used to redress international social injustice. Over-consumption has gained its own momentum. Despite the cries of those who foresee the exhaustion of resources, the poisoning of the environment, dementia in the cities and a modern socio-economic enslavement for mankind, the consumer society has no power to halt its mad gyration. It seems virtually certain that this is the final death-whirl of white technological society.

Of course, the chances are that in destroying itself the industrialized world will also drag the developing world into a common grave. Certainly the bonds which link Euro-America to much of Asia and Latin America leave little chance that much of contemporary society can survive in those continents. Africa may be different. Most of its people are still insulated from external influences. Despite all the bloodshed, millions of Africans still live in simple, ordered, humane communities, in which personal relations have priority over material possessions. African peasant communities hold and practise just those values most spurned by technological society and most sought by those trying to escape it.

The chances of Africa providing foundations for an alternative experiment in human social engineering are very slim. The cords which bind her to Euro-America are being rapidly tightened; ever more Africans accept the values of the consumer society and become its slaves. Yet confrontation of universal dimensions has already started. It is a battle between alternative systems of social life. One still hypocritically flies the banner of bastardized liberalism, freedom for the individual interpreted as an absence of communal planning, a rejection of social responsibility; the other, recognizing that this is simply camouflage for unbridled licence for the strong and unconscious slavery for the majority, realizes that freedom for the individual can only arise out of community responsibility, co-operation and control; it is by participation in a free society with the power to choose its own objectives that it visualizes genuine personal freedom being gained.

Africans have retained this concept to a greater degree than any other peoples. Whether they continue to maintain it depends on the degree to which they succeed in resisting those Euro-American influences which have brought disaster to their own societies, whilst at the same time devising the means to reduce poverty, disease and illiteracy which so far have seemed endemic to African life. There are many people in the world, especially amongst the younger generation of all continents, who seek a social order based on these same African values. The African younger generation, too, attaining maturity during the late 1970s and 1980s, will be less influenced by the effects of colonial rule. A faint chance exists here that a new start may be made by our descendants to build an alternative civilization as mankind's technological experiment begins to collapse.

If this faint hope is to be kept alive, two imperatives face Africans during the next decade. First, they must recognize that none of their problems can be solved so long as their continent remains fragmented into its present nation-states. Some wider forms of association are essential to the creation of societies capable of facing the political, social and economic challenges of this era. Secondly, in the words of Eduardo Mondlane:

A greater danger lies in the formation of new African privileged groups; the educated as opposed to the uneducated, factory-workers as opposed to peasants. To prevent concentration of wealth and services in small areas of the country and in the hands of a few, strong central planning is needed.

To which one might add some words from Amilcar Cabral:

We shall put our whole priority on agriculture. That means more than cultivation. That means realizing what people can do, can actually do. That's a question of village democracy, of village schools, of village clinics, of village co-operation.

And again:

Educate ourselves, educate other people, the population in general, to fight fear and ignorance, to eliminate little by little the subjection to nature and natural forces which our economy has not yet mastered. Fight without useless violence against all negative aspects, prejudicial to mankind, which are still part of our beliefs and traditions. Convince little by little ... that we shall end by conquering the fear of nature, and that man is the strongest force in nature ... take life seriously, conscious of their responsibilities, thoughtful about carrying them out, and with a comradeship based on work and duty done ... Nothing of this is incompatible with the joy of life, or with love of life and its amusements, or with confidence in the future and in our work ...

These are the visions which may yet inspire Africans to become the bricklayers of a second experiment in human social architecture.

Bibliography

Chapter 1   The 1960s: Decade of Disillusion

S. ANDRESKI, *The African Predicament*, London, 1969
CHIEF AWOLOWO, *Awo: The Autobiography of Chief Obafemi Awolowo*, Oxford, 1960
Path to Nigerian Freedom, London, 1947
ALHAJI SIR AHMADU BELLO, *My Life*, London, 1962
C. F. and A. B. DARLINGTON, *African Betrayal*, New York, 1968
RICHARD GREENFIELD, *Ethiopia*, London, 1965
JOHN HATCH, *A History of Post-War Africa*, London and New York, 1965
THOMAS HODGKIN and RUTH SCHACHTER MORGENTHAU, *French-Speaking West Africa in Transition*, New York, 1960
I. N. KIMOMBO and A. J. TEMU, *A History of Tanzania*, Nairobi, 1969
W. P. KIRKMAN, *Unscrambling an Empire: A Critique of British Colonial Policy 1956–66*, London, 1966
J. M. LONSDALE, *The Emergence of African Nations*, Nairobi, 1968
KWAME NKRUMAH, *Africa Must Unite*, London, 1963
Autobiography, London, 1957
ROLAND OLIVER and J. D. FAGE, *A Short History of Africa*, London, 1970
N. C. POLLOCK, *Studies in Emerging Africa*, London, 1971
NDABANINGI SITHOLE, *African Nationalism*, Oxford, 1959
VIRGINIA THOMPSON and RICHARD ADLOFF, *The Emerging States of French Equatorial Africa*, Stanford, 1960
PETER WORSLEY, *The Third World*, London, 1964

Chapter 2   Coups and Revolts

PETER BARKER, *Operation Cold Chop: The Coup that Toppled Nkrumah*, Ghana, 1969
DONALD L. BARNETT and KARARI NJAMA, *Mau Mau from Within*, London, 1966.

GEOFFREY BING, *Reap the Whirlwind*, London, 1968
CONOR CRUISE O'BRIEN, *To Katanga and Back*, London, 1962
G. M. CARTER (ed.), *Five African States*, London, 1964
MAMADOU DIA, *The African Nations and World Solidarity*, London, 1962
THOMAS HODGKIN, *African Political Parties*, London, 1961
C. HOSKYNS, *The Congo Since Independence*, London, 1965
ANDRE MANDOUZE, *La Révolution algérienne par les textes*, Paris, 1961
TOM MBOYA, *The Challenge of Nationhood*, London, 1970
KWAME NKRUMAH, *Building a Socialist State*, Accra, 1961
  Challenge of the Congo, London, 1967
KEN POST, *The Nigerian Federal Election of 1959*, Oxford, 1963
BRIAN WEINSTEIN, *Gabon: Nation Building on the Ogoové*, Cambridge, Massachusetts, 1966
JACK WODDIS, *The Roots of Revolt*, London, 1960
CRAWFORD YOUNG, *Politics in the Congo*, Princeton, 1965

Chapter 3 "Tribalism"

M. BANTON (ed.), *Political Systems and the Distribution of Power*, London, 1965
W. R. BASCOM and M. L. HERSKOVITS (eds), *Continuity and Change in African Cultures*, Chicago, 1959
BASIL DAVIDSON, *The Africans*, London, 1969
T. OLAWALE ELIAS, *The Nature of African Customary Law*, Manchester, 1956
M. FORTES and E. E. EVANS-PRITCHARD, *African Political Systems*, Oxford, 1940
MERRAN FRAENKEL, *Tribe and Class in Monrovia*, London, 1964
CLIFFORD GEERTZ (ed.), *Old Societies and New States: The Quest for Modernity in Asia and Africa*, Glencoe, 1963
JAMES L. GIBBS (ed.), *Peoples of Africa*, New York, 1965
MAX GLUCKMAN, *Culture and Conflict in Africa*, London, 1955
JOHN HATCH, *Nigeria: A History*, Chicago and London, 1970 and 1971
LUCY MAIR, *Primitive Government*, London, 1962
EZEKIEL MPHAHELE, *The African Image*, London, 1962
G. P. MURDOCK, *Africa: Its peoples and their Cultural History*, New York, 1959
B. A. OGOT and J. A. KIERAN, (eds), *Zamani*, Nairobi, 1968
R. OLIVER and G. MATHEW (eds), *History of East Africa*, Oxford, 1963
SIMON and PHOEBE OTTENBERG, *Cultures and Societies of Africa*, New York, 1960

AUDREY RICHARDS, *The Multi-cultural States of East Africa*, London, 1970

Chapter 4 Social Dilemmas

DAVID E. APTER, *The Politics of Modernization*, Chicago, 1965
SIR ERIC ASHBY, *African Universities and Western Tradition*, Oxford, 1964
ULLI BEIER, *Art in Nigeria, 1960*, Cambridge, 1960
PIERRE L. VAN DEN BERGHE, (ed.), *Africa: Social Problems of change and Conflict*, San Francisco, 1965
DUNDUZA CHISIZA, *Africa — What Lies Ahead*, New York, 1962
MAJHEMOUT DIOP, *Classes and Class Ideology in Senegal*, Paris, 1965
JACK GOODY, *Technology, Tradition and the State in Africa*, London, 1971
P. H. GULLIVER (ed.), *Tradition and Transition in East Africa*, London, 1967
GUY HUNTER, *The New Societies of Tropical Africa*, London, 1962
HILDA KUPER (ed.), *Urbanization and Migration in West Africa*, Los Angeles, 1965
ALEXANDER H. LEIGHTON *et al.*, *Psychiatric Disorders among the Yoruba*, Ithica, 1963
R. A. LEVINE, *Dreams and Deeds: Achievement Motivation in Nigeria*, Chicago, 1966
K. LITTLE, *West African Urbanization*, Cambridge, 1965
P. C. LLOYD, *Africa in Social Change*, London, 1967
        Classes, Crises and Coups, London 1971
        The New Elites of Tropical Africa, London, 1966
P. C. LLOYD, A. L. MABOGUNJE and B. AWE (eds), *The City of Ibadan*, Cambridge, 1967
JACQUES MAQUET, *Power and Society in Africa*, London, 1971
JOHN S. MBITI, *Concepts of God in Africa*, London, 1970
J. K. NYERERE, *Socialism and Rural Development*, Dar es Salaam, 1967
GEOFFREY PARRINDER, *Religion in Africa*, London and Baltimore, 1969
        West African Religion, London, 1961
R. SLOAN and H. KITCHEN (eds), *The Educated African*, London, 1962
J. SPENCER TRIMMINGHAM, *A History of Islam in West Africa*, London, 1962
VICTOR TURNER (ed.), *Colonialism in Africa*, Vol. III, London, 1971
IMMANUEL WALLERSTEIN (ed.), *Social Change: The Colonial System*, New York, 1966

Q

Chapter 5   Economic Quandaries

SAMIR AMIN, *Le Développement du Capitalisme en Côte d'Ivoire*, Paris, 1967

       Trois Expériences Africaines de Développement: Le Mali, La Giunée et Le Ghana, Paris, 1963

W. BIRMINGHAM, I. NEUSTADT and E. N. OMABOE (eds), *A Study of Contemporary Ghana*, London, 1966

MICHAEL BARRATT BROWN, *After Imperialism*, London, 1963

       From Labourism to Socialism, Nottingham, 1972

IOAN DAVIES, *African Trade Unions*, London, 1966

R. DUMONT, *False Start in Africa*, London, 1966

ECONOMIC COMMISSION FOR AFRICA, *Survey of Economic Conditions in Africa 1963–6*, United Nations

TOM J. FARER (ed.), *Financing African Development*, Cambridge, 1965

BOB FITCH and MARY OPPENHEIMER, "Ghana: End of an Illusion", *New Left Review*, No. 32, London

R. H. GREEN and ANN SEIDMAN, *Unity or Poverty?*, London, 1968

JUDITH HART, *Aid and Liberation*, London, 1973

JOHN HATCH, *Tanzania*, London and New York, 1972

M. J. HERSKOVITS and M. HARWITZ (eds), *Economic Transition in Africa*, London, 1963

GUY DE LUSIGNAN, *French-Speaking Africa since Independence*, London, 1969

J K. NYERERE, *After the Arusha Declaration*, Dar es Salaam, 1967

       Freedom and Unity, Uhuru na Umoja, Dar es Salaam, 1967

       Socialism and Rural Development, Dar es Salaam, 1967

       "Ujamaa" – The Basis of African Socialism, Dar es Salaam, 1962

E. A. G. ROBINSON (ed.), *Economic Development for Africa South of the Sahara*, London, 1963

       Seven Year Development Plan, Ghana, 1964

WILLIAM EDGETT SMITH, *We Must Run While They Walk*, New York, 1971

K. E. SVENDSEN and M. TEISEN (eds), *Self-Reliant Tanzania*, Dar es Salaam, 1969

CHARLES WILSON, *Unilever, 1945–56*, London, 1968

Chapter 6   Political Perplexities

DENNIS AUSTIN, *Politics in Ghana, 1946–60*, London, 1964

H. BIENEN, *Tanzania*, London and Princeton, 1970

GWENDOLEN M. CARTER, *Politics in Africa*, New York, 1966

       (ed.) *African One-Party States*, New York, 1962

       (ed.) *National Unity and Regionalism in Eight African States*, Cornell, 1966

CHRISTOPHER CLAPHAM, *Haile Selassie's Government*, London, 1969

L. CLIFFE (ed.), *One-Party Democracy*, Nairobi, 1967

JAMES S. COLEMAN, *Nigeria: Background to Nationalism*, Berkeley and Los Angeles, 1958

JAMES S. COLEMAN and G. A. ALMOND, *The Politics of Developing Areas*, Princeton, 1960

COLIN CROSS, *The Fall of the British Empire*, London, 1968

MICHAEL CROWDER, *West Africa under Colonial Rule*, London, 1968

RUPERT EMERSON, *From Empire to Nation*, Boston, 1962

CHRISTOPHER FYFE, *A History of Sierra Leone*, Oxford, 1962

ROBERT HEUSSLER, *The British in Northern Nigeria*, London, 1968

       Yesterday's Rulers: The Making of the British Colonial Service, Oxford, 1963

PATRICK KEATLEY, *The Politics of Partnership*, London, 1963

M. L. KILSON, *Political Change in a West African State: A Study of the Modernization Process in Sierra Leone*, Harvard, 1966

DAVID KIMBLE, *A Political History of Ghana*, Oxford, 1963

J. P. MACKINTOSH (ed.), *Government and Politics in Nigeria*, London, 1966

F. A. MAGUIRE, *Toward Uhuru in Tanzania*, London, 1970

RUTH SCHACHTER MORGENTHAU, *Political Parties in French-Speaking West Africa*, Oxford, 1964

J. K. NYERERE, *Democracy and the Party System*, Dar es Salaam, 1963

OGINGA ODINGA, *Not Yet Uhuru*, London, 1967

KEN POST, *The New States of West Africa*, London, 1964

CHRISTIAN P. POTHOLM, *Four African Political Systems*, New Jersey, 1970

RICHARD L. SKLAR, *Nigerian Political Parties*, Princeton, 1963

H. J. SPIRO (ed.), *The Primacy of Politics*, New York, 1966

VICTOR T. LE VINE, *Political Leadership in Africa: Post-Independence Generation Conflict in Upper Volta, Senegal, Niger, Dahomey and Central African Republic*, Stanford, 1967

ALEXANDER WERTH, *De Gaulle*, London, 1965

ARISTIDE R. ZOLBERG, *Creating Political Order: The Party States of West Africa*, Chicago, 1966

Chapter 7   Racialism

MARGARET BALLINGER, *From Union to Apartheid*, Folkestone, 1969

VERNON BARLETT, *The Colour of their Skin*, London, 1969

BRIAN BUNTING, *The Rise of the South African Reich*, London, 1969

COSMOS DESMOND, *The Discarded People*, London and Baltimore, 1971

C. W. DE KIEWIET, *A History of South Africa*, Oxford, 1941

I. D. MACCRONE, *Race Attitudes in South Africa*, Oxford, 1937

PHILIP MASON, *Patterns of Dominance*, London, 1970

H. J. and R. E. SIMONS, *Class and Colour Conflict in South Africa, 1850–1950*, London, 1969

A. K. H. WEINRICH, *Chiefs and Councils in Rhodesia*, London, 1971

M. WILSON and L. THOMPSON (eds), *The Oxford History of South Africa*, Vol. II, London, 1971

Chapter 8 African Soldiers

ANOUAR ABDEL-MALEK, *Egypt: Military Society*, New York, 1968

COLONEL A. A. AFRIFA, *The Ghana Coup*, London, 1966

Armed Forces of African States, Institute of Strategic Studies, London, 1966

G. CHALIARD, *Armed Struggle in Africa*, London and New York, 1969

MARTIN J. DENT, *The Military and Politics: a study of the relations between the Army and the Political Process in Nigeria, 1966–7*, London, 1968

JACQUES VAN DOORN (ed.), *Armed Forces and Society*, The Hague, 1968

S. E. FINER, *The Man on Horseback*, London, 1962

RUTH FIRST, *The Barrel of a Gun – Political Power in Africa and the Coup d'Etat*, London, 1972

W. F. GUTTERIDGE, *Military Institutions and Power in the New States*, London, 1964

MORRIS JANOWITZ, *The Military in the Political Development of New Nations: An Essay in Comparative Analysis*, Chicago, 1964

JOHN DE ST JORRE, *The Nigerian Civil War*, London, 1972

A. H. M. KIRK-GREEN, *Crisis and Conflict in Nigeria*, London, 1971

EDWARD LUTTWAK, *Coup d'Etat*, London, 1968

MAJOR-GENERAL A. K. OCRAN, *A Myth is Broken*, Accra, 1968

Chapter 9 Zambia–A Case Study

BRIAN FAGAN, *A Short History of Zambia*, London, 1966

RICHARD HALL, *The High Price of Principles*, London, 1969

Zambia, London and New York, 1965

KENNETH KAUNDA, *Zambia Shall be Free*, London, 1962

KENNETH KAUNDA and COLIN MORRIS, *A Humanist in Africa*, London, 1966

Second National Development Plan, Lusaka, 1971

Chapter 10   International Relations

MARIO DE ANDRADE, *La Poésie africaine d'Expression portugaise*, Paris, 1969

W. ATTWOOD, *The Reds and the Blacks*, London, 1967

M. J. V. BELL, *Military Assistance to Independent African States*, London, 1964

S. J. BOSGRA and C. VAN KRIMPEN, *Portugal and NATO*, Amsterdam, 1969

BASIL DAVIDSON, *The Liberation of Guiné: Aspects of an African Revolution*, London, 1969

IRVING LOUIS HOROWITZ, *The Rise and Fall of Project Camelot*, Cambridge, Massachusetts, 1968

COLIN LEGUM, *Pan-Africanism*, London, 1962

RALPH MILIBAN, *The State in Capitalist Society*, London, 1969

EDUARDO MONDLANE, *The Struggle for Mozambique*, London, 1969

ADRIANO MOREIRA, *Portugal's Stand in Africa*, New York, 1962

I. WALLERSTEIN, *The Politics of Unity*, New York, 1967

Chapter 11   Africa in the 1970s

FREDERICK S. ARKHURST (ed.), *Africa in the Seventies and Eighties*, New York, 1970

LEONARD BARNES, *Africa in Eclipse*, London, 1971
             African Renaissance, London, 1969

JOHN M. BLAIR, *Economic Concentration*, New York, 1972

BASIL DAVIDSON, *Which way Africa? The Search for a New Society*, London, 1964

W. H. FRIEDLAND and C. G. ROSBERG (eds), *African Socialism*, London, 1964

JOHN HATCH, *The History of Britain in Africa*, London and New York, 1969

COLIN LEGUM (ed.), *Africa, Handbook*, London, 1961

E. H. LEWIS (ed.), *French-Speaking Africa: The Search for Identity*, New York, 1965

LEWIS MUMFORD, *The Pentagon of Power*, New York and London, 1970 and 1971

KWAME NKRUMAH, *Dark Days in Ghana*, London, 1969

HUGH STEPHENSON, *The Coming Clash*, London, 1972

GORDON RATTRAY TAYLOR, *Rethink*, London, 1972

ALVIN TOFFLER, *Future Shock*, London and New York, 1972

Index